Wish You Weren't Here

The Black Cat Anthology of Travel Humor

Edited by

Cecil Kuhne

Black Cat
New York

a paperback original imprint of Grove / Atlantic, Inc.

Permissions on page 273.

Published simultaneously in Canada
Printed in the United States of America

FIRST EDITION

Library of Congress Cataloging-in-Publication Data
Wish you weren't here : the Black Cat anthology of travel humor / edited by
Cecil Kuhne.
     p. cm.
  ISBN-10: 0-8021-7033-1
  ISBN-13: 978-0-8021-7033-0
   1. Travel—Anecdotes. 2. Travel—Humor.   I. Kuhne, Cecil, 1952–
II. Title: Wish you were not here.
G465.W567 2007
910.2'07—dc22

2006052526

Black Cat
a paperback original imprint of Grove/Atlantic, Inc.
841 Broadway
New York, NY 10003

Distributed by Publishers Group West

www.groveatlantic.com

07 08 09 10 11 12   10 9 8 7 6 5 4 3 2 1

Wish You Weren't Here

Contents

Contents

II. Getting Around

III. Then the Wheels Fell Off

Contents

Introduction

Dave Barry, the perceptive humorist that he is, once observed about travel that "the human race is far too stupid to be deterred from tourism by a mere million years of bad experience."

Mr. Barry also adroitly noted that there is something deep within the human psyche that yearns to "introduce new bacteria into our intestinal tracts, learn new words for 'transfusion,' and have all the other travel adventures that make us want to French-kiss our doormats when we finally get home."

Who hasn't had the experience of watching a little humor unfold on the road? My wife and I one year decided to do something different for our summer vacation. The hedonistic spas, the fancy golf resorts, the cheesy cruise ships, and the pretentious journeys to the wine country no longer appealed to us. We chose instead to take a canoe trip—just the two of us—to the most remote wilderness we could find on the face of the earth.

We settled on a river flowing fast and furious between the Yukon and the Northwest Territories of Canada. Why did we do this? I'm not entirely sure. Maybe it was too much Robert Service poetry, or perhaps it was the mysterious scenes plastered on bottles of

Yukon Jack whiskey. But we were determined to go, and nothing was going to stop us. Not even the grizzly bears.

The river flowed through a vast national park, and I made the obligatory call to the rangers about the necessary precautions against *Ursus horribilis*. "What kind of firepower should we pack?" The ranger politely informed me that guns of any kind were strictly prohibited within the park, and then added, "If you're coming from the States, you'd have trouble getting one into Canada anyway."

Well, I asked, what should I do to keep from being eaten alive. "Most people bring air horns," she advised.

"Air horns?"

"Yes, you know—those little canister things that make a lot of noise."

Before our flight left, I rushed to the sporting goods store to buy a model that was about the size of a travel shave-cream dispenser.

The place we were going, I should point out, was *extremely* remote. Only a handful of parties visited the area each year because it was completely roadless. As our backcountry pilot was loading our gear into the float plane, he asked, "Where's your rifle?"

I replied with all the manliness I could muster, "Didn't bring one. The park service prohibits them, you know."

"That's sure as hell news to me. All the outfitters on the river carry 'em. The place is full of damn grizzlies. What did you bring to protect your sweet ass?"

When I told him, I thought I detected the signs of a smirk on his face. But I preferred to believe that it was a display of his great respect for the size of my cojones. Anyway, my wife and I loaded our gear into the boat and set off downstream. We did see a lot of bear tracks each night at our campsite, but we reasoned that the furry creatures were in reality very shy and simply wanted to avoid us.

We played it smart, though. We hung our food in the trees every night, just like the experts, and we never slept in clothes smothered with bacon grease. We weren't going to do something stupid like those tourists in Yellowstone—you know, the ones who slather their kids' faces with honey in the hopes of taking photos of the bears licking it off. Please, we weren't that stupid.

A few days later I ran into one of the professional guides on the river. "Does everyone here pack heat?"

"Of course—why?"

"Just wondering. I brought an air horn."

"You have got to be kidding."

I laughed nervously at my little joke and then walked back to the boat real fast.

The next day my wife and I were floating by the shore when we saw our first Grizz. He was about fifteen feet away and was nonchalantly eating berries out of a bush. He was very large.

The next day we saw another Grizz about a quarter of a mile away when he suddenly stopped to lift his nostrils in the direction of our meal on the campfire. He, too, was very large. I decided then that maybe we should start camping on the islands in the middle of the river. "You see, the river will act as a buffer against the bears," I proudly informed my wife, who I thought would be impressed by my astute precaution. She then rhetorically mused, "But the river is only two feet deep. Couldn't they just walk across and get us?" I hated that response.

Unscathed, we finished the trip a few days later. Our shuttle driver was full of questions, including the dreaded where's-your-gun query. I showed him the air horn, and he had the expression of someone who had just had cold water poured down his pants.

When we arrived home, there was an e-mail waiting, and it was from a friend who had previously counseled me on which high-powered bazooka to take. The message went like this:

You can imagine my horror when I learned after your departure that you traveled to one of the singularly most remote spots on the North American continent armed with nothing but a friggin' air horn. Are you crazy? Are you suicidal? Grizzlies burp louder than a damn air horn. Air horns are designed to ward off errant sailboats and to herald touchdowns at varsity ball games. A grizzly bear would eat your down-filled butt, scarlet orange and all, with you tooting your little horn like a VW bug going eastbound on the westbound Ventura freeway. Explain yourself very soon.

The collection of humorous travel stories you have before you comes from a panel of exceptionally talented writers armed with two critical credentials: Their tongues are planted firmly in their cheeks, and they have the marvelous ability to poke fun at themselves. These amusing essays range wide and deep across the human and the geographical spectrum.

Christopher Buckley, for example, describes a memorable trip to Belize with the tour group from hell, including a couple of senior-citizen vegans so obsessed with their digestive tracts that they spare no detail in their discussions with complete strangers. P.J. O'Rourke visits India and notes the country's primary household fuel—cow dung, which is formed into little circular patties and stuck on the sides of houses to dry, thereby solving three functions: storage space, home decor, and how to cook dinner. Nigel Barley tells of an unforgettable journey on Aeroflot, complete with mustachioed flight attendants and five meals of fried chicken variously prepared.

And, as they say, there is much, much more.

This anthology is divided into three parts. The first section— "It's the People You Meet"—deals with all those interesting individuals one inevitably encounters on the road. The second section —"Getting Around"—concerns an array of what might be called "tricky" transportation issues. And the third—"Then the Wheels Fell Off"—is devoted to all the things that can go so horribly wrong along the way.

My criteria for including each piece was simple: would it bend me over in laughter after I read it, say, ten times? I am now pleased to report that these stories passed that rigorous test with flying colors, and I'm pretty confident—no, I'm *really* confident—that they will do the same for you.

Cecil Kuhne
Dallas, Texas

I

It's the People You Meet

1

Would You Belíze?

Christopher Buckley

There are drawbacks to group travel, it occurred to me as I sat trapped in the back of the van listening to a woman I had only met an hour before acquaint me in immodest detail with the vicissitudes of her husband's lower colon. I was more interested in Belize, the small, coastal Central American country that I had always wanted, for some reason, to see, and where now I finally was. I nodded as politely as I could throughout her unbrief discourse on the virtues of Manchurian ginseng, as she eye-droppered some onto the tongue of her docile husband. I managed to keep an impassive face as she lectured me urgently that "you can't just dump everything into your liver—you've *got* to clean out the lymphs," but when she said brightly, "That's why Bill and I are into colonics," I averted my eyes in the direction of a jungle-covered Mayan hillock and thought, *It's going to be a long ten days.*

At the end of a disastrous experience traveling with F. Scott Fitzgerald, Hemingway announced to his wife his new rule: never travel anywhere with someone you don't love. That's not always practical, but I had made sure to bring along my good friend Tom. If you are going to spend ten days with a dozen people you've never met, it's prudent to bring some insurance along. As it turned out, our group was a collection of pleasant and varied people, including a bond broker who is a great-great nephew of Warren Harding; a Canadian real estate man with a passion for remote-controlled airplanes; another Canadian couple, he an accountant, she a former navigator in the RAF; a retired chief operating officer of a Big Board company; a couple of spry and engaging older ladies, one a children's portrait painter, the other a botanist; a well-read Connecticut couple, he a college administrator, she a bibliographer; and the colonically inclined California couple, who introduced themselves to everyone we came across as "Vegans." This turned out to be not a reference to a home planet in Alpha Centauri, but the word denoting strict vegetarianism. Watching them describe their draconian dietary requirements to the mystified peasant folks who cooked our meals in remote hamlets was a memorable part of the trip; you have not truly lived until you have witnessed a tank-topped blond from Los Angeles explain the evils of chicken to an emaciated Central American.

But there is this to be said in favor of group travel, especially with a pukka outfit like Butterfield and Robinson: everything is done for you—visas, transport, food, lodging, and if anything goes wrong, you get to yell at them and they're not allowed to yell back. I wish Butterfield and Robinson guided New York cab rides. *Eric, would you please tell Mr. Abouhalima to SLOW THE @#$% DOWN, GODDAMNIT!*

And there's this: you get to see a country like Belize through the eyes of a Jaime Awe. (Pronounced *Ah-weh*.) Jaime is a native Belizean, a professor of Mayan archaeology at Trent University in Ontario, smart, funny, street-wise, someone you'd want in your lifeboat.

Not that there were any lifeboats around. We were in the interior. More than half the people who go there, go for reasons having to do with the gin-clear water off Belize's coast, for the fishing, scuba diving, beaching, tanning, and general lying about. There would be some of that at the end of our trip, but now we were on our way west, climbing gradually from the mangrove swamps along the Caribbean coast, through grassy savannahs, to the foothills of the Mayan mountains in the interior. Belize doesn't have a whole lot of interior; at no point is it more than about sixty miles wide. The whole country is only slightly larger than Massachusetts, but unlike Massachusetts, it has a functioning economy and a good record on human rights, which is so rare in these parts that the country ought to be stuffed and mounted and hung above the General Assembly at the United Nations. They also speak English in Belize, so you don't have to shout at the natives in English the way you do, say, in Mexico, in order to make yourself understood.

Belize used to be British Honduras. By the time we got there, last January, the British were down to about fifty troops, owing to the fact that the United States, in a rare instance of actually accomplishing something hemispheric without making a hash of it, quietly told Guatemala to drop its idiotic, centuries-old irredentist insistence that Belize really belongs to Guatemala. That is why, despite the fact that it has been independent of the Crown since 1981, the British commandos stayed on, and will remain, conducting jungle warfare exercises, helicoptering out tourists who've stepped on fer-de-lance snakes, and performing various other vital functions, like giving the Guats the willies.

Earlier on, Belize was passed over by the *conquistadores*, probably because a lot of its coast looks like an advertisement for Off! mosquito repellent. It was finally stumbled upon by wet, disoriented, shipwrecked British sailors in the early 1600s. There followed a period of the usual rapine and plunder, with the difference that the economy was based on fishing and mahogany logging, instead of on banana or sugar or coffee plantations, so the country didn't end up being a basket case run by a lot of resentful and voluble descendants of slaves. What slavery there was was abolished in 1838, and the British magistrates, while strict, were fair, so people saw that democracy, though flawed, was better than shooting up the National Assembly every other Wednesday.

All of this was irrelevant to our purposes, since we'd come to check out the birds, who really don't care who's in charge as long as they don't govern by DDT, and to see Mayan ruins and caves. I like birds, and wish them well generally, and only shoot them about once a year; but I wouldn't say to my wife, *C'mon hon, let's go spend two weeks in Belize looking at birds.* However, if you are a bird person, then Belize is for you. Forty percent of the people who go to Chan Chich Lodge are birders, another forty percent are naturalists. Put the two together, and you've got the makings of some of the dullest conversation in any hemisphere. The remaining twenty percent, such as ourselves, come to chill out thirty-five miles from the nearest phone at a place where you can spend all day reading in a hammock listening to the plummy warbling of Oropendolas, get drunk on rum punches and then go stumble down to the nature trail and moon the electric-eye camera set up by the Wildlife and Conservation Society that snaps flash pictures of jaguars, pumas, and coatimundi with alarmed expressions on their faces. That's *really* getting to know a country.

It dawned on Tom and me that we were on something perilously close to an "eco-tour" when at the end of the first day, after a stop at the justly famed Belize zoo and after checking into our first wilderness lodge, Chaa Creek, we were taken for a short walk on the Panti trail and shown in mind-numbing detail, a bunch of trees and vines. Chocolate trees, Cohune palm trees, hog plum trees, Bayal trees, trees with black orchids (the Belizean national flower), mahogany trees, cedar trees, red gumbolino trees, fiddlewood trees, sapodilla trees. There were trees that could cure dysentery, impotence, and ringworm; purge amoebae; ward off evil spirits; make antibiotics; termite-proof Chippendale furniture; and mask filters for World War II pilots. When, two hours later, I heard the words, "Now this is another kind of gourd . . . ," I began to feel pangs of sympathy for those Brazilian cattle ranchers who are supposed to be ruining the planet. At the herbal remedy shop at the end of the Panti trail tour, one of the women bought a bottle of something that was supposed to help her husband with his marital duties. She mentioned it a couple times over dinner, which, to judge from the expression on her husband's face, may have been a couple of times too many. This is a drawback to group travel: having twelve people know that your wife thinks you need a bottle of Belizean erection tonic.

That night at Chaa Creek, a pretty collection of hibiscus-, bougainvillea- and poinsettia-covered thatched-roof bungalows set in a verdant valley—actually, pretty much everything is verdant in the jungle; if you sit down for more than five minutes, *you'll* be verdant—Jaime gave an interesting lecture on the Maya, specifically on their obsession with caves. I'll condense it for you: the Maya were *really* into caves. A good thing, too, since the whole region is filled with them, owing to the heavy rainfall eroding the porous limestone underneath. The Maya thought caves were the entrance to hell. Having grown up using the New York City subways, I immediately understood why they would think this. They left food in caves, sacrificed animals and humans in caves, buried their honored dead in caves, and ate hallucinogenic mushrooms in caves while ritually mutilating themselves, generally by piercing their tongues and penises with long, obsidian needles. I got all this from Jaime, and he has a PhD in it, so you know it's true. Jaime speculated that the Maya had disappeared due to problems resulting from population stress. My own theory was that people who eat psychotropic mushrooms and crawl into caves to perforate their tongues and penises are not going to make it to the Super Bowl.

The next day, we went into a cave. This was unquestionably the high point of the trip. Jaime told us that only about 2 percent of people who come to Belize do this, which was encouraging to hear, since, as a group trudging up the steep hill with our expensive cameras, expensive hiking boots, our fanny packs, and our multicolored clothes and cute hats, we collectively looked like a bunch of dorks. That's another problem with group touring, trying not to feel like a dork.

At any rate, we went in about three-quarters of a kilometer, however much that is, and about three hundred feet down (a hundred meters). I discovered that I am not a cave person. Despite the amazingly preserved Mayan pots we saw along the way, dating to 500–600 B.C., I kept saying to Tom, "I've seen enough. Let's go back." But Tom, being a lawyer, wanted to press on, probably sensing a massive class-action suit against Butterfield and Robinson. I was left to conclude that I was the only real dork in the group. On we went, until we came to a small opening in the damp limestone. We lowered ourselves by rope down into a chamber about one hundred and twenty feet high by seventy feet long. In the center of the packed-earth ground was a stele about the size and shape of a tombstone, surrounded by a circle of smaller ceremonial stones. This was the spot, Jaime explained, where they cut out the hearts. This produced in me intense stirrings of numinousness and wonder, as well as a keen appreciation for not having been born in Belize in 500–600 B.C.

We had lunch nearby at Checem Ha. We ate chicken with rice and red beans, coleslaw, and fried plantains, liberally covered with Marie Sharp's Hot Pepper Sauce, the ketchup of Belize, and washed it down with ice-cold Belikin beers. It was about the best meal any of us had ever had. Except for the Vegans. They complained to the lovely, toothless woman who cooked our meal about the horrors of animal fat; then they ate some rice and beans. The She-Vegan, as Tom was now privately calling her, produced a bottle of Beano, from which she made the He-Vegan take an ample spoonful. This is another downside to group travel: being made to swallow antiflatulence medicine by your wife in front of twelve people who by now have concluded that you really are a dork.

Would You Belize?

Back at Chaa Creek we talked with its owner, Mick Fleming, a hearty, burly, outgoing British expatriate. He told funny stories about a roguish jaguar hunter and Mayan tomb looter. He said that we wouldn't have to worry about banditos tomorrow. Banditos had been preying on his customers on the road to the Mayan ruins at Tikal, across the border in Guatemala. They would jump out of the bushes and stick 16-gauge shotguns in your face. They were doing it quite regularly, up to three times a week, until Mick got the Belizean Defense Forces to persuade the Guatemalan armed forces to do something about it. They'd caught them six weeks ago. I had mixed feelings, hearing this. It would be nice to say back home that we'd been robbed by banditos, but being mugged is being mugged in any language, and a 16-gauge shotgun makes a big hole whether you measure it in inches or centimeters.

The next day we drove to Tikal. Guatemala is to Belize what Ireland is to England: the butt of the jokes. The standard of living and the quality of the roads drop the moment you cross the border. Also, you see lots of soldiers, not a good sign; in ten days in Belize we saw one policeman, and I don't think he had a gun. Even the traffic cops in Guatemala seemed to have the latest submachine gun. In the last thirty-odd years, Guatemala has had an on-again, off-again civil war going that has killed a hundred thousand, about half the population of Belize, another reason Belize is not eager to be annexed by Guatemala.

Tikal was one of the great Mayan cities. It covers nine square miles, has eighteen huge temple structures and 2,080 stone roof structures. Between 1956 and 1969, one hundred scholars from the University of Pennsylvania excavated it, with some help from one thousand local laborers. They uncovered eighty of those 2,080 buildings. Jaime said that there may be as many as ten thousand other buildings underneath all that jungle. Just keeping what's been excavated from turning back into jungle is work; for instance, they have to scrape the Temple of the Lost World once a year with spatulas to ward off the green crud. They pile rocks outside the entrance to temples to protect the frescoes inside. Rocks attract snakes; snakes deter looters.

The temples are steep. A guide had recently fallen down one of them to his death. In six hours of climbing we did a year's worth of Stairmaster. Our local guide droned on in an amusing, Victorian English monotone under the hot sun—"We are now in de central acropolis, built on top of de previous structure, obeying de needs of time . . ."—as he told us what had happened here between 600 B.C. and A.D. 1000. As usual with Mayan temples, sacrifices were the main event. The victims, Luis the guide told us, "were narcotized, then degraded, de arms and leg joints dislocated, then dey were tied over the stone, decapitated, the blood collected and offered and burned with herbs." One unhappy prisoner was kept for seventeen years of bloodletting rituals before having his head cut off. They played a version of basketball, with a human skull coated with hard rubber; the losing team ended up on the sacrificial slabs. To date, archaeologists have found no evidence of any baseball strikes in Tikal.

It was a society in which you were really better off being a noble. That's true of 99 percent of civilizations, but given what went on here, being a noble at least kept the scalpel-wielding priests at arm's length. The Maya had a keen grasp of the advantages of class. If they'd had an airline, it would have been all first-class; coach passengers would have been tied to the wing, with the flight attendants coming by to poke holes in their tongues. The better neighborhoods at Tikal were strictly off-limits to the common folk. The only way you got to the top of one of those temples was if you were building it or depositing your heart on it. The nobles wore lots of jade— Lord Ah Cacao's robes contained sixteen pounds of jade—and got to eat a special diet containing more protein than the working-class schmoes, as a result of which their skeletons are on average ten centimeters longer than the others. Luis mentioned that they were given to "ritual enemas, with powdered [hallucinogenic] mushrooms." On hearing this, the Vegans began to murmur among themselves. The nobles wore beautiful headdresses of quetzal feathers and hummingbird wings. According to Luis, "They made themselves cross-eyed as a sign of beauty." I don't know how they managed that, but you can see it in the frescoes. They all do look cross.

I remember two things of Tikal. The first was a scratch of Mayan graffiti, perfectly preserved, showing a skull beside two vertical bars and two dots. Each dot represents five, each bar, one; the skull represents death. It means "twelve dead." Whether from disease, or losing at basketball, or in battle, no one knows, but there it was on the wall, twelve hundred years later.

The second was watching the sunset from the top of Temple IV. Lord Ah Cacao finished Temple IV in A.D. 741, a year before Charlemagne was born. We were almost two hundred feet up, above the jungle canopy, looking down over all of Tikal, watching the lengthening shadows and listening to a cacophony of macaws, red-lored parrots, black falcons, and howler monkeys. Hurrying back to the Jungle Lodge through the gloaming, Tom and I got briefly lost, which was not a comforting sensation in this vast, tangly agora of bats and ghosts; but soon we were swigging white cane rum with Jaime as two British women swam topless in the dirty pool.

By 1:00 p.m. the next day we were back in Belize, "civilization," as our driver smiled once we'd made it across the border. A de Havilland Twin Otter STOL (Short Takeoff and Landing) flew us to Gallon Jug, where a bus took us to a miracle of exotic hospitality built on the plaza of a Mayan ruin. Chan Chich Lodge consists of twelve thatched-roof bungalows, a very good dining room, a very good bar, nature trails, birds, jungle cats, monkeys, unexcavated ruins, a forbidding river, and that's about it. It was the brainchild of Barry Bowen, who owns the beer and Coca-Cola concession in Belize. When you control the flow of beer and Coke in a hot country, you're doing very well. He hired two ex–U.S. Special Forces

officers, and the wife of one of them, to build and run this seques-
tered Xanadu. It's run extremely well. The only complaint I heard
in our three days there was from the Vegans, who, apparently, were
simply not getting enough protein.

Jimmy Carter had been there recently, with seventeen of his
children and grandchildren, and the usual battalion of Secret Service agents. It's not quite the same as hearing that George Washington had slept there, but in the jungle you take the cachet as it
comes.

By now Tom and I had had enough tree lore to last us the nine-
ties, so we mostly lay in our hammocks reading, secure in the
knowledge that no phones would ring, the ultimate luxury. There
can't be many places on earth as lovely as the porches at Chan
Chich, entangled with hibiscus, bougainvillea, wisteria, golden
shower, wandering Jew, avocado, poinsettia, flame of the woods,
ginger, and oyster plants. Toward sunset, the birds start to go
bonkers. Ornithologists probably have a more precise term for it,
but whatever it is, it's loud, starting out as a crepuscular Vivaldi
string quartet, with the *poip-poip* of the tree frogs, and gradually
building, with a little help from the ubiquitous oscellated turkeys,
to an 1812 Overture. But it is nothing compared with what wakes
you up in the middle of the night. The first morning, Tom said to
me, somewhat shaken, "Did you *hear* that?" Yes, I shuddered. What
was that? It sounded like the Primeval Id, being denied antacid tablets. The answer—Jaime had all the answers—was several hundred
very agitated howler monkeys. "It was probably," he said, "some
male dominance issue." Whatever it was, you would not want to
get in the middle of it. No wonder the Maya went into caves and
perforated their penises.

In the midmorning heat you could walk to where the real
birdwatching action was—at the dump. The smell was a bit high,
but the mounds of ordure were covered with enough feathered
delights to keep any birder scribbling happily in his logbook. At

night, after dinner, we hung by the bar, listening to Tom and Norman, the two Vietnam-era Green Berets who built Chan Chich, with twenty or so laborers in just twenty months, for $400,000. One story they told was an object lesson on why the omens are not good for the human species.

Some Mennonites and Belizeans and Guatemalans had been illegally logging Guatemalan mahogany and hauling it over the border into Belize, on Barry Bowen's land. Tom and Norman found a pile of it worth about one million dollars. They told Bowen about it and offered to burn it. No, Bowen said, we need to let the government know about this. Thus did the Belizean government and the Guatemalan government enter in and start a game of diplomatic Ping-Pong. The Guatemalans said, We'll come and get the lumber. The Belizean government, well aware of Guatemala's smoldering lust for annexation, said, No, we'll bring it to you. Oh no, said Guatemala, no Belizean trucks on Guatemala's sovereign soil. Standoff. So, said Tom, we now have Guatemalan troops in Belize guarding the lumber while Guatemala builds a road through a nature preserve in order to get to it. He shook his head. "The lumber will have rotted by the time they get to it, and squatters will come in on the new road and settle in the biosphere." Tom and Norman had some perspective on it, anyway, having survived a previous jungle conundrum.

The next day we STOL-ed to Ambergris Cay, on the coast. It rained and was buggy, and the beaches were full of waste. It would be stretching it to call Ambergris Cay "paradise." Some went scuba diving, and reported great success, some of us hung around San Pedro, shooting pool and eating stone crab claws at Elvi's. Every time we heard a plane take off, Tom and I would look up longingly, like the people in Rick's Cafe in *Casablanca* at the flight to Lisbon. It was time to go home. We had half an hour between planes in Miami to call up the Vegans' airline and cancel their special meals.

2

The Longest Night

Tony Hawks

Some sort of music festival in the area meant that there were no vacancies in any of the bed and breakfasts in Letterfrack. Sister Magdalena left me outside a building which bore absolutely no resemblance to an old monastery, which was called The Old Monastery Hostel. A hostel, eh? I wasn't without misgivings, but at least its name maintained the ecclesiastical flavor to the day's proceedings. I went in and found nobody about. A message, chalked up on a blackboard, greeted travelers on arrival. "Welcome. Please make yourselves comfortable by the fire. Someone will be with you shortly. Everything you need is on this floor; kitchen, living room, bathrooms, and toilets. Breakfast is served at 9 a.m. downstairs in the café. Breakfast is free and includes hot organic scones, hot cereal, and organic coffee and tea. Relax, be happy, and enjoy your stay."

Too many things were organic for my liking. Without a pair of sandals, a musty aroma of henna about me, or my hair in a ponytail, I felt that I wouldn't be welcome here. I turned to my left and found myself in a large dormitory. Bunk beds seemed to be everywhere. For the first time on the trip since day one, I began to feel that I had bitten off more than I could chew. I selected a top bunk and marked out my territory by dumping my rucksack on it. I wheeled the fridge over to the window and left it there. I had made it into the dorm without anyone seeing that it was mine, and here was the opportunity to have a night off from the attention that went with being its owner. Besides, I thought it would be quite fun to let everyone in the hostel view each other with an element of suspicion, trying to establish which one of them was the idiot traveling around with a fridge. It might be the source of some healthy uneasiness.

A Chinese-looking fellow came in. I said "hello" but he didn't respond. Either his knowledge of English didn't stretch as far as "hello," or he was a git. Looking around the vast dormitory I could see the evidence, in the form of rucksacks dumped on bunks, of about fifteen other potential gits. Two nights ago, when I had lain in bed and wondered when I would next find myself "not sleeping alone," this wasn't what I had in mind.

A young American couple came in, and I realized that the dormitory was mixed. The couple were followed by a big lady who I took to be Dutch. I was working from size alone, so this was a long shot. Whatever nationality she was, she had a greater grasp of English than the Chinese chap, because when I said "hello," she said "hello" back. I smiled politely at her and then turned to him and gave a look which was designed to say "See, did that hurt?" He didn't see though, he was busy laying socks out on his bunk. It looked like he had embarked on some kind of ancient ritual in which the future could be read in the socks.

I caused at least three disapproving sharp intakes of breath from the room when I plugged my mobile phone into one of the power points to recharge it.

"Sorry," I announced, realizing that this sort of behavior was about as incompatible with organic scones as you could get.

It had to be done though, because I knew that *The Gerry Ryan Show* would want to talk to me in the morning, and besides,

enough ground had been covered now to warrant a call to Kevin
in England in order to let him know that his hundred pounds was
in some jeopardy.

"Hello, Kevin?" I said, sitting on top of a stile halfway up a mountain in the Connemara National Park.

I don't have many good things to say about mobile phones but
one plus point is the freedom they offer you to choose exciting
mountainous landscapes for your office space. A short walk from
the hostel had brought me to a spot where, to the north, I could
see moorland dominated by the Twelve Bens mountain range, and
to the west, the deeply indented Atlantic coastline with its many
inlets and creeks. I was looking forward to Kevin's next question,

"Whereabouts are you?" he obliged.

I told him, at some length.

"And what about the fridge? I suppose you dumped that days
ago?"

"No. I've still got it with me, well, not exactly at this moment,
it's back at the hostel."

"Hostel? So you're living like a King then?"

"Most of the time I am actually."

Unfortunately like the King of Tory.

"Yeah, yeah, I bet."

"I'm just warning you that it looks like I'm going to *do* this. I am
going to hitchhike round Ireland with a fridge. So you'd better start
talking to your bank manager about arranging a one-hundred-
pound overdraft."

"Look, you're not even halfway round yet. Things will go wrong.
I'm not going to start to worry until you're a couple of miles outside Dublin. The thing you forget is—"

The line went dead as the signal disappeared.

At least that's what he thought. The fact is that I had pressed the
button which cut him off. Another plus point to the mobile phone.

I didn't need a dose of cynicism just now. I shouldn't have called. Showing off. I just hadn't been able to resist it.

As I walked down the hill back to the hostel, for some reason I began singing the Johnny Nash song, "I can see clearly now the rain has gone, I can see all obstacles in my way."

I stopped and said to myself, "No, I can't. That's the beauty of this. I can't see any obstacles at all."

I had cut off the conversation with Kevin just at the moment when he had been about to point out what some of the obstacles might be. I figured that the person who didn't know that there were any obstacles, was always going to be ahead of the person who had to go around them because he or she knew where they were. This philosophy could either get me to where I wanted to be, or land me in hospital as a result of having run headlong into something which had very little give in it.

It was a straight choice. A walk down to the local pub, or an evening in the sitting room with the hardy backpacking community. For health reasons I chose the latter.

The sitting room was a large room with a dining table at one end and a great open fire dominating the other. The dining table was full of people with dyed hair and pierced noses, with their heads buried in thick paperbacks. By the fire, there were some chairs where a less formidable looking group were seated. The most comfortable looking armchair was occupied by the hostel dog, and moving him would clearly be considered sacrilege and wouldn't win me any friends. However, there was one tatty looking chair free, so I sat down in it. Immediately I felt conspicuous. It had been a bad mistake not bringing a book in with me. Everyone else appeared to be reading, and it looked as if I was there purely to keep the others from this laudable activity. Seeing that the kitchen was within easy reach through an archway, I stood up, clasped my hands and rubbed them together.

"Right," I said, like an embarrassing teacher who was trying too hard to be liked by his pupils, "does anyone want a cup of tea?"

Most ignored me completely, but some managed to look up from their reading and shake a head. The class of 4b were a tough lot. Wholesale rejection. Not a good start.

Moments later, and for the second time in a day, I found myself in somebody else's kitchen. Naturally enough, I couldn't find the tea bags anywhere. After some banging about and cursing under the breath which must have aggravated the readers in the sitting room, I was forced into popping my head round the door with the humiliating question, "Does anyone know where the tea bags are?"

There was at least one tut, and two sighs. An American guy, who was nearest to the fire, looked up at me, "Do you not have your own?"

"What?"

"You're supposed to bring your own."

"Oh, yes, of course."

I sat down, thinking that someone would find it in their hearts to offer me one of their tea bags. Initially no one did, but when I concentrated on looking really forlorn, the American girl on my right capitulated, "You can have one of my tea bags if you want. But they're lemon and ginger. Do you like lemon and ginger?"

I had no idea. Independently of each other, I had no aversion to either, but I had never experienced the two together before. Why should I have done? I didn't experiment with drugs.

"Lemon and ginger? Yes, I think so, thanks, that's very kind of you," I replied, taking the tea bag and disappearing back into the kitchen to cover it with boiling water.

On my return, the American girl watched with interest as I took my first sip. As the tea collided with my taste buds, I immediately came to the conclusion that ginger was as beneficial a partner to lemon, as mittens were to concert pianists.

"Mmm, interesting flavor," I coughed, only just refraining from

my initial instinct to spit it straight back out again. "Interesting."
What a splendidly ambiguous adjective. It was my favorite euphemism for food that I didn't like at dinner parties.

"Interesting recipe . . . interesting flavor." Interesting that you
contrived to create such a hideous, foul tasting dish.

I began to chat with the two Americans, and couldn't work out
whether they were just good friends traveling together or whether
their relationship went beyond that. I certainly didn't want to be
kept awake tonight by any noises which might clear the matter up.
There were two others sat by the fireside. One was a Swedish girl,
who joined in my chat with the Americans, and who had a large
and fresh-looking love bite on her neck, which I hoped hadn't been
the product of a night spent in this hostel. The other member of
the fireside team was a girl who I found rather pretty, and whom I
would have sat next to if the hostel dog hadn't got in there first.
She said nothing, but read constantly. However, at faintly amusing moments in our conversation, she smiled, which made me
suspect that she wasn't really reading but eavesdropping on a conversation to which she wasn't prepared to contribute.

"So what are you doing here in Ireland?" I was eventually asked
by the American guy.

I attempted to give as little away as possible but my caginess only
served to make him more inquisitive, and as the questions continued, I eventually made the mistake of revealing that I was in Ireland because of a bet.

Naturally enough, he wanted to know what the bet was. I lowered my voice and told him about the fridge business. Suddenly,
the pretty girl who was reading looked up from her book.

"Are you the guy with the fridge?" she asked.

"I am."

"You stole my lift."

"What?"

"Yesterday. You stole my lift."

Up until this moment, the coincidences in my life hadn't been that impressive. The best I had managed involved bumping into people I knew at airports. Sleeping in the same dormitory as the girl who I had pushed in front of when hitching, was probably going to edge into the lead. I owed her an apology.

"I'm so, so sorry," I said.

"It's all right."

"I would have asked the driver to stop for you, too, but there simply wasn't room."

"Because, of the fridge, right?"

"Er, yes."

"I waited two and a half hours there, you know."

All right, don't make things worse. I felt bad enough as it was.

Tina was hitching around Ireland before returning to her native Denmark to study psychology. Like so many from her part of the world, she had that disarming ability to fully participate in an English conversation without anyone else needing to make the slightest compensation for the fact that it wasn't her native tongue. She was extremely pleasant and I began to feel very bad about the hitching business. Had we been in a hotel, I could have got to my feet and said that the least I could do was buy her a drink, perhaps even order a bottle of champagne, but in present circumstances my hands were tied rather. All I could do was offer her a cup of lemon and ginger tea, provided my American supplier didn't let me down. In the event, I took her address in Denmark and promised to send her an atonement present. She smiled courteously and went off to bed. As she reached the door I had this terrible urge to call out after her, "I'll be up in a minute, darling," but I realized there was no audience for such a remark, and restrained myself.

When the conversation started to dry up, I said my good nights and made my way into the dormitory. It was dark, and I was unsure of which bunk was mine. I became conscious of the immense embarrassment I would feel were I to crawl into the wrong bunk. The big Dutch woman, Tina, and the unfriendly Chinese man were all potential victims of my disorientation and their reactions to a visitor climbing in to join them could range from a welcoming embrace to a kung fu kick to the groin or screams that this was the wrong kind of atonement present. However, I could just make out the faint outline of the fridge, which was by the window, and knew if I got to that, I could take my bearings from it and work my way back to my bunk. This was yet another first, a fridge used for navigational purposes.

I tried to undress as quietly as I could, but the more I tried, the more clumsy I became. I knocked belongings off my bunk and onto the floor, and very nearly toppled over whilst attempting to remove my jeans, getting my foot stuck in one of the legs. Each sound I was making seemed deafening. I was developing a heightened awareness of sound which wasn't going to be my ally when I shortly took on the formidable task of falling asleep.

It began well enough though, as I got comfortable rather quickly. But it soon became apparent that I was making the same mistake I make when I try to get to sleep on planes. I think too much about the whole process. As I wriggle into a newly coiled position in the inadequately proportioned airline seat, I think to myself, "Yes, that should do it . . . that's a comfortable position . . . five minutes of that and I should be right off."

Of course it is only a matter of seconds before a slight ache develops somewhere in the body and you realize that this posture isn't the gateway to uninterrupted slumber that you had hoped.

I'm not a light sleeper and have no problems in this department normally. In fact I'm good at sleeping. I sleep well. I make hardly any mistakes. If there was an Olympic event called "sleeping," I would have a good chance of being selected for the British team. Actually, I think they should introduce "sleeping" to the Olympics.

It would be an excellent field event, in which the "athletes" (for want of a better word) all lay down in beds, just beyond where the javelins land, and the first one to fall asleep and not wake up for three hours would win gold. I, for one, would be interested in seeing what kind of personality would be suited to sleeping in a competitive environment. And what a prospect—a commentator becoming excited at a competitor "nearly nodding off," or expressing disappointment at the young British lad tragically being woken by a starter's pistol, when only another five minutes in the land of nod would have won him a bronze. (And who would want to miss the slow-motion action replays?)

I looked at my watch. It was 1:30. It wasn't as if I hadn't been close to falling asleep. It had nearly happened twice. On each occasion my drift toward this peaceful state had been disturbed by a small explosion. This was the hostel's central heating system which had been spitefully designed to fire up every forty minutes. The intervals between explosions afforded enough time for one to get extremely sleepy, but not sufficiently so to avoid an abrupt awakening at the next outburst from the hostel's boilers.

At 2:00 a.m., most of those who had been lucky enough to relinquish consciousness had it restored by the noisy return of the occupant of the bunk below me. Telltale signs such as belching and singing, suggested that this man, when faced with a straight choice of what to do with his evening, hadn't gone for the healthy option. It wasn't escaping my notice that this man had made the correct decision for this situation, for as soon as he had completed a blundering and noisy shedding of his clothes, his head hit the pillow and he began snoring. Well, not quite. He was *almost* snoring. The deep breaths were there, and the accompanying snorting sounds were there, too, but only at a faint volume. It was clear this man had the potential to snore very loudly, but that this was something he preferred to warm up to. It was vital to fall asleep *before* he reached his full volume.

I failed in this regard, and one hour later he had worked his way up to a level of snoring which would have won him medals in the European Championships. All the evidence was there to suggest that in another quarter of an hour he would reach his peak, and produce snores which would rival some of the best in the world. I was alone in my concern because I could tell from the clearly audible breathing patterns of the others in the dormitory, that everyone had managed to fall asleep except me.

Being on the receiving end of snoring wasn't a new experience for me, but I had never experienced the sound coming from directly beneath me before. Somehow this made it considerably more disconcerting, and gave the distinct impression that some kind of geological upheaval was imminent. In the dead of night rational thinking vanishes, and although Ireland wasn't renowned for its earthquakes and volcanoes, at least two clamorous rumbles from beneath my bunk made me sit bolt upright in fear.

I'm against the death penalty. I believe that it is a mistake to show that killing people is wrong, by killing people. However, I'm not against the random killing of people who snore. Okay, I accept that it is harsh, barbaric, and against every decent human value, but the simple fact is that there is no other cure for snoring. People have tried myriad remedies, and none of them work. All right, you can wake them, but they're only going to fall back to sleep again and begin all over. The only truly effective way to stop someone snoring is to kill them.

I lay in my bunk considering my options. Suffocation seemed the most appropriate, but strangling I liked also. My feeling was that there wasn't a court of justice anywhere which would not be sympathetic to the mitigating circumstances of my present plight. But then, quite suddenly, he stopped. He just stopped snoring as if he had received news from a politician that a cease fire had been agreed. The silence was no comfort. I knew that this was only a temporary cessation of hostilities and that he would begin snoring again soon, so I was aware that this next period was crucial if I was going to fall asleep. I had to act now. I rolled onto my side, closed my eyes, and offered up my consciousness.

There were no takers. Evidently, mine wasn't a personality suited to sleeping under this kind of pressure. I had no place in the British Olympic sleeping team after all. It was one thing falling asleep in training, and another when you were up against the clock.

The night dragged on.

Here, in brief, are the other major events of the night:

3:30 a.m.	Drunk recommences snoring.
3:45 a.m.	Sympathy snorer on other side of dormitory starts up. (Stereo effect created.)
4:30 a.m.	Get up and go to toilet. Stub toe on corner of bunk.
4:33 a.m.	Return from toilet and stub same toe on different corner of bunk.
4:55 a.m.	Give serious consideration to shouting at the top of my voice, "LOOK EVERYONE, GET OUT OF MY ROOM!!"
5:05 a.m.	Consider suicide as an option.
5:07 a.m.	Reject suicide as an option on the grounds that it would be too noisy, and wake people up.
5:15 a.m.	Decide this night is penance for stealing Tina's lift. Give up, and resign myself to a night of no sleep.
5:16 a.m.	Fall asleep.
6:30 a.m.	Woken by Chinese-looking man's alarm clock going off.
6:31 a.m.	Decide killing is too good for Chinese-looking man. Will take contracts out on his loved ones.
8:00 a.m.	Decide to get up.
8:01 a.m.	Discover that I have an unnecessary and unwarranted erection.
8:01–8:30 a.m.	Wait for dormitory to empty.

8:32 a.m.	Dormitory almost empty. Risk getting up. Big Dutch lady sees unusual bulge in my boxers. She smiles.
8:40–9:10 a.m.	Breakfast, spent avoiding eye contact with big Dutch lady.
9:30 a.m.	Leave the premises, swearing never to stay in a hostel again, as long as I live.

The longest night was behind me.

3

Neither Here Nor There

Bill Bryson

The girl at my travel agency in Yorkshire, whose grasp of the geography of the world south of Leeds is a trifle hazy (I once asked her to book me an airplane ticket to Brussels and she phoned back ten minutes later to say, "Would that be the Brussels in Belgium, Mr. Bryson?"), had booked me into a hotel in the 742nd *arrondissement,* a charmless neighborhood somewhere on the outskirts of Calais. The hotel was opposite a spanking new sports complex, which had been built to look vaguely like a hill: It had short, cropped grass growing up its sides. Quite what the idea of this was I couldn't say because the walls sloped so sharply that you couldn't walk on the grass or sit on it, so it had no function. Its only real purpose was to enable the architect to say, "Look at this, everybody. I've designed a building with grass growing on it. Am I something?" This, as we shall see again, is the great failing of Paris architects.

The hotel was one of those sterile, modern places that always put me in mind of a hospital, but at least it didn't have the curious timer switches that used to be a feature of hotel hallways in France. These were a revelation to me when I first arrived from America. All the light switches in the hallways were timed to go off after ten or fifteen seconds, presumably as an economy measure. This wasn't so bad if your room was next to the elevator, but if it was very far down the hall, and hotel hallways in Paris tend to wander around like an old man with Alzheimer's, you would generally proceed the last furlong in total blackness, feeling your way along the walls with flattened palms, and invariably colliding scrotally with the corner of a nineteenth-century oak table put there, evidently, for that purpose. Occasionally, your groping fingers would alight on something soft and hairy, which you would recognize after a moment as another person, and if he or she spoke English, you could exchange tips.

You soon learned to have your key out and to sprint like hell for your room. The trouble was that when eventually you reemerged, it was to total blackness once more and to a complete and—mark this—*intentional* absence of light switches, and there was nothing to do but stumble straight-armed through the darkness, like Boris Karloff in *The Mummy*, and hope that you weren't about to blunder into a stairwell. And from this I learned one very important lesson: The French do not like us.

On my first trip to Paris, I kept wondering: "Why does everyone hate me so much?" Fresh off the train, I went to the tourist booth at the Gare du Nord, where a severe young woman in a blue uniform looked at me as if I were infectious. "What do *you* want?" she said, or at least seemed to say.

"I'd like a room, please," I replied, instantly meek.

"Fill this out." She pushed a long form at me. "Not here. Over there." She indicated with a flick of her head a counter for filling out forms, then turned to the next person in line and said: "What do *you* want?" I was amazed—I came from a place where *everyone* was friendly, where even funeral home directors told you to have a nice day as you left to bury your grandmother—but I soon learned that everyone in Paris was like that. You would go into a bakery and be greeted by some vast sluglike creature with a look that told you you would never be friends. In halting French you would ask

28

for a small loaf of bread. The woman would give you a long, cold stare and then put a dead beaver on the counter.

"No, no," you would say, hands aflutter, "not a dead beaver. A loaf of *bread*."

The sluglike creature would stare at you in patent disbelief, then turn to the other customers and address them in French at much too high a speed for you to follow, but the drift of which clearly was that this person here, this *American tourist*, had come in and asked for a dead beaver and she had given him a dead beaver and now he was saying that he didn't want a dead beaver at all, he wanted a loaf of bread. The other customers would look at you as if you had just tried to fart in their handbags, and you would have no choice but to slink away and console yourself with the thought that in another four days you would be in Brussels and probably able to eat again.

The other thing I have never understood about the French is why they are so ungrateful. I've always felt that since it was us that liberated them—because let's face it, the French Army couldn't beat a girls' hockey team—they ought to give all Allied visitors to the country a book of coupons good for free drinks in Pigalle and a ride to the top of the Eiffel Tower. But they never thank you. I have had Belgians and Dutch people hug me around the knees and let me drag them down the street in gratitude to me for liberating their country, even after I have pointed out to them that I wasn't even sperm in 1945, but this is not an experience that is ever likely to happen to anyone in France.

In the evening I strolled the eighteen miles to the Île de la Cité and Notre-Dame, through the sort of neighborhoods where swarthy men in striped Breton shirts lean on lampposts cleaning their teeth with switchblades and spit between your legs as you pass. But it was a lovely March evening, with just the faintest tang of spring in the air, and once I stumbled onto the Seine, at the Pont de Sully, I was met with perfection. There facing me was the Île St.-Louis, glowing softly and floating on the river like a vision, a medieval hamlet magically preserved in the midst of a modern city. I crossed the bridge and wandered up and down its half dozen shuttered streets, half expecting to find chickens wandering in the road and peasants pushing carts loaded with plague victims, but what I found instead were tiny, swish restaurants and appealing apartments in old buildings.

Hardly anyone was about—a few dawdling customers in the restaurants, a pair of teenaged lovers tonguing each other's uvulas in a doorway, a woman in a fur coat encouraging a poodle to leave *un doodoo* on the pavement. The windows of upstairs apartments were pools of warm light and from the street gave tantalizing glimpses of walls lined with books and windowsills overflowing with pot plants and decorative antiques. It must be wonderful to live on such streets on such an island and to gaze out on such a river. The very luckiest live at the western end, where the streets are busier but the windows overlook Notre-Dame. I cannot imagine tiring of that view, though I suppose in August, when the streets are clogged with tour buses and a million tourists in Bermuda shorts that SHOUT, the sense of favored ecstasy may flag.

Even now the streets around the cathedral teemed. It was eight o'clock, but the souvenir shops were still open and doing a brisk trade. I made an unhurried circuit of Notre-Dame and draped myself over a railing by the Seine and watched the *bateaux-mouches* slide by, trimmed with neon, like floating jukeboxes. It was hopelessly romantic.

I dined modestly in a half-empty restaurant on a side street and afterward, accompanied by small burps, wandered across the river to Shakespeare & Co., a wonderfully gloomy English-language bookstore full of cobwebs and musty smells and old forgotten novels by writers like Warwick Deeping. Plump chairs and sagging sofas were scattered about the rooms and on each a young person in intellectual-looking glasses was curled up reading one of the proprietor's books, evidently from cover to cover (I saw one owlish young man turn down the corner of a page and replace the book on its shelf before scowling at me and departing into the night). The bookstore had an engagingly clubby atmosphere, but how it stays in business I have no idea. Not only was the guy at the till conspicuously underemployed—only at the most considerable of intervals did he have to stir from his own book to transact a small sale—but the store's location, on the banks of the Seine in the very shadow of Notre-Dame, must surely push its rent into the stratosphere.

Anywhere else in the world Shakespeare & Co. would be a souvenir emporium, selling die-cast models of the cathedral, Quasimodo ashtrays, slide strips, postcards, and Ooh-La-La T-shirts, or else one of those high-speed cafés where the waiters dash around frantically, leave you waiting forty minutes before taking your order, and then make it clear that you have twenty-five seconds to drink your coffee, eat your rum baba, and clear off, and don't even *think* about asking for a glass of water if you don't want spit in it. How it has managed to escape this dismal fate is a miracle, but it left me in the right admiring frame of mind, as I wandered back to my hotel through the dark streets, to think that Paris was a very fine place indeed.

In the morning I got up early and went for a long walk through the sleeping streets. I love to watch cities wake up and Paris wakes up more abruptly, more startlingly, than any place I know. One minute you have the city to yourself. It's just you and a guy delivering crates of bread, and a couple of droning street-cleaning machines. (It might be worth noting here that Paris spends a hundred dollars a year per head on street cleaning compared with thirty dollars per head in London, which explains why Paris gleams and London is a toilet.) Then all at once it's frantic: cars and buses swishing past in sudden abundance, cafés and kiosks opening, people flying out of

the Métro stations like flocks of startled birds, movement everywhere, thousands and thousands of pairs of hurrying legs.

By eight-thirty Paris is a terrible place for walking. There's too
much traffic. A blue haze of uncombusted diesel hangs over every
boulevard. I know Baron Haussmann made Paris a grand place to
look at, but the man had no concept of traffic flow. At the Arc de
Triomphe alone, thirteen roads come together. Can you imagine?
I mean to say, here you have a city with the world's most patho-
logically aggressive drivers—drivers who in other circumstances
would be given injections of Valium from syringes the sizes of bicycle pumps and confined to their beds with leather straps—and
you give them an open space where they can all try to go in any of
thirteen directions at once. Is that asking for trouble or what?

It is interesting to note that the French have had this reputation
for bad driving since long before the invention of the internal com-
bustion engine. Even in the eighteenth century, British travelers
to Paris were remarking on what lunatic drivers the French were,
on "the astonishing speed with which the carriages and people
moved through the streets. . . . It was not an uncommon sight to
see a child run over and probably killed." I quote from Christopher
Hibbert's *Grand Tour,* a book whose great virtue is in pointing out
that the peoples of Europe have for at least three hundred years
been living up to their stereotypes. As long ago as the sixteenth
century, travelers were describing the Italians as voluble, unreliable,
and hopelessly corrupt; the Germans as gluttonous; the Swiss as
irritatingly officious and tidy; the French as, well, insufferably
French.

You also constantly keep coming up against these monumental
squares and open spaces that are all but impossible to cross on foot.
My wife and I, still mere children, went to Paris on our honeymoon
and foolishly tried to cross the Place de la Concorde without first
leaving our names at the embassy. Somehow she managed to get
to the obelisk in the center, but I was stranded in the midst of a

Circus Maximus of killer automobiles, waving weakly to my dear spouse of two days and whimpering softly, while hundreds and hundreds of little buff-colored Renaults were bearing down on me with their drivers all wearing expressions like Jack Nicholson in *Batman*.

It still happens. At the Place de la Bastille, a vast open space dominated on its northeastern side by the glossy new Paris Opera House, I spent three quarters of an hour trying to get from the Rue de Lyon to the Rue de St. Antoine. The problem is that the pedestrian crossing lights have been designed with the clear purpose of leaving the foreign visitor confused, humiliated, and, if all goes according to plan, dead.

This is what happens: You arrive at a square to find all the traffic stopped, but the pedestrian light is red and you know that if you venture so much as a foot off the curb all the cars will surge forward and turn you into a gooey crepe. So you wait. After a minute, a blind person comes along and crosses the great cobbled plain without hesitating. Then a ninety-year-old lady in a motorized wheelchair trundles past and wobbles across the cobbles to the other side of the square a quarter of a mile away.

You are uncomfortably aware that all the drivers within fifty yards are sitting with moistened lips watching you expectantly, so you pretend that you don't really want to cross the street at all, that actually you've come over here to look at this interesting *fin de siècle* lamppost. After another minute, 150 preschool children are herded across by their teachers, and then the blind man returns from the other direction with two bags of shopping. Finally, the pedestrian light turns green, and you step off the curb and all the cars come charging at you. And I don't care how paranoid and irrational this sounds; I know for a fact that the people of Paris want me dead.

Eventually, I gave up trying to cross streets in any kind of methodical way and instead just followed whatever route looked least threatening. So it was with some difficulty and not a little surprise that I managed to pick my way by early afternoon to the Louvre, where I found a long, immobile line curled around the entrance courtyard like an abandoned garden hose.

I hovered, undecided whether to join the line, come back later in the faint hope that it would have shrunk, or act like a Frenchman and just jump it. The French were remarkably shameless about this. Every few minutes one would approach the front of the line, pretend to look at his wristwatch, then duck under the barrier and disappear through the door with the people at the front. No one protested, which surprised me. In New York, from where many of these people came, judging by their accents and the bullet holes in their trench coats, the line jumpers would have been seized by the crowd and had their limbs torn from their sockets. Even in London the miscreants would have received a vicious rebuke: "I say, kindly take your place at the back of the line, there's a good fellow"—but here there was not a peep of protest.

I couldn't bring myself to jump the line, but equally I couldn't stand among so much motionless humanity while others were flouting the rule of order and getting away with it. So I passed on, and was rather relieved. The last time I went to the Louvre, in 1972 with Katz, it was swarming with visitors and impossible to see anything. The "Mona Lisa" was like a postage stamp viewed through a crowd of heads from another building, and clearly things had not improved since then.

Besides, there was only one painting I especially wanted to see and that was a remarkable eighteenth-century work, evidently unnoticed by any visitor but me for two hundred years among the Louvre's endless corridors. I almost walked past it myself, but something nicked the edge of my gaze and made me turn. It was a painting of two aristocratic ladies, young and not terribly attractive, standing side by side and wearing nothing at all but their jewels and sly smiles. And here's the thing: One of them had her finger plugged casually—one might almost say absentmindedly—into the other's fundament. I can say with some certainty that this was an activity quite unknown in Iowa, even among the wealthy and well traveled, so I went straight off to find Katz, who had cried in dismay fifteen minutes after entering the Louvre, "There's nothing but pictures and shit in this place," and departed moodily for the coffee shop, saying he would wait there for me for thirty minutes and no more. I found him sitting with a Coke, complaining bitterly that he had had to pay two francs for it *and* give a handful of centimes to an old crone for the privilege of peeing in the men's room ("And she watched me the whole time").

"Never mind about that," I said. "You've got to come and see this painting."

"What for?"

"It's very special."

"Why?"

"It just is, believe me. You'll be thanking me in a minute."

"What's so special about it?"

I told him. He refused to believe it. No such picture had ever been painted, and if it had been painted, it wouldn't be hanging in a public gallery. But he came. And the problem was, I couldn't for the life of me find it again. Katz was convinced it was just a cruel joke, designed to waste his time and deprive him of the last two ounces of his Coke, and he spent the rest of the day in a tetchy frame of mind.

Katz was in a tetchy frame of mind throughout most of our stay in Paris. He was convinced everything was out to get him. On the morning of our second day, we were strolling down the Champs-Elysées when a bird shit on his head. "Did you know," I asked a block or two later, "that a bird's shit on your head?"

Instinctively, Katz put a hand to his head, looked at it in horror, and with only a mumbled "Wait here," walked with ramrod stiffness in the direction of our hotel. When he reappeared twenty minutes later, he smelled overpoweringly of Brut aftershave and his hair was plastered down like a third-rate Spanish gigolo's, but he appeared to have regained his composure. "I'm ready now," he announced.

Almost immediately another bird shit on his head. Only this time it *really* shit. I don't want to get too graphic, in case you're snacking or anything, but if you can imagine a pot of yogurt upended onto his scalp, I think you'll get the picture. It was running down the sides of his head and everything. "Gosh, Steve, that was one sick bird," I observed helpfully.

Katz was literally speechless. Without a word he turned and walked stiffly back to the hotel, ignoring the turning heads of passersby. He was gone for nearly an hour. When at last he returned, he was wearing a poncho with the hood up. "Just don't say a word," he warned me and strode past. He never really warmed to Paris after that.

With the Louvre packed, I went to the new—new to me, at any rate—Musée d'Orsay, on the Left Bank opposite the Tuileries. When I had last passed it, sixteen years earlier, it had been a derelict hulk, the shell of the old Gare d'Orsay, but some person of vision had decided to restore the old station as a museum, and it is simply wonderful, both as a building and as a collection of pictures. I spent two happy hours there, and afterward checked out the situation at the Louvre—still hopelessly crowded—and went instead to the Pompidou Center, which I was determined to try to like, but I couldn't. Everything about it seemed wrong. For one thing, it was a bit weathered and faded, like a child's toy that has been left out over winter, which surprised me because it is only a dozen years old and the government had just spent $75 million refurbishing it, but I guess that's what you get when you build with plastic. And it seemed much too overbearing a structure for its cramped neighborhood. It would be an altogether different building in a park.

But what I really dislike about buildings like the Pompidou Center, and Paris is choking on them, is that they are just showing off. Here's Richard Rogers saying to the world: "Look, I put all the pipes on the *outside*. Am I cute enough to kiss or *what?*" I could excuse that if some consideration were given to function. But no one seems to have thought what the Pompidou Center should do—be a gathering place, a haven—because inside it is just crowded and confusing. The center has none of the sense of space and light and majestic calm of the Musée d'Orsay. It's like a department store on the first day of a big sale. There's hardly any place to sit and no focal point—no big clock or anything—at which to meet someone. It has no heart.

Outside things are no better. The main plaza on the Rue St. Martin is in the shade during the best part of the day and it is built on a slope, so it's dark and the rain never dries and again there's no place to sit. If they had made the slope into a kind of amphitheater, people could sit on the steps, but now if you sit down you feel as if you are going to slide to the bottom.

I have nothing against novelty in buildings—I am quite taken with the glass pyramid at the Louvre and those buildings at La Défense that have the huge holes in the middle—but I just hate the way architects, city planners, and everyone else responsible for urban life seem to have lost sight of what cities are for. They are for people. That is obvious enough, but for half a century we have been building cities that are designed for almost anything else: for cars, for businesses, for developers, for people with money and bold visions who refuse to see cities from ground level, as places in which people must live and function and get around. Why should I have to walk through a damp tunnel and negotiate two sets of stairs to get across a busy street? Why should cars be given priority over me? How can we be so rich and so stupid at the same time? It is the curse of our century—too much money, too little sense—and the Pompidou Center seems to be a kind of celebration of that in plastic.

* * *

One evening I walked over to the Place de la République and had a nostalgic dinner at a bistro called Le Thermomètre. My wife and I spent our honeymoon in the Hôtel Moderne across the way (now a Holiday Inn, alas, alas) and dined nightly at the Thermomètre because it was cheap and we had next to no money. I had spent the whole of my savings, some eighteen pounds, on a suit for the wedding—a remarkable piece of apparel with lapels that had been modeled on the tail fins of a 1957 Coupe de Ville and bell-bottom pants so copiously flared that when I walked, you didn't see my legs move—and had to borrow twelve pounds spending money from my father-in-law in order, as I pointed out, to keep his daughter from starving during her first week of married life.

I expected the Thermomètre to be full of happy memories, but I couldn't remember anything about it at all except that it had the fiercest toilet attendant in Paris, a woman who looked like a Russian wrestler (a male Russian wrestler) and who sat at a table in the basement with a pink dish full of small coins and craned her head to watch you to make sure you didn't dribble on the tiles or pocket any of the urinal cakes. It is hard enough to pee when you are aware that someone's eyes are on you, but when you fear that at any moment you will be felled by a rabbit chop to the kidneys for taking too much time, you seize up altogether. You couldn't have cleared my system with Drāno. So eventually I would zip up and return unrelieved to the table, and spend the night back at the hotel doing a series of Niagara Falls impressions. This time around, I'm pleased to say, the toilet attendant was no longer there; there actually was none at all. But just the same, I didn't take any urinal cakes.

It took me two or three days to notice it, but the people of Paris had become polite over the last twenty years. They didn't exactly rush up and embrace you and thank you for winning the war for them, but they bad certainly become more patient and accommodating. The cab drivers were still complete jerks, but everyone else—shopkeepers, waiters, the police—seemed almost friendly. I even saw a waiter smile once. And somebody held open a door for me instead of letting it bang in my face.

It began to unsettle me. Then on my last night, as I was strolling near the Seine, a well-dressed family of two adults and two teen-aged children swept past me on the narrow sidewalk and, without breaking stride or interrupting their animated conversation, flicked me into the gutter. I could have hugged them.

They still haven't got the hang of lining up in Paris. I had forgotten about this until the morning of my departure when I trudged through a gray rain to the Gare de Lyon to get a cab to the Gare du Nord and a train to Brussels. Because of the rain, there were no cabs, so I stood and waited. For five minutes I was the only person there, but gradually other people came along and took places behind me.

When at last a cab arrived and pulled up directly in front of me, I was astonished to discover that seventeen grown men and women believed they had a perfect right to try to get in ahead of me. A middle-aged man in a cashmere coat who was obviously wealthy and well-educated actually laid hands on me. I maintained possession by making a series of aggrieved Gallic honking noises—"Mais, non! Mais, non!"—and using my bulk to block the door. I leaped in, resisting the chance to catch the pushy man's tie in the door and let him trot along with us to the Gate du Nord, and told the driver to get me the hell out of there. He looked at me as if I were a large, imperfectly formed turd, and with a disgusted sigh engaged first gear. I was glad to see some things never change.

4

Falling Off the Map

Pico Iyer

Another cheerful day in Cuba. I wake up in the Hotel Pernik in Holguín and get into an elevator to go to breakfast. The elevator groans down a few feet, then stops. I press a button. The button falls off. I ring a bell. There is silence. I kick the door. The elevator groans up to the floor just left. Outside, I can hear excited cries. *"Mira!" "Dime!" "El jefe!"* A little later, the doors open, just a crack, and I see a bright-yellow head, and then a black face with a beard. "Don't worry," the face assures me. "You cannot move." The doors clang shut again, and I hear a crowd gathering outside, more "Pssts" and cries. Every now and then, the doors open up a few inches and a new face peers in to wave at me and smile. Then I hear a voice of authority, and as a chain gang of men strains to push open the doors, a teenager gets up on a stepladder and, methodically, starts to unscrew the whole contraption.

Twenty-five minutes later, I am released upon the Pernik dining room. My British guidebook, not generally bullish on things Cuban, waxes rhapsodic about the hotel's fare. "Eat and drink extremely well," it says. The Pernik, it adds, has "a long and appetizing menu featuring steak in many forms, good fish and chicken, and fresh fruit and vegetables—even including avocado." Not today, it seems. "What would you like?" a smiling waitress asks. "What do you have?" "Nothing." "No eggs, no tea, no avocado?" "Nothing. Only beer." At the next table, a waitress is prizing open a bottle top with a spoon. The "typically cavernous Eastern European dining hall" is full of happy diners this morning, but not, it seems, of food.

Outside, my school friend Louis and I run into a woman from Aruba who is here to find her grandmother. The grandmother, unfortunately, is lost, but the Aruban has decided in the meantime to smuggle out a '56 Chevy. "Here the people have no salt, no sugar, only one piece of bread a day," she informs us as she gets into our car, "but this is a paradise compared with Aruba." Where are we from? England. "Ah," she sighs, "like Margaret Snatcher, the crime minister," Louis, a Thatcher devotee, accelerates. We drop her off at the airport and head for Santiago. Only four hours as the Nissan flies.

Driving along the one-lane roads, past sunlit fields of sugarcane, we pass billboards honoring the great revolutionary heroes (Martí, Guevara, O'Higgins), signs declaring SPEED IS THE ALLY OF DEATH, lonely ceiba trees, and goat-drawn carts. Flying Pigeon bicycles are everywhere, and vintage Plymouths, and hissing, rusted buses. Sometimes we stop to pick up hitchhikers, and Louis serenades them with passages from *The Waste Land,* ditties from the Grateful Dead, and—his latest attraction—manically pantomimed scenes from *The Jerk.* Bicycles, chickens, children swarm and swerve across the roads. I remember the time in Morocco when, on our way to the airport, he hit a dog. The dog bounded off unhindered; our Citroën limped to a halt.

Then, suddenly, out of nowhere, a bicycle swerves in front of us, there is a sickening thud, and our windshield shatters, splattering us with glass. I cannot bear to get out to see what has happened. But somehow, miraculously, the boy on the bicycle has been thrown out of the path of the car and gets up, only shaken.

A crowd forms, and, a few minutes later, a policeman appears. "We're so sorry," I tell him. "If there's anything we can do. . . ."

"No problem," he says, patting me on the shoulder. "Don't worry. These things happen. We're sorry if this has spoiled your holiday in Cuba."

Spoiled our holiday? We've almost spoiled the poor boy's life!

"Don't worry," he assures me with a smile. "There is just some paperwork. Then you can go on."

A car comes up, and two more imposing cops get out. They take some notes, then barrel up towards us. "These boys," says one. "No, no. It was entirely our fault." "These young boys," he goes on. "You will just have to fill out some forms, and then you can be on your way."

Soon we are taken to a hospital, where a young nurse hits me on the wrist. Then she asks me to extend my arms, to touch my nose, to touch my nose with my eyes closed. Luckily, it is a big target: I pass with flying colors.

Then we are taken to the local police station, a bare, pink-walled shack in the town's main plaza. Inside, a few locals are diligently observing a solitary sign which requests them to SPEAK IN A LOUD VOICE.

Across from us sits our hapless victim, next to a middle-aged man. Sizing up the situation, we go over to him. "Look, we can't apologize enough for what we did to your son. It was all our fault. If there is any. . . ."

"No, no, my friends." He smiles. "Is nothing. Please enjoy your time in Cuba." Louis, overwhelmed, presents the family with a box of Dundee Shortbread, purchased, for just such occasions, at the Heathrow Duty-Free Lounge. A festive air breaks out.

Then we are ushered into an inner office. A black man motions me to sit before his desk and hand him my passport. "So, Señor Pico." "My surname, actually, is Iyer." "So your father's name is Pico." "No, my father's name is Iyer." "But here it says Iyer, Pico." "Yes. My family's name is Iyer." "So your mother's name is Pico."

"No. My father's name is Iyer." "So your mother's name is. . . ." This goes on for a while, and then a baby-faced cop with an Irish look comes in. He claps a hand on Louis's shoulder. Where are we from? England. "No wonder he looks like Margaret Thatcher," he exclaims, and there is more jollity all around. Then he leans forward again. "But you are from India, no?" Yes. "Then tell me something." His face is all earnest inquiry. "Rajiv Gandhi is the son of Indira Gandhi?" Yes. "And the grandson of the other Gandhi?" "No. He is the grandson of Nehru. No relation to the other Gandhi." "No relation, eh? Not a grandson of the other Gandhi?" The Irishman shakes his head in wonder, and the black man sits back to take this thunderbolt in. Then he resumes typing out his report six times over, without benefit of carbons.

Finally, he turns to Louis. "So your family name is Louis," he begins. "No, no," I break in, and add, "he cannot speak Spanish." There is a hasty consultation. Then the Irishman pads off, only to return a few minutes later with a trim, round-faced boss with glasses and a tie. "*Guten Tag*," cries the police chief, extending a hand toward me. "No, no," I say. "It's him." The police chief spins around. "*Guten Tag*," he cries, greeting Louis like a long-lost friend and proceeding to reminisce about a "*Freundin*" he once knew in Leipzig. Things are going swimmingly now. "Margaret Thatcher, very sexy woman!" exclaims the Irishman. "Rajiv Gandhi is not the grandson of the other Gandhi," explains the black man to a newcomer. "*Aber, diese Mädchen.* . . ." the police chief reminisces. We could almost be at a Christmas dinner, so full of smiles and clapped shoulders is the room. "If this were anywhere else," Louis whispers, "if this were England, in fact, and a foreigner hit a local boy, they'd probably be lynching him by now."

At six o'clock—it is clear that the police plan to make a day of it—the police chief invites us to dinner at the town's only hotel. Guests of the police, he says. We sit down, and Louis spots a glass of beer. He orders one, and drinks it. Then another. Then another.

The chief orders more beers all round, then proposes a toast to *Die Freundschaft*. The waitress drops off a few beers. "She worked in Czechoslovakia for four years," the chief proudly informs us. "How is the weather now in Prague?" Louis asks her in Czech. "I worked for four years in a Trabant factory," she answers. The police chief, exultant, proposes more toasts to *Die Freundschaft*.

"Paraguay is the only place in the world where you win at blackjack even if you're only even with the bank," offers Louis.

"*Gut, gut, sehr gut!*" cries the chief, more animated than ever.

We renew a few pledges to eternal friendship, then get up and return to the police station, which is sleepy now in the dark.

Louis sits down and promptly slumps over. A group of policemen gathers round him to peer at his handless watch.

Then, suddenly, he sits up. "I'm feeling really terrible," he announces and, lurching out to the terrace, proceeds to deposit some toasts to *Die Freundschaft* in the bushes.

The police chief, anxious, comes over. "I'm sorry," I explain. "We haven't eaten properly for a few days, we were somewhat dehydrated already, and he's probably anyway in a state of shock." With a look of infinite tenderness, the chief summons a lieutenant, and, one on either side of Louis, they take him to the hospital.

Ten minutes later, the team returns, all smiles.

"How are you feeling?"

"Great. All better now."

"Good."

Louis slumps over again, and I maintain our vigil for the man from the car rental firm who is due to take us to Santiago. He was expected at two-thirty. It is now nine-fifteen.

Suddenly, a policeman walks into the room and summons me urgently over. I hurry to his side. Maybe he will give us a lift? "You are an Indian?" he says.

"Yes."

"Then tell me something." He points to a TV. "Two months ago, we saw Rajiv Gandhi being burned. Why did they not put his body in the ground?"

What is the Spanish word for "cremation"? I wonder wildly. *"Cremación,"* I try.

"Cremation, eh? Is that right? Thank you," he says, and walks out.

A little later, Louis gets up again and staggers to the terrace. More toasts to *Die Freundschaft* go down the drain.

"I'm really sick," he says. "I can't move. Just get me a bed."

I relay the request to the police chief.

For the first time all day, his commitment to our friendship seems to flag. *"Hier gibt es kein Bett!"* he barks. *"Das ist nicht Hotel! Das ist nicht Krankenhaus!"*

"Jawohl, mein Herr," I say, and we go on waiting for the car rental man.

Suddenly, headlights sweep into the plaza, and a car pulls up. I hurry outside. A man gets out, with an air of great briskness, and I hurry over to him. "So you are Indian?" he says. "Yes." "Then tell me something, please. When Rajiv Gandhi died, why did they not put his body in the ground?"

"Cremation," I reply with tired fluency, and, satisfied, he gets in his car and drives away.

Watching this open-air university in action, the police chief is shamed, perhaps, by his earlier brusqueness. "Once," he tells me in German, "I traveled for six hours by train to Dresden to meet my roommate's sister."

"Ach ja?"

At 11:15 p.m., the car rental man appears, and we return to the inner office to do some paperwork. "So—your name is Pico?" "Well, my family name is Iyer." "So your father's name is Pico." "No. . . ."

At 1:15 a.m., we pull up at last in front of the Casagranda Hotel in Santiago ("simultaneously dirty and suffocating," sings my guidebook), a famous old joint recently closed for fumigation, where we have a four-day reservation, paid for in advance in London. I leave

Louis comatose in the back of our new car, sundry revelers singing and banging drums around him in the street. Inside the hotel, an enormous man is sitting next to a wooden cash register. When he sees my voucher, he looks unhappy. Party girls in backless dresses and well-coiffed boys stroll down the pitch-black staircase from the rooftop cabaret. A couple of them sit on a couch in the lobby and gaze expectantly in my direction. The enormous man looks desperate. I look worse. He picks up a telephone and starts dialing.

Thirty minutes later, he has found us alternative accommodations. At 2:15 a.m., a convoy of two cars, including one spokesman for the house of Gandhi, one new rental car, and one immobile investment banker, pulls up at the Hotel Gaviota. As soon as it does, a young boy rushes out. "Welcome," he cries, in English. "How was your trip? Welcome to the Hotel Gaviota! It's great to see you!"

"Thanks."

"We have some Welcome Cocktails all ready for you! What will it be? A cuba libre? A daiquiri? Some *ron?* What would you like?"

"My friend cannot move."

"No problem. A Welcome Cocktail will help. It's on the house!"

"But he's already heard Margaret Thatcher impugned, almost killed a boy, and been taken to a hospital by a police chief speaking German."

"Sure!" says the boy. "That's why he needs a Welcome Cocktail. Please! My friends are waiting!" He points to the bar, where two young bloods are sitting hopefully in the dark.

I go over to Louis, now propped up in the lobby, and break the news to him.

He does not look overjoyed.

"The thing is, unless you order a Welcome Cocktail, I don't think you'll get a room."

"Okay, okay, just get me some mineral water." Realizing that this could entail a long wait—yesterday we had stopped in a small town to ask two boys for water and been told, "For water you must go to the next town! Only forty-five kilometers away!"—I go to the desk to do some paperwork. On one side is a sign that advises, CRAZY LOVE IS NOT TRUE LOVE. On the other, a stack of Cubatur brochures. *"Ven a vivir una tentación!"* Come to live out a temptation!

Proprieties observed, we follow our host on the ten-minute walk to our suites, made-for-mobster caverns from the fifties, with mirrors all round, and enormous makeup areas for showgirls.

"This is okay?" the young boy asks.

"Sure," I say. But one thing still bothers me: why doesn't he care about the fate of Rajiv Gandhi?

5

Around the World in a Bad Mood

John Krich

That last week in Nepal, we'd begun a contest to pick the most Easternized Westerner. Which meant the phoniest—and we had no trouble turning up qualified entrants. The saddest part of it was that those dollar-a-day Buddhaheads who were most sincere were also the most implausible. The kids who'd turned thoroughly Sherpa or Hindu or Han, from cloth-capped, hash-dizzied noggin to chappal-sandaled, road-powdered toes, were the kids who'd actually changed the least. While these blissful vagrants had tossed aside their competitive wits in scorn of European ambitions, Asia's edge-of-survival game had served to revive, even glorify, their baser instincts. A change of costume merely helped establish an Oriental *mise-en-scène* in which the Occidentals could act out whatever they liked, offend who they liked. Our contestants were wolves in monks' clothing.

So far, the candidate for top honors was a vision I'd stood beside in the Poste Restante line of the urine-scented Kathmandu "royal mail" office. Though the light was poor to nonexistent, I noticed that this youth was not satisfied with the usual Indian pajamas, but had dyed his velveteen vest and his cheesecloth bloomers a translucent pink. He'd even doused his curly hair with henna to color-coordinate his Little Bo Peep coif with his outfit. His shoes were gold-braided Sultan's slippers, with toes curled like flames and pointing up as he pranced. Both arms, and his neck, were a gallery, displaying one of the subcontinent's largest private collections of ivory bracelets, Shiva charms, and holy-eye pendants. Over his curls, he'd planted a lopsided shepherd's skull cap, also pinkish. As a finishing touch, he clutched a full-length Biblical staff, which he rocked like a baton while he chanted, *"Shanti, shanti"* until I began to suspect this was the name by which he was getting his letters from home.

The pink prancer had nearly been matched by the lost Christian Iris had spied one morning doing his ablutions with outcasts in the sunken pit of a Nepalese public bath. How pale he looked beside his fellow scrubbers, how much more of him there was to scrub, stripped to his loincloth! And so raw and newborn, so foolishly pure, amidst the blackened spigots and sandstone statuettes! What could these people, and their sculpted deities, have made of his grappling with toothpaste and Prell shampoo?

Returning to India, we would soon find more entrants thanks largely to the Indian border patrol. Awaiting the midnight shuttle from the Nepalese border to the Indian plains along with a medium-sized village that slept, ate, and presumably multiplied in the shelter of our first Indian railway platform, Iris and I were girding ourselves against the scramble for seats that was the station house populace's recurrent form of uprising. Just as the train arrived, pulled by a steam engine, we were beckoned by a single, hyper-skinny constable. He was truly a figure out of Gilbert and Sullivan, shrunken inside an outlandish sailor's suit, pointing at us with his umbrella. He plucked foreigners off the platform like a garbage-picker plucks old paper in the park.

"You will follow on after me, please!"

"But we've got to get on this thing. . . ." Already, as the train slowed, whole families were catapulting through the windows of the second-class carriages. And we'd fought through three swarming queues just to get our tickets!

"Yes, yes . . . have no concern." We were led, against the human tide, toward the front of the train. The policeman, or whatever he was, deposited us in an empty, European-style compartment with two wooden benches facing barred windows. I was sure this had to be some sort of rolling pokey, and Iris bridled at being segregated from all that folklore in the other cars. But we were just the first victims of the round-up. In order of appearance, came a shaggy blond Dutchman in homespun vest and blue jeans; a swollen-eyed, big-hipped girl in overalls who turned out to be the daughter of the Mexican ambassador to somewhere; a New Zealander who puffed a corn-cob pipe and dressed like a Boy Scout; and a set of lanky twins, with red hair in pony tails and Irish brogues, outfitted entirely in the floppy white winding sheets favored by the inhabitants of the region. While the rest of us sat meekly on the benches, these yogic Dubliners spotted sagging nets above us and clambered up, quick as mountain lions. Using their knapsacks for pillows, they stretched out for a comfortable snooze.

"That's a smart way to use the luggage racks," Iris commented.

"Loo-gage racks?" sneered the louder of the twins. "These aren't loo-gage racks, Missy. These are the bogies. You know, the sleepers, me gal. That's all the Indian railways ever provide, unless you're a maharani. Good to bring along a bed roll, except you don't need one in this heat, do you?"

"No," I answered. "And you won't have much time to sleep."

"How's that?"

"We'll be changing trains." I was eager to spout the information that had taken me an hour to squeeze from an indifferent clerk. "From Raxaul transfer at Muzaffarpur, take the Evening Mail to Siliguri, transferring to Local for Siliguri Junction, transfer point for Rayna, transferring once again for Patna Junction, thence by steamer across the Ganges to Patna Central. . . ."

"Ay, the time-honored roundabout."

"It's labyrinthine," the second echoed with a whisper. "The ol' Minos and the Minotaur bit."

"Muzzy-froo-froo!" The Dutch hippie came out of his stupor. "I wouldn't take a bath in Muzzy-froo-froo!"

"But who was kind enough to make us these reservations?" the Irishman wanted to know.

"The porkie pies," his alter ego answered.

"Handy of them."

"But why us?"

"Don't ask why." The voice of the veteran.

Still, rumors were exchanged. Broken English was no obstacle.

"Maybe they isolate us. Like a cancer," said the Dutchman. "Like foreign matter."

"We've been kidnapped by a white slave ring!" suggested the Mexican number, who's name was Rita. "It's *muy* exciting!"

"No, no, dear child, they simply have orders to protect us," the New Zealander explained.

"They don't want us to lose our stashes," the hippie joked.

"Ay, that's it!" confirmed the spokesman twin. "We heard about robberies along this line. Lots of pickpockets, I heard tell. The tourist bureau's just keeping us out of harm's rather large way!"

This theory was confirmed by the officer when he rejoined us. But some doubts were left because he answered all questions with that characteristically Indian twist of the neck that meant yes and no at the same time. He was practiced at being noncommittal. With his bobby's demeanor and gold epaulets, he belonged in the River Thames Patrol. His eyebrows were massive, his skin the color of a rubber ball, and he was so wizened he looked as though he'd been stuffed, at birth, in a crawlspace between two tenements. However, when Indians frantically tested the heavy door to our berth, the officer shooed them away with a hummingbird's trill of Hindi and a general waving about of his closed umbrella.

Before the train pulled out, an hour late, he was joined by two stockier men gripping ancient wood-barreled rifles. Rejects from the Ghurkas, perhaps.

As the tracks curved, I could see hairy legs dangling through the windows of the cars behind us, plastic shoes slipping off, braceleted forearms snatching for air, corners of attaché cases. I was relieved not to be in that wriggling midst, but also disoriented. Unpopulated, unproblemed, what was Mother India anyhow? Just another plain to roam, another verse of "Happy Trails to You." But if we weren't part of the Indians' India, we were in another one that was just as genuine, that served as a great haven for cast-offs and scroungers, the India that was their vast stage.

The Dutch fellow beside me was an unabashed performer. The favored English words in his dialogue were "joint," "pipe," and "roach." They were his *raisons de voyager;* he was returning from Kathmandu well supplied. He kept pulling perfectly rolled, hash-dosed cigarettes from his vest pocket. He seemed completely oblivious of our armed escort, but it turned out he knew something we didn't. After passing the smoke around, he got up and presented a fresh one to the border patrol. The offer of "ganja" brought out their first crooked smiles. They smoked the joint like pros. When the first sergeant's rubber face cracked, all decorum vanished. His troop got the giggles.

Their tipsiness only added to the confusion of our many switch-overs. Each time, we replayed a worn melodrama. Suspense was provided by the fact that no one seemed to know where our next train was coming from. How many tracks did we have to hop in the middle of the steamy night? Was it right that the police chased Indians off the platform benches so we could sit there? Would the Indians notice if we refused to take their places? And would our escort be looking after us on the next train? Did we want them to? The wait was always longer than scheduled. The policemen would procure us our bench, disappear, return only after the next train had sat and shuddered awhile and we'd gotten prepared to pile into the dark caverns of cars. We would count the bodies sleeping in their wraparound dhoti sheets and surmise the train was already full-up. Then the police would usher us to another empty mail car near the locomotive. In the meantime, the Mexican girl would regale whoever would listen with an account of her many roadside liaisons.

"It was so hard to leave him there in Pokhara! Those nights on the mountainside, I'll never forget them! *Amor* Himalaya! *Mi querido!* We know each other too briefly, we are like the wind, no? . . . But it is good to be free also, like the wind."

"That's our credo all the way," said the brash twin.

"I am much woman!" Rita took her cannonball breasts in her cupped hands. "My boyfriend's waiting for me in Delhi, but you know what I say? 'While Juan's away, Rita will play!'"

"Have another hit of this," the Dutch boy encouraged. "It will make you shake hands with oblivion."

"Ay, it packs a karmic wallop!"

"Yummy! . . . I told myself, 'Rita, be strong. Don't cry. It's not worth it to shed another tear for a man in this lifetime, Rita.' I want to be reincarnated as a tree or a flower. Something pretty, but without sex! . . . There was this Italiano boy I suntan beside at Paradise Beach. That boy in Mykonos was the worst. He made Rita cry so much—and I only know him two days! Two days in the sun! We did not need clothes. We did not need words. This time, it was not so hard to go."

At each layover, the Irish partners busied themselves at the refreshment carts that soon surrounded our bench. A wobbling kerosene lamp lit a pan filled with month-old oil in which a bearded vendor kept various forms of rigid dough floating. The Indians went ape for these greasy turnovers. "Pure Ghee Products!" the signs in town always boasted. "Lovely Sweets! Most Fine in Bengal! Try Once, Return Forever! Sweets!"

"Mmmmm! Quite tasty, ay?" The Irishmen compared notes through the night. None of the rest of us dared touch anything so thrice-fried. "Remember the pun in Bombay? Ay, the South! That's where they really cook things up!"

"Yes, India's a goor-met treat, it is! It's a rolling banquet!" Apparently, changing trains every fifteen minutes was how they got to see the menu. "It's a goor-met treat for the four-star tourists and tchai-shop set alike!"

I preferred the approach of the New Zealander, who, between refilling his pipe, asked for sips from my iodine-dosed canteen. But I grew uneasy when he started in, "The Brits left the railways, all right, but they didn't bother telling the locals how to run it. . . ."

"It can't be all that hard." I'd learned that "locals" was just the postcolonialists' euphemism for "natives."

"No, but they've got a knack for complication," he mused, without having to say who "they" was. "This your first time on the subcontinent?"

"Yes. . . . But I've already been in Calcutta."

"Right. Nasty heap, that is. . . . Did you go and queue up for one of those student discounts?"

"Uh-huh. Took us all day."

"Ever seen so much paper stacked in one room, and so little being done about it? It's no surprise they don't have any to spare for wiping your arse."

I wasn't quite sure of his logic, but it was three in the morning.

"You'll be grateful to the Brits by the time you're through."

"How so?"

"At least, they built things. At least, they left something behind. Otherwise, what would there be?"

"Just Indians, I guess. And a few thousand temples."

"Yes, that's about it—if that's your cup of Darjeeling. Of course, there wouldn't be airfields, or railways, so I don't know how you'd get to see them."

I didn't know why he was here, a fifth column among the idolators, unless it was to tamp down his pipeful and feel superior. I didn't have time to find out, either, because our final baton pass of trains turned frenetic and sloppy. The umbrella man had his assistants round us up and follow him toward the front of our latest steam-drawn city. While we counted the boxloads of snoring bodies from the platform, the doleful sergeant moved through the darkened cars at the same pace as our chain-gang shuffle. He was doing a bedcheck, and soon called for the aid of our honor guard. They trotted through the pajama party, rifles at their sides. We waited obediently for their return, senses dulled, with nowhere in particular to escape. We watched them flush a newcomer out of the bogeys the way hunters flush out a pheasant.

"Vast is it?" This bird knew how to squawk. "Don't touch me, crazy *polizei!*"

Their prize catch was wrestled onto the platform, though neither he nor the Indians put much serious effort into the tussle. His name, we'd soon learn, was Rolf. He was a large-boned Swiss with fierce eyes and a stiff, unwashed shock of black hair. His lumberjack's build and swagger were particularly conspicuous beside his Munchkin captors. Though Rolf was dressed like a saddhu, the quilt of sewn handkerchiefs that made his pants and vest were stretched to bursting by his milk-fed frame. His clothes were but doilies atop a volcano. From the little else Rolf carried, it was obvious that these homespuns were his only set. They would no doubt be traded somewhere down the road for any new disguise that was appropriate to the local climate or religion. Tonight, he was a gunsel in angelic robes.

"Vat you do with me? You take me from good sleep, understand?" The Indian *carabinieri* first recoiled from Rolf, then attempted to bound him in with shrugging shoulders. "Ach, you vant to protect me, is dat it? From my dreams, ja? Ach, I vas sleeping good. When I go to toilet, I ask Indians to vatch my bags, ja? I been in India long time. Never got a thing took. Not even a cigarette, you hear?"

Whatever the time of night, Rolf wouldn't go quietly, like the rest of us, especially when he saw that he had an audience. Besides, he knew these patrolmen would gladly kick their fellow country-men about, but would never dare raise an umbrella against a European.

"Why you can't leave me alone? Why you not let me sleep? Dis is crazy, man. You know vat is crazy? Fucking policeman." Still, they nudged him in our direction. "Ach, come on now. You vant to be crazy, I let you. I go vit you, okay? Rolf is good boy, ja! . . . Only I never got a thing took. I don't got suspicion for Indians like you got! Ach! Come on!"

Any hopes I had of staking out a quiet spot for some shut-eye in our next cattle bin were dashed when Rolf met voluptuous Rita. They were a perfect match, with years of global gossip to exchange. It was hard to say which of them had been away from home longer, if they could be said to have a home. Rolf was conversant in every subject Rita raised: home remedies for malaria, the least crowded beaches in Goa, the best villages to score dope in Gilgat and Swat, the right price for a bottle of Johnny Walker Red in the black mar-kets of Rangoon. The *chica* in coveralls didn't mention any of her former lovers; perhaps she was thinking of Rolf as her next victim. But he wasn't looking for anyone or anything, just looking around. Rolf was complete. He had to be dependent on the world he'd left behind only when the pages for visas and customs stamps in his Swiss passport were filled. This was his one complaint in life.

"Cheap Swiss bastards don't give me enough fucking pages! Let me see yours. Ja! You see dat? Six more pages than me. And Ameri-cans get as many as they like. They know how to use the staples, man. It folds like an accordion! Now I'm running out again. Got to make a big scene at ze consulate. Othervise, go home again. Lucky I vent to Lumbini to cross border to Nepal." He'd detoured a hundred miles and several days' journey from the usual entry point. "Ja, I remember from the last time, the customs stamp it is smaller in Lumbini. I vas right! See dat? I save half a page, ja!" Lumbini was also Buddha's birthplace.

"You're *loco,* boy," Rita was batting her lashes. She preferred to talk about her latest case of "Delhi belly" and tease him with implications of how the ailments had restricted other activities in her lower region.

"Ach, I don't care!" And he didn't. "I eat anything! I trink everything! Hand it over, man!" Rolf's words were blown from his mouth. "I vas never sick. Just like I never got nothing took. If you are living amongst ze people, ja, zen vat can happen to you? Only vat happens to the people. Ach! I am happy."

He pronounced it "hoppy" and I believed him. Rolf was comfortable no matter where he was because he was an overgrown pup, a perennial child who saw the world with a child's easily replenished amazement. Despite his protests, he was tickled by the way he'd been pirated from his berth; it was one more delightfully illogical gambit. He bridled over the escort service only because he wanted back in the absurd playpen. "I travel every place. Never had no protection! I see everything. I need to eat and zen sleep. Othervise, I need nothing. Except ze fucking passport!"

Dawn was coming. Our last leg was also the shortest. We knew this route had run out of trains when the police stayed behind; after all that official coddling, they shoved us out through the window. But we hadn't reached the end of the line. To get there, we had to cross one formidable river and to do that, we had to let ourselves be carried along by a morning commuters' stampede. Down a well-trod gulley we all slid, toward an antique steamer with two decks and the same number of charred smokestacks. The quay was no more than a series of gangplanks that bowed under the hordes and didn't seem capable of holding them all. Rolf acted as leader of our pack, holding his walking stick in the air so we could keep near it, and clearing a path toward the ferry as though his free arm was a machete. Aboard, Rolf led us up a set of stairs that no one else seemed to be testing, then onto a covered upper deck, with glossy hardwood floors that made it look like a dancing pavilion. There were luscious, tasseled red armchairs placed generously about, just for us. With Rolf there, we thought nothing of falling into them. He didn't check his ticket, or care what sort of contraption was now conveying him. He found a local English-language newspaper on the galley by his lounger, as if left there by his valet, and started to declaim from it: "Yesterday forenoon Madame Home Secretary Sri Devi Nanu Ram addresses ze All-Bihar Women's Conference concerning ze governmental program aimed at smashing area-wide ignorance of birth control methods and vas received cheerily. . . ."

I had a perfect seat for my first look at the Ganges. It was being revealed in a murky, purple light. The surface was shallow and unbroken. The granulated water showed no current at all. Yet a single oarsman at the prow of a crushed slipper of a barge was working his way slowly, slowly against serious resistance. He was far up shore, nearly stilled, as I tracked his progress, mesmerized by the oar he drove through the river like a musician drawing a bow. No, the musical equivalent of the Mother Ganga and its navigators was not an instrument of pluck but of drone: the tamboura, harmonic ground of the ages. At the rate he was going, it would take the oarsman all day to move up the riverbank a thousand feet.

Somewhere near Patna, downstream, they were supposed to be building a bridge. Later, in New Delhi, I would be treated to a documentary film all about it. The work had begun with enthusiasm. Only the second human attempt to span the Ganges! Squadrons of barefoot women built up the pylons with buckets of mud. Slowly, so slowly. Gangs drove the supports into the shallows with well-timed heave-hos. Slowly, so slowly these human pile drivers worked. And where was the bridge now? I saw only long, low dunes of Himalayan silt. Slowly, slowly, said the Ganges. How dare I be bothered about having lost one short night's sleep?

Predictably, a team of conductors, or bo's'ns, came and asked for our claim stubs to the easy chairs. We were the only occupants of the first-class section and none of us had first-class tickets—only white skin and audacity. Again, Rolf was pried from his coziness. This time, he was not alone. We had to push our way toward the back of the ferry and find space on the aft deck. No armchairs here.

The old coal-burner started up. For over an hour, we drifted toward Patna. All that time, the tireless Scottish engine dumped its Victorian soot into the breeze and down onto the second-class passengers at the stern. The soot fell on the freshly starched kurtas and neatly kept account books of the spectacled clerks. It fell on the lavender rags of the beggars. It fell on the painted limbs of a family of naked pilgrims, interfering with the daily cleansing they effected through a shuffling of the few brass bowls and cups that were their only possessions. It fell on the Indians' seering, staring, scowling faces. The faces told me, "You see! The coal furnace's discharge can't get at our souls!"

But the atmosphere was less clouded by imported pollutants than it was by desires gone nowhere. The cross-legged commuters on our ferry's back this day carried with them the delicate dreams that were the oldest expression of man's elevation from beastliness. Yet they were still forced to live like beasts. The Indians I met loved to talk glowingly about their great, wise civilization, but none of that grandiloquent respect for the whole seemed to be accorded to the human constituents. The people bore every indignity for the sake of their culture's continuing cohesion. It wasn't a fair bargain. What did all the touted spiritual pre-eminence do for the Indian flesh? My own life may have been riddled and ruled by objects, by possessions. These people's lives were riddled and ruled by the lack of them. It wasn't just the scarcity of water that made the Ganges sacred. It was the pervasive filth of existence. Anything that refreshed momentarily, that tore off the dirt of living near the earth, was worthy of worship. At the very least, non-being was preferable to being because it was *clean*.

I cast about for my comrades, for the comic visions of the night. They'd been separated, dispersed, gone as silent as the river. Even Rolf had crumpled into a pile of World War I life jackets. Our group status had vanished. No armed guard, or color barrier, protected us. Foreign matter no longer, we were a dilute in the turgid stream of India.

Already, the day was a kiln. Nothing could escape its slow burn. The stares pointed at me were black, blacker, blackest. The insistent dust had to be constantly flicked away. So, too, did the light. The great Indian light blew like glittery grit from one victim to the next. The light: capricious and uncomfortable like the dust. The light: refracted and tortured like the people. The light: cleansing and purgative like the river.

We eat, we breathe, we die. In that sense, each society purports only to its own expertise of eating, breathing, dying. Why had I come to see this one? The holy men were so busy painting themselves they almost forgot to be holy. It is their task to be holy. The babus and the desk clerks smirked. It is their task to smirk. They do it for the benefit of all, though in order to smirk so effectively, their task includes being against the benefit of all. Dawn on the Ganges had afforded me a moment of pure, uncorrupted sight. A veritable karmic wallop. Then came the Indian questions: Who knows what you see? Would someone else see it the same? What does it matter in the long run? What, after all, is the *good* in seeing?

6

Little Bit and the America

Ludwig Bemelmans

"Look, what a lovely day we have for sailing." I said, pointing my pen toward the lit-up greenery outside the open window. The birds sang in the trees, and the sun shone on a deck of brightly colored luggage tags which I was filling out. Under "S.S. *America*" I had carefully lettered my name, and I answered the gay question of "Destination?" with "Cherbourg."

I was about to fill out a new tag when I noticed Barbara's silence. She was standing at the window, staring at me. I saw clearly the symptoms of wanting something, symptoms long known to me and always the same. I remembered that the day before she had said something about a dog, but I had been called away before I could talk about it at length.

For the most part, Barbara is a sweet and normal child; when she wants something, she changes. The child is then under great stress. A trembling of the lower lip precedes the filling of the beautiful eyes with tears. I am allowed to see these hopeless eyes for a moment, and then, as a spotlight moves from one place to another, she averts her gaze and slowly turns, folds her arms, and looks into the distance, or if there is no distance, at the wall. The crisis is approaching. She swallows, but her throat is constricted; finally, with the urgency of a stammerer, and with her small hands clenched, she manages to convey a few dry words. The small voice is like a cold trumpet. The last word is a choking sound. There is a long, cold silence.

On the morning of sailing I recognized the first stage of this painful condition that overcomes her from time to time. I could tell it by her eyes, her mouth, the position she stood in, the peculiar angles of her arms and legs. She was twisted in an unhappy pose of indecision. Not that she didn't know precisely what she wanted: she was undecided about how to broach the subject.

After the tears, the gaze into the distance, the silence, Barbara blurted out, "You promised I could have a dog."

I steeled myself and answered, "Yes, when we get back from Europe you can have a dog."

An answer like that is worse than an outright no. The mood of "I wish I was dead" descended on Barbara. She stared coldly out of the window, and then she turned and limply dragged herself down the corridor to her room, where she goes at times of crisis. She closed the door not by slamming it, but with a terrible, slow finality. One can see from the corridor how she lets go of the handle inside—in unspeakably dolorous fashion; slowly the handle rises, and there is the barely audible click of the mechanism. There is then the cutting off of human relations, a falling off of appetite, and nothing in the world of joy or disaster matters.

Ordinarily the comatose state lasts for weeks. In this case, however, Barbara was confronted with a deadline, for the ship was sailing at five that afternoon and it was now eleven in the morning. I usually break down after three or four weeks of resistance. The time limit for this operation was five hours.

She decided at first to continue with standard practice, the manual of which I know as well as I do the alphabet.

From the door at the end of the corridor came the sound of heartbreaking sobs. Normally these sobs last for a good while, and then, the crisis ebbing off, there follows an hour or two of real or simulated sleep, in which she gathers strength for renewed efforts. This time, however, the sobs were discontinued ahead of schedule and were followed up by a period of total silence, which I knew was taken up with plotting at the speed of calculating machinery. This took about ten minutes. As the door had closed, so it opened again, and fatefully and slowly, as the condemned walk to their place of execution, the poor child, handkerchief in hand, dragged along the corridor past my room into the kitchen. I never knew until that morning that the pouring of milk into a glass could be a bitter and hopeless thing to watch.

I am as hardened against the heartbreak routine as a coroner is to postmortems. I can be blind to tears and deaf to the most urgent pleading. I said, "Please be reasonable. I promise you that the moment we get back you can have a dog."

I was not prepared for what followed—the new slant, the surprise attack.

She leaned against the kitchen doorjamb and drank the last of the milk. Her mouth was ringed with white. She said in measured and accusing tones, "You read in the papers this morning what they did in Albany."

"I beg your pardon?"

"They passed a law that all institutions like the A.S.P.C.A. are to be forced to turn dogs over to hospitals, for vivisection—and you know what will happen. They'll get her and then they'll cut her open and sew her up again over and over until she's dead."

"What has that got to do with me?"

"It has to do with the dog you promised me."

"What dog?"

"The dog that Frances wants to give me."

Frances is a red-headed girl who goes to school with Barbara. "I didn't know Frances had a dog."

Barbara raised her eyebrows. "You never listen," she said, and as if talking to an idiot and with weary gestures she recited,

"Poppy, I told you all about it a dozen times. Doctor Lincoln, that's Frances's father, is going to Saudi Arabia to work for an oil company, and he had to sign a paper agreeing not to take a dog, because it seems the Arabs don't like dogs. So the dog has to be got rid of. So Doctor Lincoln said to Frances, 'If you don't get rid of her, I will.' Now you know how doctors are—they have no feelings whatever for animals. He'll give her to some hospital for experiments."

I resumed filling out baggage tags. When I hear the word "dog" I see in my mind a reasonably large animal of no particular breed, uncertain in outline, like a Thurber dog, and with a rough dark coat. This image was hovering about when I asked, "What kind of dog is it?"

"Her name is Little Bit."

"What?"

"Little *BIT*—that's her name. She's the dearest, sweetest, snow-white, itsy-bitsy, tiny little toy poodle you have ever seen. Can I have her, please?"

I almost let out a shrill bark.

"Wait till you see her and all the things she's got—a special little wicker bed with a mattress, and a dish with her picture on it, and around it is written 'Always faithful' in French. You see, Poppy, they got Little Bit in Paris last year, and she's the uniquest, sharpest little dog you've ever seen, and naturally she's housebroken, and Frances says she's not going to give her to anybody but me."

I was playing for time. I would have settled for a Corgi, a York-shire, a Weimaraner, even a German boxer or a Mexican hairless, but Little Bit was too much. I knew that Doctor Lincoln lived some thirty miles out of the city, and that it would be impossible to get the dog to New York before the ship sailed.

"Where is the dog now?" I asked with faked interest.

"She'll be here any minute, Poppy. Frances is on the way now—and oh, wait till you see, she has the cutest little boots for rainy weather, and a cashmere sweater, sea green, and several sets of leashes and collars—you won't have to buy a thing."

"All right," I said, "you can have the dog. We'll put it in a good kennel until we return."

The symptoms, well known and always the same, returned again. The lower lip trembled. "Kennel," she said—and there is no actress on stage or screen who could have weighted this word with more reproach and misery.

"Yes, kennel," I said and filled out the baggage tag for my portable typewriter.

"Poppy—" she started, but I got up and said, "Now look, Barbara, the ship leaves in a few hours, and to take a dog aboard you have to get a certificate from a veterinary, and reserve a place for him, and buy a ticket."

To my astonishment, Barbara smiled indulgently. "Well, if that's all that's bothering you—first of all, we're going to France; the French, unlike the English, have no quarantine for dogs, and they don't even ask for a health certificate. Second, you can make all the arrangements for the dog's passage on board ship, after it sails. Third, there is plenty of room in the kennels. I know all this because Frances and I went down to the U.S. Lines and got the information day before yesterday."

I stared into the distance. At such times I feel a great deal for the man who's going to marry Barbara. With all hope failing I said, "But we'll have to get a traveling bag or something to put the dog in."

"She has a lovely little traveling bag with her name lettered on it, 'Little Bit.'"

The name stung like a whip. "All right then." I wrote an extra baggage tag to be attached to the dog's bag.

Barbara wore the smug smile of success. "Wait till you see her," she said and ran out of the room. In a moment she returned with Frances, who, I am sure, had been sitting there waiting all the while. The timing was perfect.

Little Bit had shoebutton eyes and a patent-leather nose and a strawberry-colored collar; she was fluffy from the top of her head to her shoulders and then shorn like a miniature Persian lamb. At the end of a stub of a tail was a puff of fluff, and other puffs on the four legs. She wore a pale blue ribbon, and a bell on the collar. I thought that if she were cut open most probably sawdust would come out.

A real dog moves about a room and sniffs its way into corners. It inspects furniture and people, and makes notes of things. Little Bit stood with cocksparrow stiffness on four legs as static as her stare. She was picked up and brought over to me. I think she knew exactly what I thought of her, for she lifted her tiny lip on the left side of her face over her mouse teeth and sneered. She was put down, and she danced on stilts, with the motion of a mechanical toy, back to Frances.

I was shown the traveling bag which was like one of the pocketbooks that WAC colonels carry.

"We don't need that tag," said Barbara. "I'll carry her in this. Look." The pocketbook, which had a circular opening with a wire screen on each end for breathing purposes, was opened; Little Bit jumped into it, and it was closed. "You see, she won't be any bother whatever."

The bag was opened again. With a standing jump Little Bit hurdled the handles of the bag and stalked toward me. Tilting her head a little, she stood looking up, and then she again lifted her lip over her small fangs.

"Oh, look, Barbara!" said Frances. "Little Bit likes your father— she's smiling at him."

I had an impulse to sneer back but I took the baggage tags and began to attach them to the luggage. Then I left the room, for Frances showed signs of crisis; her eyes were filling, and the heartbreak was too much for me. Little Bit was less emotional. She ate a hearty meal from her *Tourjours fidèle* dish and inspected the house, tinkling about with the small bell that hung from her collar.

It was time to go to the boat. The luggage was taken to a taxi, and Little Bit hopped into her bag. On the way I thought about the things I had forgotten to take care of, and also about Little Bit. It is said that there are three kinds of books that are always a success: a book about a doctor, a book about Lincoln, and a book about a dog. Well, here was Doctor Lincoln's dog, but it didn't seem to hold the elements of anything except chagrin. I wondered if Lincoln had ever had a dog, or a doctor, or if Lincoln's doctor had had a dog. I wondered if that side of Lincoln, perhaps the last remaining side, had been investigated as yet or was still open.

We arrived with Doctor Lincoln's dog at the customs barrier, and our passports were checked. The baggage was brought aboard. In our cabin we found some friends waiting. Frances and Barbara, with Little Bit looking out of her bag, inspected the ship. The gong sounded, and the deck steward sang out, "All ashore that's going ashore!" The passengers lined up to wave their farewells. The last of those that were going ashore slid down the gangplank. Good-bye, good-bye—and then the engine bells sounded below, and the tugs moaned and hissed, and the ship backed out into the river.

There are few sights in the world as beautiful as a trip down the Hudson and out to sea, especially at dusk. I was on deck until we passed the Ambrose Lightship, and then I went down to the cabin.

Little Bit was lying on a blotter, on the writing desk, and watching Barbara's hand. Barbara was already writing a letter to Frances, describing the beauty of travel and Little Bit's reactions. "Isn't she the best traveling dog we've ever had, Poppy?"

The cabins aboard the *America* are the only ones I have ever been in that don't seem to be aboard ship. They are large—more like rooms in a country home—a little chintzy in decoration, and over the portholes are curtains. In back of these one suspects screened doors that lead out to a porch and a Connecticut lawn rather than the ocean.

I put my things in place and changed to a comfortable jacket. I said, "I guess I better go up and get this dog business settled."

"It's all attended to, Poppy. I took care of it," said Barbara and continued writing.

"Well, then you'd better take her upstairs to the kennels. It's almost dinnertime."

"She doesn't have to go to the kennels."

"Now look, Barbara—"

"See for yourself, Poppy. Just ring for the steward, or let me ring for him."

"Yes, sir," said the steward, smiling.

"Is it all right for the dog to stay in the cabin?" I asked. The steward had one of the most honest and kind faces I have ever seen. He didn't fit on a ship either. He was more like a person that worked around horses, or a gardener. He had bright eyes and squint lines, a leathery skin, and a good smile.

He closed his eyes and announced, "Dog? I don't see no dog in here, sir." He winked like a burlesque comedian and touched one finger to his head in salute. "My name is Jeff," he said. "If you want anything—" And then he was gone.

"You see?" said Barbara. "And besides, you save fifty dollars, and coming back another fifty, makes a hundred."

I am sure that Little Bit understood every word of the conversation. She stood up on the blotter and tilted her head, listening to Barbara, who said to her, "You know, Little Bit, you're not supposed to be on this ship at all. You musn't let anybody see you. Now you hide, while we go down to eat."

There was a knock at the door. Silently Little Bit jumped to the floor and was out of sight.

It was the steward. He brought a little raw meat mixed with string beans on a plate covered with another plate. "Yes, sir," was all he said.

Barbara was asleep when the first rapport between me and Little Bit took place. I was sitting on a couch, reading, when she came into my cabin. By some magic trick like an elevator going up a building shaft, she rose and seated herself next to me. She kept a hand's width of distance, tilted her head, and then lifted her lip over the left side of her face. I think I smiled back at her in the same fashion. I looked at her with interest for the first time—she was embarrassed. She looked away and then suddenly changed position, stretching her front legs ahead and sitting down flat on her hind legs. She made several jerky movements but never uttered a sound.

Barbara's sleepy voice came from the other room. "Aren't you glad we have Little Bit with us?"

"Yes," I said, "I am." I thought about the miracles of nature, how this tough little lion in sheep's pelt functioned as she did; with a brain that could be no larger than an olive, she had memory, understanding, tact, courage, and no doubt loyalty, and she was completely self-sufficient. She smiled once more, and I smiled back: The relationship was established. Life went on as steadily as the ship.

On the afternoon of the third day out, as I lay in my deck chair reading, Barbara came running. "Little Bit is gone," she stammered with trembling lower lip.

We went down to the cabin. The steward was on all fours, looking under beds and furniture. "Somebody musta left the door open," he said, "or it wasn't closed properly and swung open, and I suppose she got lonesome here all by herself and went looking for you. You should have taken her up to the movies with you, Miss."

"She's a smart dog," said Barbara. "Let's go to every spot on board where she might look for us."

So we went to the dining-room, to the smoking-room, the theater, the swimming pool, up the stairs, down the stairs, up on all the decks and around them, and to a secret little deck we had discovered between second and third class at the back of the ship, where Little Bit was taken for her exercise mornings and evenings and could run about freely while I stood guard.

A liner is as big as a city. She was nowhere.

When we got back the steward said, "I know where she is. You see, anybody finds a dog naturally takes it up to the kennels, and that's where she is. And there she stays for the rest of the trip. Remember, I never saw the dog, I don't know anything about her. The butcher— that's the man in charge of the kennels—he's liable to report me if he finds out I helped hide her. He's mean, especially about money. He figures that each passenger gives him ten bucks for taking care of a dog, and he doesn't want any of us to snatch. There was a Yorkshire stowing away trip before last; he caught him at the gangplank as the dog was leaving the ship—the passenger had put him on a leash. Well, the butcher stopped him from getting off. He held up everything for hours, the man had to pay passage for the dog, and the steward who had helped hide him was fired. Herman Haegeli is his name, and he's as mean as they come. You'll find him on the top deck, near the aft chimney, where it says 'Kennels.'"

At such moments I enjoy the full confidence and affection of my child. Her nervous little hand is in mine, she willingly takes direction, her whole being is devotion, and no trouble is too much. She loved me especially then, because she knows that I am larcenous at heart and willing to go to the greatest lengths to beat a game and especially a meany.

"Now remember," I said, "if you want that dog back we have to be very careful. Let's first go and case the joint."

We climbed up into the scene of white and red ventilators, the sounds of humming wires, and the swish of the water. In yellow and crimson fire, the ball of the sun had half sunk into the sea, precisely at the end of the avenue of foam that the ship had ploughed through the ocean. We were alone. We walked up and down, like people taking exercise before dinner, and the sea changed to violet and to indigo and then to that glossy gunmetal hue that it wears on moonless nights. The ship swished along to the even pulse of her machinery.

There was the sign. A yellow light shone from a porthole. I lifted Barbara, and inside, in one of the upper cases, was Little Bit, behind bars. There was no lock on her cage.

No one was inside. The door was fastened by a padlock. We walked back and forth for a while, and then a man came up the stairs, carrying a pail. He wore a gray cap, a towel around his neck, and a white coat such as butchers work in.

"That's our man," I said to Barbara.

Inside the kennels he brought forth a large dish that was like the body of a kettledrum. The dogs were barking.

"Now listen carefully, Barbara. I will go in and start a conversation with Mr. Haegeli. I will try to arrange it so that he turns his back on Little Bit's cage. At that moment, carefully open the door of the cage, grab Little Bit, put her under your coat, and then don't run—stand still, and after a while say, 'Oh, please let's get out of here.' I will then say good evening, and we both will leave very slowly. Remember to act calmly, watch the butcher, but don't expect a signal from me. Decide yourself when it is time to act. It might be when he is in the middle of work, or while he is talking."

"Oh, please, Poppy, let's get out of here," Barbara rehearsed.

I opened the door to the kennel and smiled like a tourist in appreciation of a new discovery. "Oh, that's where the dogs are kept," I said. "Good evening."

Mr. Haegeli looked up and answered with a grunt. He was mixing dog food.

"My, what nice food you're preparing for them. How much do they charge to take a dog across?"

"Fifty dollars," said Mr. Haegeli in a Swiss accent. There are all kinds of Swiss, some with French, some with Italian, and some with German accents. They all talk in a singing fashion. The faces are as varied as the accents. The butcher didn't look like a butcher—a good butcher is fat and rosy. Mr. Haegeli was thin-lipped, thin-nosed, his chin was pointed. In the light he didn't look as mean as I expected; he looked rather fanatic, and frustrated.

"How often do you feed them?"

"They eat twice a day and as good as anybody on board," said Mr. Haegeli. "All except Rolfi there—he belongs to an actor, Mr. Kruger, who crosses twice a year and brings the dog's food along." He pointed to the cage where a large police dog was housed. "Rolfi, he is fed once a day, out of cans." He seemed to resent Rolfi and his master.

"You exercise them?"

"Yes, of course—all except Rolfi. Mr. Kruger comes up in the morning and takes him around with him on the top deck and sits with him there on a bench. He doesn't leave him alone. There is such a thing as making too much fuss over a dog."

I said that I agreed with him.

"He tried to keep him in his cabin—he said he'd pay full fare for Rolfi, like a passenger. He'll come up any minute now to say good night to Rolfi. Some people are crazy about dogs." Mr. Haegeli was putting chopped meat, vegetables, and cereal into the large dish. "There are other people that try to get away with something—they try and smuggle dogs across, like that one there." He pointed at Little Bit. "But we catch them," he said in his Swiss accent. "Oh yes, we catch them. They think they're smart, but they don't get away with it—not with me on board they don't. I have ways of finding out. I track them down." The fires of the fanatic burned in his eyes. "I catch them every time." He sounded as if he turned them over to the guillotine after he caught them. "Ah, here comes Mr. Kruger." he said and opened the door.

Kurt Kruger, the actor, said good evening and introduced himself. He spoke to Mr. Haegeli in German—and Mr. Haegeli turned his back on Little Bit's cage to open Rolfi's. The entire place was immediately deafened with barking from a dozen cages. The breathless moment had arrived. Barbara was approaching the door, but the dog-lover Kruger spotted Little Bit and said, "There's a new one." He spoke to Little Bit, and Little Bit, who behaved as if she had been carefully rehearsed for her liberation, turned away with tears in her eyes.

Mr. Kruger and his dog disappeared.

Mr. Haegeli wiped his hand on his apron and went back to mixing the dog food. The chances for rescuing Little Bit were getting slim.

"Where do you come from, Mr. Haegeli?"

"Schaffhausen. You know Schaffhausen?"

"Yes, yes," I said in German. *"Wunderbar."*

"Ja, ja, beautiful city."

"And the waterfall!"

"You know the Haegeli Wurstfabrik there?"

"No, I'm sorry."

"Well, it's one of the biggest sausage factories in Switzerland— liverwurst, salami, cervelat, frankfurters, boned hams—a big concern, belongs to a branch of my family. I'm sort of a wanderer. I like to travel—restless, you know—I can't see myself in Schaffhausen." He looked up. He was mixing food with both hands, his arms rotating.

"I understand."

"Besides, we don't get along, my relatives and I. All they think about is money, small money—I think in large sums. I like a wide horizon. Schaffhausen is not for me."

"How long have you been traveling?"

"Oh, I've been two years on this ship. You see, I'm not really a butcher but an inventor."

"How interesting! What are you working on?"

At last Mr. Haegeli turned his back on the cage in which Little Bit waited. "Well, it's something tremendous. It's, so to say, revolutionary."

"Oh?"

"There's a friend of mine, a Swiss, who is a baker, but you know, like I'm not a real butcher, he is not exactly a baker—I mean, he knows his trade but he has ambition to make something of himself—and together we have created something that we call a frankroll." He waited for the effect.

"What is a frankroll?"

"It's a frankfurter baked inside a roll. We've everything here to experiment with, the material and the ovens. I make the franks and he makes the rolls. We've tried it out on the passengers. Mr. Kruger, for example, says it's a marvellous idea. I might add that the experimental stage is over. Our product is perfect. Now it is a question of selling the patent, or licensing somebody—you know the way that is done. You make much more that way."

"Have you tried?"

Mr. Haegeli came close, the inventor's excitement in his eyes now. "That is where the hitch comes in. On the last trip I saw the biggest frankfurter people in America—they're in New York. Well, the things you find out! They were very nice. The president received us and looked at the product and tasted it. He liked it, because he called for his son and a man who works close to him. 'I think you've got something there,' said the old man. I think with him we would have had clear sailing, but he had one of these wisenheimers for a son."

As Haegeli talked he forgot completely about the dogs. He gesticulated with hands that were sticky with hash, using them as a boxer does when he talks with his gloves on. Standing close to me, he held them away lest dog food soil my clothes. He stood exactly right, with his back turned to the spot where Barbara was slowly reaching to the door of Little Bit's cage. It was all foiled again by the return of Mr. Kruger and Rolfi. Mr. Kruger kissed his dog good night and stood waiting while Rolfi slowly walked into his cage. He said to Rolfi that it was only for two more nights that he had to be here, he wished us a good night also, and after a final good night to his dog he went.

"Where was I?" said the butcher.

"With the frankroll, the old man, and the wise-guy son."

"Right. Well, the son was looking at our product with a mixture of doubt, so he took a bite out of it, and in the middle of it he stopped chewing. 'Mmmm,' he said. 'Not bad, not bad at all. But—' He paused a long time, and then he said, 'What about the mustard, gentlemen?'

"I said, 'All right, what about the mustard?'

"So the wise guy says, 'I'm a customer. I'm buying. I'm at a hotdog stand. I watch the man in the white jacket. He picks up the frankfurter roll that's been sliced and placed face down on the hot plate—he picks it up in a sanitary fashion—and he takes the skinless frank with his prong and puts it in the roll and hands it to me. Now, I dip into the mustard pot, or maybe I decide on a little kraut, or maybe I want some condiments or relish. Anyway, I put that on the frank—' He held out his hand.

"So I said, 'What's all that got to do with our frankroll?'

"So Junior says, 'A lot. Let me explain. It's got no appeal. Practical maybe, but to put the mustard on the hot dog the customer would have to slice the frankfurter bun first, and that leads us straight back to the old-fashioned frankfurter and the old-fashioned roll. The frankroll may be practical, but it's got no sizzle to it. No eye appeal, no nose appeal—it's no good.'

Well, the old man was confused, and he got up and said that he'd like to think about it, and then he said he'd like to show us the factory. Well, you'd never think how important a thing a frankfurter is. There are two schools of thought about frankfurters, the skin frank and the skinless. These people specialize in skinless ones—because the American housewife prefers them without skin—but did you know that the skinless comes with skins and have to be peeled? This factory is spotless. There is a vast hall, and at long tables sit hundreds of women, and music plays, and they all have in their left hand a frankfurter, and in the right a paring knife, and all day long they remove the skins from the frankfurters—an eight-hour day. And at the end of the room is a first-aid station, because at the speed at which they work there is a great deal of laceration. The man in charge—"

"Oh, please, Poppy, let's get out of here!" Barbara broke in.

"The man in charge explained that in spite of elaborate safety precautions there was a great deal of absenteeism on account of carelessness. They had people who were working on a machine to skin the frankfurters. 'Now if you could invent a frankfurter-skinning device,' said the old man to me, 'you'd be a millionaire overnight.' Well, we're not licked yet. The beauty of working on a ship is that you have everything on board. One of the engineers is working with us on a skinning machine, and I have another outfit lined up for the frankroll."

The light in Mr. Haegeli's eyes faded. He wiped his hand again on his apron, and I shook it, and slowly we walked out on deck and down the first flight of stairs to A deck. I said to Barbara, "Run for your life, for by now he has discovered that Little Bit is gone."

We got to the cabin. Little Bit smiled on both sides of her face, and she bounced from floor to chair to dresser. There was a knock on the door—the thrill of the game of cops and robbers had begun. Little Bit vanished.

Barbara asked innocently, "Who is it?"

It was the steward. "Did you find her?"

Barbara smiled.

"You got her back?"

Barbara nodded.

"Well, for heaven's sake, keep her out of sight. That crazy butcher is capable of anything—and I got a wife and family."

"From now on the dog must not be left," I said to Barbara. "She must go with us wherever we go, to the dining-room, on deck, to the lounge, and to the movies. And you can't carry her in that bag—you have to cover her with a scarf or have her inside your coat."

Barbara started going about as if she carried her arm in a sling. The steward averted his eyes whenever he met us, and he didn't bring any more dog food.

Mr. Kruger said, "The kennel man suspects you of having removed the dog from the kennel."

"We did."

"Good," said the actor. "Anything I can do, I will."

"Well, act as if you didn't know anything about it. How is Rolfi?"

"Oh, Rolfi is fine. You know, he's never bitten anybody in his life except that kennel man."

Mr. Kruger offered to get Little Bit off the boat. He had a wicker basket in which he carried some of Rolfi's things, and he would empty that, except for Rolfi's coat, and in that he would carry Little Bit off the *America,* for the butcher would follow us and watch us closely, and if he didn't find the dog before he'd catch us at the customs.

"Isn't he a nice man—Mr. Kruger? People always say such mean things about movie actors," said Barbara.

Camouflaged in a scarf, Little Bit rested on Barbara's lap during meals. On the deck chair she lay motionless between my feet, covered by a steamer rug. She traveled about under Barbara's coat, and she took her exercise on the secret afterdeck, while I watched from above.

After the morning walk, the next day, the steward knocked. He looked worried. "The butcher was here," he said, "and went all over the room. He found the dish with those French words and the dog's picture on it, on the bathroom floor."

"How could we be so careless?" I said, my professional pride hurt.

"And of course he saw the bag with *Little Bit* printed on it. I said I didn't know nothing about any dog."

We doubled our precautions. Little Bit's mouth was down at the edges with worry. I contemplated what to do. After all, there were only two more days, and if the worst happened we could sit

upstairs with Little Bit, the way Mr. Kruger sat with Rolfi. I said
to Barbara, "Perhaps it would be best to pay the passage and have
it over with."

The symptoms were back "No, you can't do that. Think of the
poor steward and his family!"

"Well, we could settle that, I think, with the butcher. I don't like
to cheat the line—"

"Well, Poppy, you can send them a check afterward, if that wor-
ries you, or drink a few extra bottles of champagne, or buy something in the shop."

Knock on the door.

"Who is it?"

"The purser, sir."

"Please come in."

The door opened. Behind the purser stood Mr. Haegeli.

"Just wanted to look and see if everything is all right. Are you
comfortable, sir?"

"Everything is fine."

"By the way, sir, we're looking for a small white dog that's been
lost. We wondered if by any chance it's in here."

"Come in and look for yourself."

"That's quite all right, sir. Excuse the intrusion. Good evening."
The purser dosed the door.

"What a nice man!" said Barbara.

The butcher was excluded from pursuing us in the public rooms
of the ship; he couldn't follow us to the movies or the dining room.
But he seemed to have spies. "What a lovely scarf you have there,
Miss," said the elevator boy, and after that we used the stairs. The
butcher came on deck in a fatigue uniform and followed us on the
evening promenade around deck, during which Little Bit sat inside
my overcoat, held in place by my right hand in a Napoleonic pose.
We made four turns around deck. I leaned against the railing once,
holding Little Bit in place, so that I could stretch my arms; Barbara

was skipping rope, and the maneuver fooled him. He ran downstairs, and we caught him as he emerged from near our cabin—he had made another search. We saw his shadow on the wall near the stairs several times. He seemed to be nearing a nervous breakdown. Mr. Kruger told us that he had sworn we had the dog and meant to find it at any cost. There was one more night to go, and the next day the ship would dock.

At ten Barbara would deliver Little Bit to Mr. Kruger, and we would fill the bag in which she traveled with paper tissue, tobacco, soap, extra toothbrushes, razor blades, dental floss, and other things. which can all be bought in Europe but which for some droll reason one always takes along.

Little Bit was fed from luncheon trays which we ordered for ourselves in the cabin instead of going down to lunch.

The steward was shaking. "I don't know," he said, "when that guy butchers, or when he takes care of the other dogs. He's hanging around here all the time. I hope you get off all right."

On the last afternoon on board I became careless. Some passengers and a bearded ship's officer were watching the last game of the deck-tennis tournament, and others were lying this way and that in their deck chairs, forming a protective barricade. Barbara had checked on the butcher—he was busy aft, airing some of his charges.

I thought it safe to take Little Bit out of my coat and place her on deck so that we all could relax a bit. She had been there but a moment when I heard a cry. "Ha," it went. It was the "Ha" of accusation and discovery, chagrin and triumph, and it had been issued by Mr. Haegeli. who stood with both arms raised. Fortunately he was not a kangaroo and was therefore unable to jump over the occupied deck chairs. I gathered up Little Bit, and we were safe for a few seconds. By now I knew the ship's plan as well as the man who designed her. We went down two decks on outside stairs, entered through a serving pantry, climbed one inside service stair, and then nonchalantly walked to the bar. I sat down and rang for the steward. I ordered something to drink. In a little while Barbara, with her lemonade in hand, said, "He's watching us through the third window!"

I swept my eyes over the left side of the room, and his face was pressed against the glass, pale and haunting. He kept watch from the outside, and ran back and forth as we moved around inside.

We went down to dinner. When we came back I got a cigar. He was outside the bar. As I went to the saloon to have coffee he was outside that window.

"Don't give Little Bit any sugar," Barbara said. "He's watching us."

The floor was cleared for dancing, and we got up to walk back to the library. There is a passage between the main saloon and the library off which are various pantries and side rooms, and it has no window. In a corner of it is the shop, and on this last evening people stood there in numbers buying cartons of cigarettes, film, small sailor hats, miniature lifebelts, and ship models with "S.S. *America"* written on them. Here I suddenly realized the miraculous solution of our problem. It was in front of me, on a shelf. Among stuffed Mickey Mice, Donald Ducks, and teddy bears of various sizes stood the exact replica of Little Bit—the same button eyes and patent-leather nose, the fluff, the legs like sticks, the pom-pom at the end of the tail and the blue ribbon in its hair.

"How much is that dog?" I asked the young lady.

"Two ninety-five."

"I'll take it."

"Shall I wrap it up, sir?"

"No, thanks, I'll take it as is."

"What are we going to do now, Poppy?"

"Now you keep Little Bit hidden, and I'll take the stuffed dog, and we'll go into the library."

There we sat down. I placed the stuffed dog at my side and spoke to it. The butcher was on the far side of the ship, but he almost went through the window. He disappeared and ran around to the other side. I had arranged the toy dog so that it seemed to be asleep at my side, partly covered by Barbara's scarf. I told her to take Little Bit down to the cabin and then come back, and we'd have some fun with the butcher.

When she came back Barbara took the toy dog and fixed its hair and combed the fluff. Then I said, "Please give me the dog." We walked the length of the ship on the inside. The butcher was sprinting outside, his face flashing momentarily in the series of windows.

At the front of the ship we went out on deck. I held the dog so that the pom-pom stuck out in back, and I wiggled it a little, to give it the illusion of life. It took the butcher a while to catch up. He walked fast—we walked faster. He almost ran—we ran. He shouted, "Mister!" I continued running. As we came toward the stern I asked Barbara, "Can you let out a terrible scream?"

"Yes, of course," said Barbara.

"One—two—three—*now.*"

She screamed, and I threw the dog in a wide curve out into the sea. The butcher, a few feet away, gripped the railing and looked below, where the small white form was bobbing up and down in the turbulent water. Rapidly it was washed away in the wake of the *America*.

We turned to go back into the saloon.

We left the butcher paralyzed at the stern. He wasn't at the gangplank the next day.

Little Bit landed in France without further incident.

7

Birth of a Mountain Climber

Eric Newby

When Hugh arrived from New York ten days later I went to meet him at London Airport. Sitting in those sheds on the north side which still, twelve years after the war, gave the incoming traveler the feeling that he was entering a beleaguered fortress, I wondered what surprises he had in store for me.

His first words after we had greeted one another were to ask if there was any news from Arnold Brown.

"Not a thing."

"That's bad," he said.

"It's not so disastrous. After all, you have done some climbing. I'll soon pick it up. We'll just have to be careful."

He looked pale. I put it down to the journey. Then he said: "You know I've never done any *real* climbing."

It took me some time to assimilate this.

"But all that stuff about the mountain. You and Dreesen. . . ."

"Well, that was more or less a reconnaissance."

"But all this gear. How did you know what to order?"

"I've been doing a lot of reading."

"But you said you had porters."

"Not porters—drivers. It's not like the Himalayas. There aren't any "tigers" in Afghanistan. No one knows anything about mountaineering."

There was a long silence as we drove down the Great West Road.

"Perhaps we should postpone it for a year," he said.

"Ha-ha. I've just given up my job!"

Hugh stuck out his jaw. Normally a determined-looking man, the effect was almost overwhelming.

"There's nothing for it," he said. "We must have some lessons."

Wanda and I were leaving England for Istanbul on 1 June. Hugh and I had just four days to learn about climbing.

The following night after some brisk telephoning we left for Wales to learn about climbing, in the brand new station wagon Hugh had ordered by post from South America. He had gone to Brighton to fetch it. Painted in light tropical colors it had proved to be rather conspicuous in Hammersmith. Soon it had been covered with swarms of little boys and girls whose mothers stood with folded arms silently regarding it.

We had removed all the furniture from the drawing room to make room for the equipment and stores. Our three-piece suite was standing in the garden under a tarpaulin. The drawing room looked like the quartermaster's store of some clandestine force. It was obvious that Hugh was deeply impressed.

"How long have you been living like this?"

"Ever since we can remember. It's not all here yet. There's still the food."

"What food?" He looked quite alarmed.

"Six cases of Army ration, compo. in fibre boxes. It's arriving tomorrow."

"We can always leave it in England. I don't know about you but food doesn't interest me. We can always live off the country."

I remembered von Dückelmann, that hardy Austrian forester without an ounce of spare flesh on him, who had lost twelve pounds in a fortnight in Nuristan.

"Whatever else we leave behind it won't be the food."

"Well, I suppose we can always give it away." He sounded almost shocked, as if for the first time he had detected in me a grave moral defect. It was an historic moment.

With unconcealed joy my wife watched us load some of the mountaineering equipment into the machine.

"We'd better not take all of it," said Hugh. "They might wonder why we've got so much stuff if we don't know how to use it."

Over the last weeks the same thought had occurred to me constantly.

"What about the tent?"

The tent had arrived that morning. It had been described to me by the makers as being suitable for what they called "the final assault." With its sewn-in groundsheet, special flaps so that it could be weighed down with boulders, it convinced me, more than any other single item of equipment, that we were going, as the books have it, "high." It had been specially constructed for the curious climatic conditions we were likely to encounter in the Hindu Kush.

"I shouldn't take *that,* if I were you," said my wife with sinister emphasis. "The children tried to put it up in the garden after lunch. Whoever made it forgot to make holes for the poles."

"Are you sure?"

"Quite sure. You know it's got those poles shaped like a V, that you slip into a sort of pocket in the material. Well, they haven't made any pockets, so you can't put it up."

"It's lucky you found out. We should have looked pretty silly on Mir Samir."

"You're going to look pretty silly at any rate. I shouldn't be surprised if they've done the same thing to your sleeping bags."

"Have you telephoned the makers?"

"That's no use. If you send it back to them, you'll never see it again. I've sent for the little woman who makes my dresses. She's coming tomorrow morning."

We continued to discuss what we should take to Wales.

"I should take your Folboat," said Hugh. "There's bound to be a lake near the inn. It will be a good chance of testing it BEFORE YOU PASS THROUGH THE GORGES. The current is tremendously swift."

I had never had any intention of being either drowned or ritually mutilated in Mahsud Territory. I told him that I hadn't got a Folboat.

"I was almost certain I wrote to you about getting a Folboat. It's a pity. There's not much time now."

"No," I said, "there isn't."

It was nearly midnight when we left London. Our destination was an inn situated in the wilds of Caernarvonshire. Hugh had telephoned the proprietor and explained to him the peculiar state of ignorance in which we found ourselves. It was useless to dissemble: Hugh had told him everything. He was not only an experienced mountaineer, but was also the head of the mountain rescue service. It is to his eternal credit that he agreed to help us rather than tell us, as a more conventional man might have done, that his rooms were all booked.

We arrived at six o'clock the following morning, having driven all night, but already a spiral of smoke was issuing from a chimney at the back of the premises.

The first thing that confronted us when we entered the hotel was a door on the left. On it was written EVEREST ROOM. Inside it was a facsimile of an Alpine hut, done out in pine wood, with massive benches round the walls. On every side was evidence of the presence of the great ones of the mountain world. Their belongings in the shape of ropes, rucksacks, favorite jackets and boots were everywhere, ready for the off. It was not a museum. It was more like the Royal Enclosure. Sir John and Sir Edmund might appear at any moment. They were probably on the premises.

"Whatever else we do I don't think we shall spend much time in the *Everest Room*," said Hugh, as we reverently closed the door. "For the first time I'm beginning to feel that we really do know damn all."

"EXACTLY."

At this moment we were confronted by a remarkably healthy-looking girl.

"Most people have had breakfast but it's still going on," she said.

The only other occupant of the breakfast room was a compact man of about forty-five, who was eating his way through the sort of breakfast I hadn't been able to stomach for ten years. He was wearing a magnificent sweater that was the product of peasant industry. He was obviously a climber. With an hysterical attempt at humor, like soldiers before an attack, we tried to turn him into a figure of fun, speaking in whispers. This proved difficult, as he wasn't at all comic, just plainly competent.

"He looks desperately healthy." (His face was the color of old furniture.)

"Everyone looks healthy here, except us."

"I don't think it's real tan."

"Perhaps he's making a film about mountain rescue."

"How very appropriate."

"Perhaps he'll let us stand in, as corpses."

After breakfast the proprietor introduced us to the mystery man. We immediately felt ashamed of ourselves.

"This is Dr. Richardson," he said. "He's very kindly agreed to take you out and teach you the rudiments of climbing."

"Have you ever done any?" asked the Doctor.

It seemed no time to bring up my scrambles in the Dolomites, nor even Hugh's adventures at the base of Mir Samir.

"No," I said firmly, "neither of us knows the first thing about it."

We had arrived at seven; by nine o'clock we were back in the station wagon, this time bound for the north face of the mountain called Tryfan.

"Stop here," said the Doctor. Hugh parked the car by a milestone that read "Bangor X Miles." Rearing up above the road was a formidable-looking chunk of rock, the *Milestone Buttress*.

"That's what you're going to climb," said the Doctor. "It's got practically everything you need at this stage."

It seemed impossible. In a daze we followed him over a rough wall and into the bracken. A flock of mountain sheep watched us go, making noises that sounded suspiciously like laughter.

Finally we reached the foot of it. Close-to it didn't seem so formidable. The whole face was scarred by the nailed boots of countless climbers.

"This thing is like a bypass," said the Doctor. "Later in the season you'd have to queue up to climb it. We're lucky to have it to ourselves."

"If there's one thing we don't need it's an audience."

"First of all you've got to learn about the rope. Without a rope climbing is suicide. It's the only thing that justifies it. Chris told me what you're planning to do. If anything happens on that mountain, it may not get into the papers, and at least no one else will have to risk their necks to get you off if anything goes wrong. If I thought that you were the sort of people who would take risks, I wouldn't have come with you today."

He showed us how to rope ourselves together, using the proper knots; the bowline for the leader and the end man; the butterfly noose, a beautifully symmetrical knot, for the middleman; how to hold it and how to coil it so that it would pay out without snarling up, and how to belay.

"You never move without a proper belay. I start to climb and I go on until I reach a knob of rock onto which I can belay. I take a *karabiner*? (he produced one of the D-shaped steel rings with a spring-loaded clip) "and attach a sling to the loop of rope round my waist. Then all I have to do is to put the sling over the knob of rock, and pass the rope under one shoulder and over the other. If possible, you brace your feet against a solid block. Like that you can take the really big strain if the next man comes off.

"When the second man reaches the leader, the leader unclips the *karabiner* with the sling on it, and the second man attaches it to his waist. He's now belayed. The second man gives his own sling to the leader who goes on to the next pitch. Like this."

"What I don't see," I whispered to Hugh, "is what happens if the leader falls on the first pitch. According to this he's done for."

"The leader just mustn't fall off."

"Remind me to let you be leader."

The Doctor now showed what I thought was a misplaced trust in us. He sent us to the top of a little cliff, not more than twenty feet high, with a battered looking holly tree growing on it. "I want you to pretend that you're the leader," he said to Hugh. "I want you to belay yourself with a sling and a *karabiner* to the holly tree. On the way up I am going to fall off backwards and I shan't tell you when I'm going to do it. You've got to hold me." He began to climb.

He reached the top and was just about to step over the edge when, without warning, he launched himself backwards into space. And then the promised miracle happened, for the rope was taut and Hugh was holding him, not by the belay but simply with the rope passed under one shoulder and over the other. There was no strain on the sling round Hugh's waist at all, his body was like a spring. I was very impressed—for the first time I began to understand the trust that climbers must be able to have in one another.

"Now it's your turn," said the Doctor.

It was like a memorable day in 1939 when I fell backwards off the fore upper topsail yard of a four-masted barque, only this time I expected Hugh to save me. And he did. Elated we practiced this new game for some time until the Doctor looked at his watch. It was 11:30.

"We'd better get on to the rock. We wouldn't normally but there's so little time and you seem to be catching on to the roping part. Let's go. We'll take the *Ordinary Route*. You may think it isn't much but don't go just bald-headed at it. I'm going to lead. It's about two hundred feet altogether. We start in this chimney." He indicated an inadequate-looking cleft in the rock face.

It seemed too small to contain a human being at all but the Doctor vanished into it easily enough. Like me, he was wearing nailed boots, not the new-fangled ones with rubber vibram soles. I could hear them screeching on the rock as he scrabbled for a foothold. There was a lot of grunting and groaning then he vanished from sight. Hugh went next. It was easier for him as he was very slim. Then it was my turn. Like a boa constrictor swallowing a live chicken, I wriggled up it, with hideous wear and tear to my knees, until I emerged on a boulder slope.

"Now we begin," said the Doctor.

"What was that, if it wasn't the beginning?"

"The start. This is the beginning."

"How very confusing."

The worst part was what he called "Over the garden wall," which entailed swinging round a projection, hanging over a void and then traversing along a ledge into a cave.

"I wish he'd wear rubbers," I said to Hugh, as the Doctor vanished over the wall with a terrible screeching of tricounis. "It's not the climbing I object to, it's the noise."

There was still a twenty-foot chimney with a tree in it up which we fought our way and, at last, we lay on the top panting and admiring the view which was breathtaking. I was very impressed and proud. It wasn't much but I had done my first climb.

"What do you call this?" Hugh said, warily. "Easy, difficult or something in between?"

"Moderate."

"How do they go? I've forgotten."

"Easy, moderate, difficult, very difficult, severe, very severe, exceptionally severe, and excessively severe."

"Oh."

While we were eating our sandwiches the Doctor began to describe what he called "The Free Rappel." More than a year has passed since, for the first and last time, I practiced this excruciatingly painful method of descending the face of a mountain. Even now I am unable to remember it without a shudder. Like the use of the bayonet, it was something to be learned, and if possible, forgotten for ever.

"You first," said the Doctor. In dealing with him we suffered the disadvantage that he wasn't retained at some handsome fee to teach us all this. He was in fact ruining his holiday, in order to give us a slightly more than even chance of surviving.

"Put a sling round the tree and run the double rope through it; now pass it round your right thigh, between your legs; now up the back and sling it over your left shoulder so that it falls down in front. That's right. Now walk backward to the edge, keep the rope taut. Now keep your legs horizontal and walk down."

I walked down. It would have been perfect if only the face of the cliff had been smooth; unfortunately it was slightly concave, which made it difficult to keep my legs at right angles to the face. I failed to do so, slipped, and went swinging backward and forward across the face like a pendulum, with the rope biting into my groin.

"Well, you've learned one lesson," Hugh said cheerfully, when I reached the bottom after disengaging myself from the rope and swarming down in a more conventional manner.

"If it's a question of doing that again or being castrated by Mahsuds, I'll take the Mahsuds. My groin won't stand up to much more of this."

"You must be very sensitive," Hugh said. "Lots of girls do it."

"I'm not a girl. There must be some other way. It's impossible in thin trousers."

After a large, old-fashioned tea at the inn with crumpets and boiled eggs, we were taken off to the *Eckenstein Boulder*. Oscar Eckenstein was a renowned climber at the end of the nineteenth century, whose principal claim to fame was that he had been the first man in this or any other country to study the technique of holds and balance on rock. He had spent his formative years crawling over the boulder that now bore his name. Although it was quite small, about the size of a delivery van, his boulder was said to apparently embody all the fundamental problems that are such a joy to mountaineers and were proving such a nightmare to us.

For this treat we were allowed to wear gym shoes.

Full of boiled egg and crumpet, we clung upside down to the boulder like bluebottles, while the Doctor shouted encouragement to us from a safe distance. Occasionally one of us would fall off and land with a painful thump on the back of his head.

"YOU MUST NOT FALL OFF. Imagine that there is a thousand-foot drop under you."

"I am imagining it but I still can't stay on."

Back at the inn we had hot baths, several pints of beer, an enormous dinner, and immediately sank into a coma. For more than forty hours we had had hardly any sleep. "Good training," was Hugh's last muffled comment.

By this time the waitresses at the inn had become interested in this artificial forcing process. All three of them were experienced climbers who had taken the job in the first place in order to be able to combine business with pleasure. Now they continued our climbing education.

They worked in shifts, morning and afternoon, so that we were climbing all the time. We had never encountered anything quite like them before. At breakfast on the last day, Judith, a splendid girl with auburn hair whose father had been on Everest in 1933, told us what she had in mind. "Pamela and I are free this afternoon; we're going to do the *Spiral Stairs* on Dinas Cromlech. It's an interesting climb."

As soon as we could get through our breakfast we looked it up in the Climbing Guide to the Snowdon District, Part 6.

"Dinas Cromlech," said the book,

is perhaps the most impressive cliff on the north side of the Llanberis Pass, its massive rhyolite pillars giving it the appearance of some grim castle . . . all routes have surprising steepness . . . on the whole the rock is sound, although on first acquaintance it may not appear to be so.

Spiral Stairs was described as "Very difficult" and as having "an impressive first pitch with good exposure." At the back was a nasty picture of the Cromlech with the routes marked on it. Besides *Spiral Stairs* there was *Cenotaph Corner, Ivy Sepulchre,* and the *Sexton's Route.* It sounded a jolly spot.

"I wish we were doing *Castle Gully.* It says here, 'a pleasant vegetable route.'"

"They might have decided on *Ivy Sepulchre,*" said Hugh. "Just listen to this. 'Two hundred feet. Exceptionally severe. A very serious and difficult climb . . . loose rock overhangs . . . progress is made by abridging type of lay-back movement, an occasional hold of a doubtful nature appearing *now* and *then.*' He doesn't say what you do when it doesn't."

"What's a lay-back?"

"You were doing a lay-back when you fell off the Eckenstein Boulder."

"This is only the beginning, it gets worse. 'At this point the angle relents. . . .'"

"Relents is good," I said.

"'. . . to a small niche below the conspicuous overhang; no belay. Start the overhang by bridging. The climbing at this point is exceptionally severe, strenuous, and in a very exposed position.' It goes on and on! 'A short groove leads to the foot of an old rickety holly tree and after a struggle with this and the crack behind it, a good hold can be reached on the left wall.'"

"I wonder why everything seems to end with a rickety old holly tree."

We decided to have a quiet morning. Just then the other two girls appeared loaded with gear.

"Hurry up," they said, "we've got to be back by half past twelve. We're going to take you up *The Gauge*. You made a nonsense of it, the Doctor said. And you've both got to lead."

That afternoon, as Judith led the way up the scree from the road towards the base of Dinas Cromlech, we felt that if anything the guide book, in spite of its somber warnings, had not prepared us for the reality. It was as if a giant had been smoothing off the sides of a heap of cement with a trowel and had then lost patience and left it half finished. Its most impressive feature was a vast, right-angled wall, shiny with water and apparently smooth.

"*Cenotaph Corner*," said Judith, "Hundred and twenty feet. When you can do that you really will be climbers."

It seemed impossible.

"Joe Brown led it in 1952, with Belshaw. Joe's a plumber in Manchester. He spends every moment he can here. You remember how awful it was last winter when everyone's pipes were bursting? In the middle of it he left a note on the door of his house: 'Gone climbing. Joe Brown.' People nearly went mad."

"Where is he now?"

"In the Himalayas."

We looked at what he had climbed with awe.

There were already three people on *Spiral Stairs*. I could see what the book meant by "good exposure." At that moment one of them was edging his way round the vertical left-hand edge of *Cenotaph Corner*.

"That's the part that always gives me a thrill," said Pamela, the other girl. "Pity. Let's not wait, let's do *Ivy Sepulchre* instead."

"Oh, Pamela, do you think we ought to? It may be too much for them."

She made us sound like a couple of invalids out on the pier for an airing. Nevertheless, this was no time for stubborn pride. I asked Hugh if that was the climb we had been reading about at breakfast. He said it was.

"I think Judith's right," I said. "It may be too much for us."

As we waited in the cold shadow under the lee of the *Cenotaph*, Judith explained what we were going to do.

"The beginning's rather nasty because of that puddle. It makes your feet slippery just when they need to be dry. We'll climb in two parties. Pamela will lead Hugh, I'll lead you. The first part's seventy feet; round the edge of the *Cenotaph* it's very exposed and you'll feel the wind. Don't come on until I shout and you feel pressure on the rope. I'll be belayed then. Even if you come off you won't fall far."

"What happens if someone does come off? You can't just leave them hanging."

"Send for the fire brigade," said Judith.

Both girls were shuffling their boots on the rock like featherweight boxers. Then Pamela was gone, soon to be followed by Hugh. After what seemed an eternity it was Judith's turn. I had her belayed but at this stage it wasn't much use: I remembered the Doctor's warning. "The leader must not fall off." Then she vanished. I continued to pay out the rope. There was a long interval and I heard her shout very distantly to come on and the rope tautened.

It was impossible to get onto the rock without getting at least one foot wet.

Very slowly I worked my way out to the corner of the *Sepulchre*. As I edged round it into what seemed to be empty space I came on to the part with good exposure, the part that always gave Pamela a thrill. Below me was a huge drop to the rocks and as I came round the wind blew my hair into my eyes.

Two more pitches and we were on the top. I felt a tremendous exaltation. Sitting there on a boulder was a man in a bowler hat and white collar smoking a pipe.

"Early closing in Caernarvon," Judith said.

"He looks like an undertaker to me."

"We shall have to hurry, it's Pamela's day to serve tea." We went down a wide gully, then raced down the scree to the car. The others were waiting for us. The girls were pleased, so were we. Only the man with the bowler hat weighed on my mind. I asked Hugh if he had seen him.

"Which man? We didn't see a man."

"Now you're making me feel like one of those schoolteachers at Versailles."

"We saw the other party, but we didn't see a man in a bowler hat."

As we were leaving for London, Judith gave me a little pamphlet costing sixpence. It showed, with the aid of pictures, the right and wrong ways of climbing a mountain.

"We haven't been able to teach you anything about snow and ice," she said, "but this shows you how to do it. If you find anything on the journey out with snow on it, I should climb it if you get the chance."

"I wish we were coming with you," she added, "to keep you out of trouble."

"So do we," we said, and we really meant it. Everyone turned out to say good-bye. It was very heartwarming.

"You know that elderly gentleman who lent you a pair of climbing boots," Hugh said, as we drove through the evening sunshine towards Capel Curig.

"You mean Mr. Bartrum?"

"Did you know he's a member of the Alpine Club? He's written a letter about us to the Everest Foundation. He showed it to me."

I asked him what it said.

"He wrote, 'I have formed a high opinion of the character and determination of Carless and Newby and suggest that they should be given a grant toward the cost of their expedition to the Hindu Kush.'"

II

Getting Around

8

Weird Karma

P. J. O'Rourke

I never went to India in the old days, when people were going there to get mystical, meditate their heads off, and achieve the perfect state of spirituality that we see embodied even now in George Harrison and Mia Farrow. I guess I wasn't evolved enough to follow my bliss. And, come to think of it, I don't have the kind of bliss you'd care to tailgate.

I never went to India at all until this past summer, and then, instead of meditating, I took a daft, relentless road trip organized by Land Rover as part of an around-the-world test of its new Discovery sport-utility vehicle. Four journalists, 3 Land Rover employees, and a photographer were put into 2 vehicles and sent 1,700 miles over 6 days from Islamabad, Pakistan, to Calcutta, through the most populous part of the subcontinent at the hottest time of the year.

The equivalent would be to drive U.S. Route 1 from the outlet shops of Freeport, Maine, to downtown Miami in August. Consider if the driver had never been to America before. What would he think, after being Blockbustered, Safewayed, Chevroned, Shelled, Dodged, Nissaned, Wal-Marted, Dress Barned, Gapped, Burger Kinged, Dairy Queened, and Taco Belled? Would he have a good impression of the United States? No. Would he have an accurate impression? That's another matter.

Yet even the most accurate impressions may be deeply confusing. You can come back from India in tune with the godhead, I suppose, or you can come back realizing you know nothing about India—or, possibly, anything else. I attained reverse enlightenment. I now don't understand the entire nature of existence. My conscious mind was overwhelmed by a sudden blinding flash of . . . oncoming truck radiator.

Nirvana, from the Sanskrit word meaning "blow out," is the extinction of desires, passion, illusion, and the empirical self. This happens a lot in India, especially on the highways. Sometimes it's the result of a blowout, literally. More often, it's the product of a head-on crash.

We did our driving mostly on the Grand Trunk Road, the "river of life" and "Backbone of all Hind" made famous in Kipling's *Kim*. The Grand Trunk begins near the Khyber Pass, ends just short of the Bay of Bengal, and dates back to at least the fourth century B.C. For the greater part of its 1,600-mile length, the Grand Trunk runs through the broad, flood-flat Ganges plain. The road is straight and level and would be almost two lanes wide if there were such things as lanes in India. The asphalt paving—where it isn't absent—isn't bad. As roads go in the developing world, this is a good one. But Indians have their own uses for the main thoroughfare spanning their nation. It's a place where friends and family can meet, where they can set up charpoy beds and have a nap and let the kids run around unsupervised. It's a roadside cafe with no side—or tables, or chairs—where the street food is smack-dab on the street. It's a rent-free function room for every local fete. And it's a piece of agricultural machinery. Even along the Grand Trunk's few stretches of tollbooth-cordoned "expressway," farmers dry grain on the macadam.

The road is a store, a warehouse, and a workshop. Outside Chandigarh, on the border of Punjab and Haryana states, a blacksmith had pitched his tent on a bridge. Under the tent flaps were several small children, the missus working the bellows, and the craftsman himself smoking a hookah and contemplating his anvil, which was placed fully in the right of way. The road is also convenient for bullock carts, donkey gigs, horse wagons, pack camels, and the occasional laden elephant—not convenient for taking them anywhere, just convenient. There they stand, along with sheep, goats, water buffalo, and the innumerable cows sent to graze on the Grand Trunk. I watched several cows gobbling cardboard boxes and chewing plastic bags. There may be reasons besides sanctity that the Indians don't eat them.

With all this going on, there's no room left for actual traffic on the Grand Trunk. But here it is anyway, in tinny, clamorous, haywired hordes—Mahindra jeeps made with machine tools used on World War II Willys, Ambassador sedans copied from '50s English models, motorcycles and scooters of equally antique design, obsolete Twinkie-shaped buses, and myriads of top-heavy, butt-spring, weaving, swaying, wooden-bodied Tata trucks, their mechanicals as primitive as butter churns.

India's scientists had, just before our arrival, detonated several nuclear devices, yet everywhere around us was Indian technology that seemed more akin to the blunderbuss than to the A-bomb. The Tatas, Ambassadors, Mahindras, and whatchamacallits were coming right at us, running all day with horns on and all night with lights off, as fast as their fart-firing, smut-burping engines would carry them. The first time I looked out the windshield at this melee, I thought, *India really is magical. How can they drive like this without killing people?*

They can't. Jeeps bust scooters, scooters plow into bicycles, bicycles cover the hoods of jeeps. Cars run into trees. Buses run into ditches, rolling over on their old-fashioned rounded tops until they're mashed into chapatis of carnage. And everyone runs into pedestrians. A speed bump is called a "sleeping policeman" in England. I don't know what it's called in India. "Dead person lying in the road" is a guess. There's some of both in every village, but they don't slow traffic much. The animals get clobbered, too, including the sacred cows, in accidents notable for the unswerving behavior of all participants. Late in our trip, in Bihar state, the car in front of us hit a cow—no change in speed or direction from the car, no change in posture or expression from the cow.

But it's the lurching, hurtling Tatas that put the pepper in the *masala* and make the curry of Indian driving scare you coming and going the way last night's dinner did. The trucks are almost as wide as they are long and somewhat higher than either. They barrel down the road taking their half out of the middle, brake-less, lamp-less, on tread-less tires, moving dog-fashion with the front wheels headed where the rear wheels aren't. Tatas fall off bridges, fall into culverts, fall over embankments, and sometimes just fall, flopping onto their sides without warning. But usually Tatas collide with one another, in every possible way. Two Tatas going in opposite directions ahead of us snagged rear wheels and pulled each other's axles off. And Tatas crash not just in twos but in threes and fours, leaving great, smoking piles of vaguely truck-shaped wreckage. Inspecting one of these catastrophes, I found the splintered bodywork decorated with a little metal plaque: "LUCKY ENGINEERING."

In one day of travel, going about 265 miles from Varanasi to the border of West Bengal, I recorded 25 horrendous Tata wrecks. And I was scrupulous in my tallying. Fender benders didn't score; neither did old, abandoned wrecks or broken-down Tatas. Probable loss of life was needed to make the list. If you saw just one of these pileups on I-95, you'd pull in to the next rest stop—clutch foot shivering, hand palsied upon the shift knob—saying "Next time, we fly."

In India, you shout to your car mates "That's number 19! I'm winning the truck-wreck pool for today!"

As we drove from Lahore, Pakistan, to the Indian border, it was clear that we were approaching a land of mysteries. We went down the only connecting road between two large and important countries and, suddenly, there was nothing on the Grand Trunk. No one was going to or fro. They can't. "Pakistani and Indian nationals are only allowed to cross the border by train," says my guidebook. This utter lack of traffic has not prevented the establishment of fully staffed customs posts on both sides of the border.

Getting out of Pakistan was a normal third-world procedure. A customs official explained the entire system of Pakistani tariff regulation and passport control by rubbing his thumb against his forefinger.

"Fifty dollars," he said. I opened my wallet, foolishly revealing two $50 bills. "One hundred dollars," he said.

Things were very different on the Indian side. The rules concerning the entry of two Land Rovers and a trailerful of spare parts into the country occupy a book large enough to contain the collected works of Stephen King and the unabridged Oxford English Dictionary.

The Land Rovers had already passed the customs inspections of 13 nations, including Bulgaria and Iran, without hindrance, delay, or more than moderate palm-greasing. The Indian officials, upon hearing this, clucked and wagged their heads in sympathy for the hundreds of brother customs agents from London to the deserts of Baluchistan who had lost an opportunity to look up thousands of items in a great big book. Everything had to come out of the cars and the trailer. Everything had to go through a metal detector, even though the detector didn't seem to be plugged in. And everything had to come back through an X-ray machine that the customs agents weren't watching because they were too busy looking up items in a great big book.

All this took four hours, during which the seven or eight agents on duty met each hint at bribery with the stare you'd get from an octogenarian Powerball winner if you suggested the 25-year pay-out option. The fellow who was recording, in longhand, everything inside our passports did take two cigarettes, but he wouldn't accept a pack.

None of the cases, trunks, or bags—unloaded and reloaded in 105-degree heat—was examined, except for a wrench set. Perhaps there is one wrench size that requires a special permit in India. Our tire pressures had to be checked, however, in case the all-terrain radials were packed with drugs. The Indian-government tire gauge wasn't working, so we offered ours. We were halfway through checking the tires when we realized that nobody was accompanying us. I walked around behind the customs building to take a leak and found drugs to spare. I was pissing on $1,000 worth of wild marijuana plants.

By the time we left customs it was late afternoon. The staggering traffic and whopping crowds of India materialized. We still had 250 miles to go that day to stay on schedule. A brisk pace was required. Think of it as doing 60 through the supermarket parking lot and the school playground.

This is the India ordinary travelers never see—because they're in their right minds and don't drive down the Grand Trunk. And we didn't see much of it ourselves. The scenery was too close to view, a blur of cement-block shops and hovels in unbroken ranks inches from the fenders. But my map showed only open country with occasional villages meriting the smallest cartographic type size. There are a lot of people in India, some 970 million. I don't know what they want with the atomic bomb; they already have the population bomb, and it's working like a treat. And yet India, with a population density of 745 people per square mile, is not as crowded as the Netherlands, which packs 940 people into that same space. But nobody comes back from Holland aghast at the teeming mass of Dutch.

Indian crowding is not the natural result of baby-having but the unnatural result of too many people tied to the land by tradition, debt-bondage, caste, and illiteracy. Business and industry is pushed into the road by subsistence agriculture, which takes up a lot more room than making a living with a laptop, a phone, and a fax.

Life is jammed tight in India to keep it out of the picnic-blanket–sized rice field that's the sole means of support for a family of 10. Every inch of land is put to purpose. At the bottom of a 40-foot-deep abandoned well, which would be good for nothing but teenage suicides in America, somebody was raising frogs. Public restrooms in Calcutta employ the space-saving device of dispensing with walls and roofs and placing the urinal stalls on the sidewalk. No resource goes to waste, which sounds like a fine thing to advocate next Earth Day, except in the real world of poverty, it means that the principal household fuel of India is cow flop. This is formed into a circular patty and stuck on the side of the house, where it provides a solution to three problems: storage space, home decor, and how to cook dinner.

Therefore, what makes a drive across India overwhelming (and odoriferous) isn't population, it's poverty. Except it's even more complicated than that. It always is in India. The reason for those ranks of shops and houses along the Grand Trunk—and for the cars, trucks, and buses bashing into one another between them—is the money from an expanding economy that people now have to buy and build these things. And the reason for the great smoldering dung funk hanging over India is that people now have something to cook over those fires. The chaos of India is not just poverty's turmoil, it's also prosperity's stew.

When India gained its independence in 1947, the nation's political elite instituted an economic system that combined the perplexities of the capitalist old-boy network with the intricacies of socialism and then added the extra something we'd experienced going through customs. (Britain has a lot of paperwork and is a rich country, so if India has a lot of paperwork, it will be a rich country also.) The result was known as the "license-permit-quota raj." *The Economist* once said, "This has no equal in the world. In many ways it puts Soviet central planning to shame." Indian industries were trapped and isolated by the government. Like an aunt locked in the attic, they got strange. Hence the Tata trucks, the Ambassador sedans, and the motorcycles that Evel Knievel would be afraid to ride.

But by 1992 India had begun to surrender to free-market reforms. Imports were allowed, foreign investment was encouraged, and customs regulations were (amazing as this seems after having been through Indian customs) simplified. The Indian economy has been growing at about 7 percent a year ever since. As many as 200 million people now make up the Indian middle class—a number roughly equal to the total middle class of the United States. There are plenty of flat bellies in India but few of the distended kind that announce gross malnutrition. And the beggars, whom Western visitors have been taught to expect in legions, arrive only in platoons. A kid selling trinkets in Agra was irked to be mistaken for such. "I'm not a beggar," he said. "You want to buy, you get. Eighty rupees."

The quaint, old India is still there, however, just beyond the clutter of the Grand Trunk Road. In West Bengal we visited a beautiful farm village full of amusing thatch architecture and cute peasant handcrafts. Here the handsome patina of tradition glowed upon lives that were quiet, calm, and as predictable as the lifelong poverty, semiannual famine, and the dowry needed to marry off the 10-year-old daughter.

The villagers were friendly enough. But what if carloads of French tourists pulled into my driveway and took happy snaps while I scrubbed down the barbecue? I preferred the messy hopes on the Grand Trunk.

Maybe—on a brief trip, anyway—it's better to make no attempt to understand India. Just go to the beauty spots like the rest of the international rubberneckers and stand agape, getting your tonsils sunburned. We tried that, too. (Land Rover needed PR photos with something other than wrecked trucks in the background.)

We took a side journey into the Himalayan foothills, to Shimla, the colonial hill station that was the summer capital of British rule. It's built at a higher elevation than Kathmandu. The road up was like the Grand Trunk except at the same angle as your basement stairs and in the shape of used gift-wrap ribbon on Christmas morning.

Shimla is a mulligatawny of concrete and roof tin, with the only charming parts being the leftovers of colonial oppression. Along the Mall there's a row of dusty shops that the British—seeing mountains all around them and not knowing what else to do—built in Alpine-style. The parade ground has views to die for (or die of, if you lean against the flimsy railings). Atal Bihari Vajpayee, the prime minister of India, was headed to town. Preparation consisted of a minor government functionary's loudly testing the PA system:

HELLO HELLO HELLO HELLO HELLO HELLO HELLO
HELLO HELLO HELLO HELLO HELLO HELLO HELLO
HELLO HELLO HELLO ONE TWO THREE FOUR FIVE
SIX SEVEN EIGHT NINE TEN MICROPHONE TESTING
HELLO HELLO HELLO HELLO HELLO HELLO HELLO
HELLO HELLO HELLO HELLO HELLO HELLO HELLO

For an hour. This was the crowd warm-up. The speech must have been a dilly. Meanwhile, behind handsome batik curtains, tribal women in full native dress with nose jewelry the size of baby shoes were repairing the pavement.

Back on the Grand Trunk, we visited the Taj Mahal, an impressive pile built with public funds in Agra while a famine scourged the countryside. The Taj was commissioned by Shah Jahan to memorialize his favorite wife, who died in 1631 giving birth to their fourteenth child. If Jahan had really wanted to show his love, he could have cut back on the Viagra.

And we saw the holiest place of all, Varanasi, where millions of pilgrims descend the ghats into the Ganges, using its waters to purify themselves of sins, as well as to carry away the funeral pyres of friends and relatives. Everybody but me made a sunrise trip to see these sacred rites. I stayed in bed. No death before breakfast, please. Plus, there's the matter of barging in on other people's religious ceremonies: Yo, is that the Holy Eucharist? Cool! Can I taste?

And once you got started looking at religions in India, how would you know when to stop? There are Buddhists, Muslims, Sikhs, Jains, Parsis (Zoroastrians), Christians, Jews, and 800 million Hindus.

I am confused enough by the material surface of India without delving into its metaphysical foundation garments. Hinduism is said to have 330,000,000 gods, which is fine by me if folks want that many. But such multiplication of divinity can't help but add to the profound obscurity of Indian culture, as do the 17 officially recognized languages and the intricate caste system that somewhat resembles American ideas about social class, except you can't touch Wayne Huizenga because he founded Waste Management, Inc.

Everything in India seems to be a brain-teaser. Just getting dressed is a riddle. This is how you put on a sari: Take a piece of cloth 4 feet wide and 25 feet long and tuck one corner into your underpants. Turn around clockwise once. Tuck the upper hem into your underpants. Make a pleat by holding the fabric between your thumb and little finger, spreading your hand, extending the fabric around your forefinger and bringing it back to your thumb. Do this eight times. Tuck the top of the pleats into your underpants. Turn around clockwise again, and throw everything that remains over your left shoulder. (And I still looked like hell.)

Each little detail of India is a conundrum. Painted above door frames you see the Sanskrit character for the sacred, meditative *om,* bracketed by a pair of swastikas. The swastika is really just a Hindu symbol for self-energization and the accomplishments of life (the Nazis swiped it for the Aryan look). Nonetheless, the message over the doors seems to read *"Sieg heil* inner peace *sieg heil."*

Which isn't too far wrong at the moment. The current coalition government in India—the one that likes atomic bombs—is headed by the Bharatiya Janata Party. The BJP is avidly nationalistic and espouses Hindu fundamentalism—sort of like Pat Buchanan and Ralph Reed but with 330,000,000 Jesuses. And the BJP believes in rigid observation of the caste system, so it's like Pat and Ralph have gotten together with the people who do the Philadelphia social register. Or worse, because the most influential support for the BJP comes from the Rashtriya Swayamsevak Sangh, the RSS, a secretive, hard-line Hindu brotherhood that was almost certainly responsible for the assassination of Mahatma Gandhi, and whose half-million members wear matching khaki shorts to early-morning rallies and make funny, stiff-armed salutes. One reputed RSS leader, K. S. Sudarshan, has said, "We don't believe in individual rights because we don't think we are individuals."

Modern India is, in ways, an unattractive place. But things could be worse. And the BJP seems determined to make them so. The country has a population greater than those of North and South America combined. Its land area exceeds France, Germany, Great Britain, Iraq, Japan, Paraguay, and Ghana put together, and its citizens are that similar. They get along as well as everybody at the UN does. India is as complicated as the earth. Indeed, if a person were to announce his nationality as "earthling," there would be a one-in-six chance that he was Indian. To all this, the BJP responds with a slogan: "One nation, one people, one culture."

Just when you think you're not getting India, you start to get it even less. East of Varanasi, in Bihar state, we encountered a

Communist rally. Hundreds of agitated-looking agitators waved red flags and brandished staves. We were a ripe target for the anger of the masses—eight capitalist prats in fancy Land Rovers with a trailerful of goodies protected by only a tarp. We were ignored. It seems the ideological fury of the Communist Party of India (Marxist-Leninist) is directed primarily at the Communist Party of India (Marxist).

The latter runs Calcutta. According to my guidebook, "they have somehow succeeded in balancing rhetoric and old-fashioned socialism with a prudent practicality. . . . Capitalism is allowed to survive, but made to support the political infrastructure."

Not that you'd know this by driving into Calcutta, where the infrastructure doesn't look like it could support another flea. Certainly the Howrah Bridge over the Hooghly River couldn't. It carries 60,000 motor vehicles a day, and they were all there when we tried to get across at 5 p.m.

I spent the next four days trying to accomplish something in India. If you're going to be confounded by the country, you can't go as a tourist. Tourism is a pointless activity. Pointless activity is a highly developed craft in India. You could spend months touring the country, busy doing fuck-all. Meanwhile, the Indian government and business bureaucracies are busy doing fuck-all of their own. You could accidentally come back thinking you'd caught the spirit of the place. If you intend to be completely baffled, you have to try to accomplish something. Any task will do. For instance, the Land Rover Discoverys and the trailer had to be put into a cargo container in Calcutta and shipped to Australia. This should take 20 minutes. Adjusting the clock to official Indian Daylight Wasting Time, that's four days,

First, the port was closed. Well, it wasn't really closed. I mean, it is sort of closed because the Port of Calcutta has silted in and is nearly useless. Only about three ships were there. This doesn't keep hundreds of stevedores, shipping clerks, and port officials from coming to work, of course. But there were city-council elections that day, with attendant rioting. So the police had to suppress voters and weren't available for harassment at the port.

Then the port was closed because it was Sunday.

Then our shipping agents got into an argument about when to pick us up at the hotel the next day. Not that they disagreed with one another.

"We will go to get them at 9:30 in the morning," one said.

"Oh, no, no, no, no," said another. "It must be 9:30 in the morning."

"How can you talk like this?" said a third, stamping his foot. "The time for us to be there is 9:30 in the morning."

We had about 10 shipping agents. There's no such thing as hiring an individual in India. In a Bihar village it took the services of two shops, four shopkeepers, and a boy running for change for me to buy a pack of cigarettes.

While I waited for the port to open, I wandered the streets of Calcutta. The city is a byword for squalor, but parts of Washington, D.C., are dirtier (Congress, the White House), and Calcutta smells no worse than a college dorm.

The poverty is sad and extensive, but at least the families living on the streets are intact—talking to one another instead of to themselves. I did see some people who seemed really desperate, addled and unclean. But these were American hippies getting mystical at Calcutta's Dum Dum airport. I was standing in the ticket line behind an Indian businessman, who stared at the hippies and then gave me a stern look, as if to say "These are *your people*. Isn't there something you can *do?*"

Calcutta's pollution is more visible than it's fashionable for American pollution to be—smoke and trash instead of microwaves and PCBs. The food sold on its streets may be unidentifiable, but it's less likely than New York City hot dogs to contain a cow asshole.

The crowding is extreme, but you get used to it. You get used to a lot of things in India—naked ascetics; 100 sheep being herded through downtown traffic; costumed girls parading in single file linked by electric wires, one carrying a car battery and the rest with blue fluorescent tubes sticking out of their headdresses.

I was waiting to cross the busiest street in Calcutta when a four-story temple complex on wheels went by, complete with high priest, idols, acolytes, clouds of incense, blazing torches, and banging gongs. And what I noticed was that I hadn't noticed it. Imagine the pope (and quite a bit of St. Peter's) coming down Broadway at rush hour and you thinking *Should I wait for the walk signal?*

There's a certain pest factor in Calcutta, caused mostly by roving market-bearers who double as shopping touts. But it's not without its entertainment value. Bearer number A49 from New Market told me to avoid the other bearers because they would get me into their shops and cut my throat. Lesser merchants, squatting on the street, sell everything from new Lee jeans to brightly colored pebbles and pieces of broken mirrors. The poster wallah's selection included photographs of kittens tangled in balls of yarn and a rendering of the goddess Kali holding a severed human head by its hair.

In the midst of this was the Oberoi Grand Hotel, its guards stationed at the gate with sticks to use on touts and beggars. At the Oberoi everything was efficient, crisp, clean, pukka (except when the electricity went out). The Indians inside seemed as perplexed by the India outside as I was. I told Alex, the restaurant manager, about the muddle at the port. "Oh, this country," he said. "There are no two ways around it."

We had parked the Land Rovers and trailer in the hotel's courtyard. The shipping agents came by to inform us that everything in the vehicles had to be clean and packed exactly as described on the customs documents. We set about amending 1,700 miles' worth of dirt and equipment disorder. It was 100 degrees in the courtyard. Removing the trailer tarp, we discovered an ax had come loose from its lashings and punctured a container of beef stew and a can of motor oil. The trailer bed was awash in oil and what Hindus euphemistically call "brown meat."

On Monday we went back to the port, where the customs inspectors ignored everything about our cleanliness and packing except the ax. "What is this?" asked the chief inspector.

"An ax," we said.

The officials conferred at length and decided it was so. Then there was a seven-hour delay because of an engine serial-number discrepancy. The customs inspectors were worried that we'd stolen one of the Discoverys from Land Rover. "*We're* from Land Rover," we said. "These are the only Discoverys in Asia, and they can't be stolen because they're both right here." The inspectors returned to their office cubicles to ponder this. We sat on the dock.

I asked one of our shipping agents why so many of the Tata drivers had decorated their front bumpers with one dangling shoe.

"Oh, for the heck of it," he said.

Finally, the Land Rovers were rolled into the cargo container. I stayed on in Calcutta for a few more days, in awe at a dundering flux of a place that seemed in total disarray but where I couldn't even get lost because everyone with a clean shirt spoke English. In the midst of the street stampede (not a figure of speech, considering the sacred cows), there are young hawkers with what look like shoeshine boxes. What's offered for sale, though, isn't a wingtip buff. The youths crouch in the hubbub, juggling the tiny wheels and springs of wristwatches, setting timepieces running again. There is a whole street in Calcutta lined with tiny stalls where artisans with soldering irons rearrange the logic on the latest computer circuit boards.

Indian journalist and novelist Gita Mehta says her country produces 5 million university graduates a year. That's four times the number of bachelor degrees awarded annually in the United States. Yet nearly 48 percent of all Indians are illiterate, and almost two-thirds of Indian women are. It is the smartest country in the stupidest way.

You walk by a newsstand—a "newssquat," to be precise—and see the *Calcutta Telegraph*, the *Calcutta Statesman*, the *Asian Age*, the *Times of India*, and stacks of newspapers in Hindi, Bengali, and other languages. A *Telegraph* feature section contained a "KnowHow" pullout on particle physics. A *Statesman* op-ed page had an article on energy efficiency: "The heat rate of the power plant, in layman's terms, refers to how much kilo calorie of heat is required to produce 1 kwh of power." You think you're in a nation of Einsteins. Then you look up from your newspaper and see a man walking along wearing a bucket upside down over his head.

9

Boats and Planes

Pete McCarthy

"So, Liam, what river do you think Luxor stands on?"

"Er, the Danube?"

The sun's shining and the gorse is blooming as I head back towards Cork airport. A day shy of two weeks and I finally manage to override the perpetual search mode on the repmobile radio by pressing the same button I've been frantically jabbing at for a fortnight. One day someone will reinvent twiddling a dial to find channels and be hailed as a technological genius.

The decline of the Catholic Church's influence in the last two decades has coincided with the rise of the phone-in on Irish radio, where a nation confesses its darkest heresies and most startling sexual unorthodoxies to a new priesthood of silver-tongued disc jockeys. Radio confers a cathartic anonymity, and a sense of self-justification, that can't be had from confessing the same stomach-churning filth to a steely-hearted alleged celibate in a Saturday night confessional, while your neighbors sit in rows outside, adjusting their underpants and trying to listen.

"Now, Kathleen, you're on your way to Sligo for your twenty-first. Can you tell me who wrote *The Importance of Being Earnest*?"

"Er, Ernest . . . Ernest . . . Ernest Hemingway?"

These days, you can normally rely on Irish talk radio for an engrossing catalog of out-of-court settlements for testosterone-crazed bishops, or guilt-ridden farmers owning up to serial gusset-twanging with semi-literate babysitters. Instead, I've got round two of the morning quiz. And the Sixteenth Rule of Travel says: *However Exotic the Country, the Local Radio Phone-in Quiz Induces in the Traveler a Sudden and Dramatic Downturn in the Will to Live.* But passing through Bandon half an hour from the airport things take a turn for the better, with news of a plan to put a great big light on the top of Croagh Patrick, Ireland's holiest mountain up there in County Mayo. The light would shine out across the world, or at any rate Mayo, as a symbol of Ireland's faith. The organization behind this controversial plan turns out to be a bloke called Gerry, who seems to have it well thought through.

"So, Gerry, have you thought how you'll be getting the power up there?"

"Well, we've considered all the possibilities, like, but the best way will be if we dig a trench there, right up the side."

"A trench up the side of Croagh Patrick, Gerry?"

"That's it, yeah."

"So have you talked to the fella with the digger yet?"

"Er, well now, I've got me own digger, y'see."

"So what'll you be putting up there on the top of the mountain then, Gerry? Will ya—"

"Just a, y'know, a great big light, like."

"Will there not be a burger bar or some other kind of refreshment outlet?"

"Ah, sure, no, just a picnic will be nice."

"What did St. Patrick have to drink up there? Do we know that, Gerry?"

As I pull into the airport poor Gerry's taking a terrible drubbing from enraged listeners accusing him of blasphemy, congenital idiocy, and ignorance of the fact that the top of Croagh Patrick is under cloud 90 percent of the time. Gerry's morale goes into free fall, perhaps because work on the sacrilegious trench has already begun, and he's thinking it might be quite hard now to go back and fill it in. Maybe he's already bought the electric cable.

I park the repmobile in a potholed wasteland among dozens of its clones and head for the terminal.

Apart from once absentmindedly eating a whole packet of stale crisps in the Dar es Salaam departure lounge before looking in the bottom of the bag for crumbs and discovering it was full of live ants, I can think of few travel experiences more depressing than returning a hire car to an airport dealership. The desk will be unmanned as you approach, because the partially trained company representative has seen you coming and hidden behind the counter in the hope that you'll drop the keys in the box and go away. This way they can post you a prepaid credit card slip, which is infinitely preferable to standing there watching your reactions as you read the bill.

After standing my ground for two or three minutes, a young man suddenly pops up from underneath the counter, feigning surprise. According to his label, his name is Ruaraigh; and he's very red. Either he's already embarrassed at the answers he's about to give me, or he's got someone down there with him.

"Ah, hiya, heh, didn't see you there just now. Looking for some fax paper. Can I help ya at all?"

Standard industry practice then prevails, as Ruaraigh denies all knowledge of my, or the repmobile's, existence, and elaborately fails to find the paperwork.

"Sorry about the delay there, Mr. McCarthy."

I've already done the mental sums on this one. Thirteen days, call it two weeks, at what was it? Twenty-two pounds ninety-five pence a day. Say £165 a week. Add on some tax, and there are always some insurance extras the bastards haven't told you about, £380, say £400 tops, which still seems a lot for cheap seats, no central locking and pariah status, but there you go, that's the world we live in.

"Here it is now, Mr. McCarthy. Sorry about the hold-up, like."

But instead of a simple invoice saying "Car Two Weeks 400 quid" the printer is pummeling out unfeasible columns of figures on, at the last count, three sheets of corporate paper. It's taking on the look of the extras on a Keith Richards hotel bill. As the machine runs out of puff, Ruaraigh rips off the account, detaches the side perforation and glances at it, before passing it to me with a nervous grin.

"Jeezus, Mary, and Joseph, that can't be right!"

The anguished howl comes from nearby, where a big woman in a state of shock, and inappropriate velour leisurewear, has just received her bill at the ironically-named Budget counter. I glance down at mine and feel physically sick.

"Six hundred and thirty-two pounds?"

"Yes, sir. Six hundred and thirty-two pounds thirty-four pence. But that's punts remember, Mr. McCarthy, sir."

Everything's turning woozy with the nausea. For a moment I can't think straight. Punts? What's he on about? Perhaps it's rhyming slang and he's talking about his bosses.

"So, if you allow for the exchange rate, sir, that's only. . . ."

"Six hundred and thirty-two pounds to hire a tiny bloody embarrassment of a car for two weeks? Why the hell is car hire so expensive in this country?"

"Well, sir, it's not two weeks, it's only thirteen days."

"That's right, so there should be at least a day to knock off then, shouldn't there? This can't be right."

"Well, sir, no, sir, because you got the first week at the weekly rate, which was, let's see, £210 plus tax, but the second week isn't a week at all now, if you follow me, it's only six days, and at the daily rate, I'll just check on the calculator, that'll be £223.95 plus tax."

"So, it's more for six days than a week?"

"That's right, sir, yes, because of the discount, you see, sir."

"But can't I just pay for a week and give you a car back a day early and then everyone gains, don't they?"

"I can't do that, sir, not unless you hang on to it until tomorrow, and then it'll be cheaper all right. Would you like to do that?"

"But, bloody hell, what are all these extras anyway?"

"Well, sir, there's £11 a day insurance."

"What?"

"Ah y'see, you initialled for that, here and here. It's fully comprehensive and there's tax here and here and here."

And on it goes. A litany of charges. Optional insurance, special insurance, roadside insurance, home contents insurance, booking fee, room service, adult video, gas bill, optional tip, and two Four Seasons pizzas, all adding up to the final breathtaking total.

"But what's this here?"

"The daily rate, sir. That's the special BBC rate."

"But I'm not working for the bloody BBC."

"Well, the computer has you down as BBC, Mr. McCarthy."

"I'm not from the BBC. I worked for them here once a couple of years ago. That's all."

"Well, that'll be it then. It'll be in the computer and you qualify for that rate."

"But it's £30 a day. I booked at £22.95."

"Well, that is the special BBC rate, sir."

"Seven quid a day more than the standard rate?"

"Seems to be, sir, heh, heh. I'd say it's time they renegotiated that deal now. They probably haven't looked at it for a long time there."

Suddenly a shifty youth with spots, jug ears, and a company polo shirt materializes from out the back and hands a slip of paper to Ruaraigh.

"Look, what I'll do, Mr. McCarthy, is I can put in a request to Head Office to bump your rate down from the BBC rate to the normal rate, like. I can't promise anything now, but maybe they'll send you through a discount on the old credit card."

"Thanks, Ruaraigh. I appreciate that."

"But the thing is, sir"—looking ominously at the paper Jug-ears has slipped him—"it seems there's damage to the car, sir."

"But there can't be. I only just bloody parked it outside."

"I know that, sir, but our operatives have just been checking it out, sir."

Jug-ears is out the back, staring like a vindictive gargoyle.

"And there's a cracked windscreen, sir."

"A tiny crack, yes, the size of a match head. A pebble hit it but I've got your comprehensive insurance."

"You still have to pay the first £75 of any claim, Mr. McCarthy."

I'm near to tears now, realizing the only thing round here that's comprehensive is the way I've been stitched up.

"And the tank's not full, neither, sir. So there'll be £7.50 for petrol. You're always better off filling up before you bring it back because we have to charge top whack."

The bloody thing hadn't been full when I drove it away. Hire cars never are. The needle drops from full to three-quarters when you've barely left the airport, because behind the phony smiles of the front desk, in airport car parks all over the world, spaced-out jug-eared school-leavers, whose meals taste of nothing but petrol, are sucking on siphon pipes to swindle you.

"So that makes it £714.84 to be exact."

Less non-BBC discount, of course, if it comes through. I could have bought a car for less.

The flight, on the other hand, was £21.30 one way, Cork–London, one of the new no-frills deals that makes you wonder how they can afford a pilot who's passed his test. Just before take-off, but well after take-off time, the family we've all been waiting for finally turns up. I spotted them in the bar earlier: three kids, mum and dad, and an out-on-parole brother-in-law, all in various combinations of

Manchester United replica kit, except for mum, who's gone for Glasgow Celtic, though I think one of her tattoos is United.

Seats on these flights are unreserved, like being in a bus, or the casualty department of a hospital. The family, who are clearly in high spirits, having presumably given Social Services the slip earlier in the day, base themselves a few rows up to my right; the eldest boy though, a nine-year-old sociopath, is banished down the aisle to sit next to me. When he complains, then shrieks, his uncle—carry-on beer in hand ready for take-off—comes down and threatens him, then gives him a can of Coke and a family-size bag of what smell like prawn cocktail and Russian cigarette-flavor cheesy corn snacks. The kid chugs the Coke and guzzles the technicolor chemicals in the few minutes we're sitting on the tarmac, then as we begin to taxi, he starts wailing, "Ma, Ma, Ma" in a monotone crescendo that goes unnoticed by the increasingly lively, and indeed armwrestling, family group up front. He blurts out the words, "Ma, I'm gonna do a sick," just a split second before blurting out the Coke and cheesy snacks from, I can't help noticing at such close range, nose and gob simultaneously. Fortunately a woman across the aisle is quick to react with a no-frills sick bag, and I get away with minor traces of splashback.

As we gain altitude and my pebble-dashed chinos begin to crisp up nicely, I consider the reasons for this hiatus in my journey. I'm planning to spend a lot more time traveling round the west of Ireland, but not in a hire car; and I can't make the Loch Derg pilgrimage before they open for business in June. And anyway work calls.

Well, not work exactly, but one of the management-imposed charades that plague many industries these days, and television more than most. Every few months the senior executives at BBC and Channel 4 and ITV leave to take up similar jobs at a rival channel, where they immediately sack the existing staff and bring in their mates from their last job. They then cancel programs, and commission focus groups of unemployable daytime TV-watchers with personality disorders to try and find out what viewers want.

Meanwhile, writers are summoned from all over the country to dream up ideas for vibrant, new, original programs, which are then ditched in favor of the braindead pet, cookery, gardening, and home improvement shows that have come to dominate the British airwaves. This time I'm considering pitching an idea about two sick dogs who swap homes. While they're away they get looked after by sexy vets, and their gardens and kennels have makeovers. Then they die and get barbecued by Ainsley Harriott. I'll need about a month in England for meetings with various chancers, charlatans, and posh boys calling themselves producers, then I can go back to Ireland for as long as I like.

As we come in to land at Stansted there is a vicious fracas involving the three-year-old in the middle of the row in front of me, who has spent the entire flight standing on her seat slam-dancing and head-butting the shoulder of the woman in the window seat. The child's mother, sitting in front of Sick Boy—now working his way through his second Snickers bar with 7-Up chasers—is an odd one, and no error.

Thirty-something, white and Irish, she's dressed in a full-length embroidered biblical gown with striped pyjamas showing underneath, desert sandals, and a blue nativity-play headdress. The whole ensemble is nicely complemented by two-inch-thick orange foundation—like one of those scary women at a department store cosmetics counter—pouting pink lip gloss, and Dusty Springfield mascara, which appears to have been applied with a table tennis bat.

In England, we're used to being able to place people socially at a glance and it's frustrating when, as with this woman, the totality of the image simply does not compute. The best I can come up with for now is that she's from one of those obscure fundamentalist Christian sects who don't believe in books or paracetamol. The poor woman has probably endured baptism by immersion, possibly in red-hot coals, and has been forced to practice serial polygamy with thin blokes with white beards and crocheted hats in poorly heated outbuildings in places like Sligo and Suffolk.

This lifestyle has clearly had its effect on the child, who is disturbed, and enjoying every minute of it. For the duration of the flight, her mother has half-heartedly attempted to control her by repeating the mantra, "Do you want a smack?" fifty or sixty times. Or perhaps it was "some smack." It's hard to be sure. In any case, mum was the one who got the smacks: first, when the child carefully considered the hard-edged plastic toy she'd been given to placate her, then launched it at her mother's face from a distance of two feet; and a second time, when, without warning, she landed a sickening right cross to her jaw. You got the feeling that once she got her on her own back at the ashram, she'd really lay into her.

"So what was that on the plane about a smack?"

"Nothing, dear."

"Come here a minute would you, mother?"

As the wheels come down and we're preparing to land, mum, the woman by the window, and two hosties are still trying to force the kid to sit and fasten her seatbelt, while she emits a stomach-churning keen. At any rate, it's stomach-churning for Sick Boy. This time he dispenses with the formality of a warning. He simply honks once, like a poorly goose, then chunders with tremendous violence. Foaming Snickers fragments hit the back of the nativity headdress like a flock of starlings. Then the kid's mother runs down the aisle and belts him.

The glamor of airline travel is beginning to wear off. Next time I'll recapture the serene atmosphere of my childhood.

I'll go back to Ireland on the ferry.

A little more than six weeks later and I'm in a pub in Wales waiting for the night ferry to Cork. It's more than two decades since I last arrived in Cork by boat, and I have a strong sense of what I can only describe as nostalgic anticipation. For reasons I cannot fathom, the telly in the corner above the bar was showing Jimi Hendrix in black and white when I came in. He was playing "Purple Haze" then. He's doing "Hey Joe" now. Look—there's Noel Redding standing next to him. The half-dozen men in the pub are watching as if they're a new act. Perhaps driving to the ferry has somehow taken me through a time warp to the 1960s. This bar contains no indication that the last thirty years have happened. The most modern things in it are Formica and pork rinds. I've never understood the appeal of a snack that has hair growing out of it.

Hope the car's safe outside. It's a big tank of a Volvo saloon, nearly twenty years old, chunky, blue, deeply unfashionable, and it only cost £290. How do you like that then, Ruaraigh? Less than a week's hire price. I found it in Brighton in a little back-street garage up from the station. I test-drove it, knocked him down from £400, did the deal, and drove off. Six hundred yards away the clutch failed, the gears wouldn't change, and it broke down in the middle of the Old Shoreham Road. I had to call the AA—the Automobile Association, not Alcoholics Anonymous. As I hadn't yet worked out how to open the hood, it was quite embarrassing. The AA man didn't disguise the fact that he thought I was a twat. Yet, when I was a kid, they used to salute you if you were a member. What went wrong there then?

Still, it's a bargain, I keep telling myself, especially if you don't count the £720 I've spent so far on repairs. Plus tax, road test fees, punitive insurance, add Ruaraigh's bill—and the non-BBC discount never materialized, by the way—and I'm almost two grand down already. And I'm not even in Ireland. As I've said, I'm in bloody Wales.

When I came in I had to ask three times for a pint before the barmaid understood me. They've never liked me, the Welsh. I went to a Wales–England rugby game at Cardiff Arms Park once, too crowded to move, and at half-time the people on the tier above us pissed on us for being English. I tried to explain I was a fellow Celt, but had to settle for turning my collar up.

Oh Christ, Hendrix has finished now and Marmalade are on, singing "Ob-La-Di, Ob-La-Da." This can't be what all the telly's like down here, can it? Mind you, these blokes don't seem to notice. They're up playing darts now, four of them, big buggers, with enormous beer bellies poking through skin-tight leisure tops. That one there, you can see the shape of his navel through it, and Christ, can they swear. These people swear more than the Irish. The only words I can hear as they're throwing the arrows are swear words. The barmaid's swearing now, too. They probably think I'm some terrible ponce, sitting here with an English accent and writing things down. Hope they don't come over.

"Hey, what are you writing, butt? Give us a look, will you?"

"Oh, it's nothing. Just some stuff about what fat bastards you are. Hey, come on, lads, only joking. . . ."

Nah, smashing people the Welsh. St. Patrick came from here, didn't he? There you are then. Nancy Sinatra's on now; this is all getting a bit weird. Better not have any more to drink till I'm on the boat. Walk to the door. Whatever you do, don't look back. They might take it as a sign of weakness.

10

The Bus Plunge Highway

Tom Miller

To reach the town of Febres Cordero I took a bus to Guayaquil—
at 1.6 million, the country's most populous city. The 150-mile
ride started smoothly despite my apprehension. Bus rides through
Latin America have always induced fear in me, brought on by years
of reading one-paragraph bus-plunge stories used by newspapers in
the States as fillers on the foreign-news page. The datelines change,
but the headlines always include the words *bus plunge,* as in 12 DIE IN
SRI LANKA BUS PLUNGE, or CHILEAN BUS PLUNGE KILLS 31. "We can count
on one every couple of days or so," an editor at *The New York Times*
once told me. "They're always ready when we need them." Never
more than two sentences long, a standard bus-plunge piece will usually include the number feared dead, the identity of any group on
board—a soccer team, church choir, or school bus—and the distance
of the plunge from the capital city. The words *ravine* and *gorge* pop
up often. Most of the stories come from Third World countries, the
victims comprising just a fraction of the faceless brown-skinned
masses. "A hundred Pakistanis going off a mountain in a bus make
less of a story than three Englishmen drowning in the Thames," noted
foreign correspondent Mort Rosenblum in *Coups & Earthquakes.* Is
there a news service that does nothing but supply daily papers with

bus-plunge stories? Peru and India seem to generate the most coverage; perhaps the wire services have more stringers in the Andes and Himalayas than anywhere else.

If an Ecuadorian bus driver survives a plunge fatal to others, according to Moritz Thomsen in *Living Poor*, "he immediately goes into hiding in some distant part of the country so that the bereaved can't even up the score. There are rumors of whole villages down in the far reaches of the Amazon basin populated almost entirely by bus drivers. This is probably apocryphal. . . ."

If you anticipate a bus trip in Latin America, go through the following checklist prior to boarding:

- Look at the tires. If three or more of the six tires (most buses include two rear sets of two each) are totally bald, the probability of bus plunge increases. Visible threads on the tires means a blowout is imminent.
- Does the bus have at least one windshield wiper? Good. If it's on the driver's side, so much the better. Try to avoid buses whose windshields are so crowded with decals, statues, and pictures that the driver has only a postcard-sized hole through which to see the future. Shrines to saints, pious homilies, boastful bumper stickers, and religious trinkets do not reflect the safety of a bus. Jesus Christ and Che Guevara are often worshipped on the same decal. This should give neither high hopes nor nagging suspicion.
- The driver's sobriety isn't a factor. The presence of his wife or girlfriend is. If she's along, she will usually sit immediately behind him, next to him, or on his lap. He will want to impress her with his daring at the wheel, but he will also go to great lengths not to injure her. If he has no girlfriend or wife, the chances of gorge-dive increase.
- You can't check the bus for brakes. Once I asked a driver in Guatemala about the brakes on his bus. "Look," he said, "the bus is stopped, isn't it? Then the brakes must work."

- On intercity buses, seats are often assigned before boarding. Refuse the seat directly behind the driver or in the front right. If your ride takes place during the day, you'll be subjected to at least one heart-skip a minute as your bus casually passes a truck on an uphill blind curve or goes head-to-head with an oncoming bus. At night, the constant glare of approaching headlights will shine in your eyes. At any hour, the driver's makeshift radio speaker will dangle closer to your ears than you'd like.
- Always have your passport ready. Random military inspections take place when you least expect them. I once delayed a bus full of cross-country travelers for ten minutes a couple of miles outside Esmeraldas, on the Pacific Coast south of Colombia, while frantically searching first for my bag atop the bus, then my passport within the bag.

In defense of Latin-American buses: They go everywhere. *Everywhere.* No road is so dusty, bumpy, unpopulated, narrow, or obscure that a bus doesn't rumble down it at least once every twenty-four hours. The fare is very little—Cuenca to Guayaquil costs less than three dollars—and, barring plunges, they almost always reach their destination. If your window opens, you'll get a view of the countryside unmatched in painting or postcard. Your seatmate may be an aging *campesina* on her way home or a youthful Indian on his first trip to the big city. Dialects of Spanish and Quichua unknown to linguists float past you. Chickens, piglets, and children crowd the aisles or ride on top.

At Cuenca's *terminal terrestre,* the bus station, I had a choice of taking a regular bus or an *aerotaxi* to Guayaquil. The former travels slower, hence theoretically safer. The latter, a small twenty-four-seater, whizzes along far faster, has less leg room, and is more plunge-prone. I resisted the odds and took an *aerotaxi.*

The trip, five and a half hours long, begins at eighty-four hundred feet above sea level, climbs somewhat higher, and descends to a sea level straightaway for the final ninety minutes or so. The advantage of the drive toward Guayaquil is that the precipitous ravine usually falls off on the left side of the two-lane road; the disadvantage is that you're headed downhill most of the way. Guard railings, few and far between, relieved a bit of my fear, except when the downhill section was bent outward or was simply broken off. For the better part of the first hour we followed a cattle truck, which moved only slightly faster than its cargo could have managed on its own.

The cattle turned off at Azogues, and we pushed on deep into the province of Cañar. The temperature dropped. I looked out the left side onto the clouds surrounding peaks nearby and distant. The thin air above the clouds in the Andes gave the sunlight colors unknown below. Only occasionally did our driver attempt a suicide squeeze—overtaking someone around a blind curve—and we settled into a quiet passage. Crude signs advertised local cheeses. Small piles of *toquilla* straw lay on the ground near doorless houses where women sat in the entrances weaving Panama hats. Julio, the driver, knew all the potholes and bumps on that road and managed to hit every one. Pepe, his helper—the driver's assistant is almost always a younger brother, son, or nephew—fidgeted with the radio until he found a distant station whose static muffled a brass band. We passed Cañari Indians heading home; in front the father, directly behind him his wife, behind her a passel of kids, and bringing up the rear a burro and a goat. Each party in the procession was connected to the one behind by a rope tied around the midsection. A dog yipped alongside.

We descended into the thick of the clouds and Julio downshifted. The white line down the center of the curving two-lane road was his only guide; even the hood ornament had disappeared into the clouds. After five minutes he slowed further and then stopped. Pepe walked through the *aerotaxi* collecting money. I nudged Horacio next to me. "What's this for?"

"We're at the shrine," he replied. "Each driver stops at this shrine along the way and leaves some money. It's their way of asking God's blessings for a safe journey." Often the saints are next to a police checkpoint so that the driver can make two payoffs at once. Offering insurance money to some saint required a gargantuan leap of faith, but if it would assure us a trip free of bus plunge, I wanted in. I coughed up a few *sucres*.

Pepe trotted across the road to leave our money at the shrine when suddenly a half-dozen Indian faces appeared out of the clouds pressing against the windows. "*¡Choclos! ¡Choclos! ¡Diez cada uno!*" They were selling sweet corn cooked with onion, cheese, and egg for slightly more than ten cents each. Two barefoot Indian women in felt hats and thick mud-stained ponchos slipped onto the bus and walked up and down the aisle. "*¡Choclos! ¡Choclos! ¡Nueve cada uno!*" The price had gone down some. Another vendor with a glazed look in her eyes and a baby in her arms rapped desperately on a window trying to get a passenger to open it. Her shrill voice seemed as distant as her eyes. Pepe returned, and the Indians withdrew into the Andean mist.

Bus drivers' assistants throughout Latin America display keen skills at hopping on and off moving buses, keeping track of which passenger is due how much change for his fare, pumping gas, climbing through a window to the roof to retrieve some freight before the bus stops, and changing blowouts. Pepe performed all these feats in the course of the run to Guayaquil, and excelled at hopping on the bus when it was already in second gear. Trotting apace of the bus, he first took a short skip on the ground to get the spring in his feet, then a short jump at a forty-five-degree angle calculated to land him on the first step while he grasped a metal bar next to the doorway. His motion appeared so fluid and effortless, he seemed to be simply stepping onto a bus in repose.

The right rear tire blew out on the southern edge of the town of Cañar. Julio pulled into an abandoned service station and Pepe had us back on the road within ten minutes. In more restful moments he sat on a makeshift seat between Julio and the door. The only job forbidden him was highway driving, and even then he was allowed to maneuver the bus around the terminals.

The ride down the western face of the Andes settled into a relatively peaceful journey once the tire was changed and the saint paid off. We went through long stretches where the only hint of life was an occasional *choza,* a straw thatched hut, set back from the road. Valleys with streams and rivers flowing toward the Pacific held small towns. Our descent to sea level was practically complete and we entered a different climate, province, and culture. Bribing the saint had worked; we had passed the bus-plunge zone safely.

11

On the Road, Again

Tony Horwitz

Three deserts block my circumnavigation of the rest of the continent: the Gibson, the Great Sandy, and the Great victoria. I choose the Gibson—Ernest Giles's desert—and plot the following course:

1. Fly to Ayers Rock, thus bypassing the ill-fated patch of scrub where the rented Ford found its resting place a few months ago.
2. Hitch west along the unsealed Gunbarrel Highway, a desert track into 600 miles of townless, empty desert. The most direct route to Western Australia and the most desolate. I want to get Way Out There.
3. Proceed via the goldfields all the way to Perth, where I will arrive in a week's time, before moving up the coast to Broome and Darwin.

It's all as clear and effortless as running my finger along the map. If I stick to this itinerary and don't linger too long in any one place, I can cover the rest of the continent in the time I have before returning to work.

The only hitch, so to speak, is that I need permission to cross the Aboriginal lands west of Ayers Rock. One call and I'm there.

BUREAUCRAT:	Mr. Horwitz, are you sure you want to do this? We're talking about a desert track, not the Autobahn.
MR. HORWITZ:	What's the problem? Isn't there any traffic?
BUREAUCRAT:	Heaps, Mr. Horwitz. Three cars a day on average.
MR. HORWITZ:	I reckon I'll risk it.
BUREAUCRAT:	Suit yourself. I'll give you a permit for ten days.

Ten days! A camel could hump it to Western Australia faster than that.

But after three hours of burning roadside heat, the only thing that's moved west all day is the angle of the sun. Now, instead of roasting my face and arms, it's blowtorching the back of my neck. Another few hours and I'll have a body coat as red as Ayers Rock.

The first sign of traffic is a cloud of dust on the western horizon, coming from the direction of Docker River, which is where I'm headed. It's a four-wheel drive that looks like one of those mythical beasts I read about in outback motoring guides, equipped with two extra tires on the roof, a spare everything in the boot, and enough food and water to survive a nuclear holocaust. Or a three-day dust storm, which is what the driver appears to have just traveled through.

"The only cars I saw going your way were broken down." The driver's voice is muffled, as if someone's shoveled sand into his lungs. "Anyway, the cars are so filled with jerry cans of petrol that they wouldn't have room for an extra body."

An hour later, I decide to start walking. If I don't, I'll melt right here on the road within view of the Rock. The problem is, which way? It's six miles back to the Ayers Rock resort, and a bit further to the Olgas, on the way to Docker River. Which way? I'll start walking back to the resort and stick out my finger at any car that passes, going east or west. If the rides so decree, I will retreat to the Stuart Highway and go south toward Adelaide, entering Western Australia by crossing the Nullarbor Plain. The long way around, but so be it. Let the rides decide.

An hour later, a van winds down from the Olgas, heading east. I run across the road and point my finger back toward Alice. The van slows, a side door swings open, and a hand pulls me into the tenth reunion of an astronomy class from Tokyo.

"How you do?" says a grinning young woman named Atsuko. She is the only member of the group who speaks any English. "We, how do you say, go bush? And you?"

"Bush. Great. Yeah, I go bush, too." And off we drive, east, back the way I came.

Inside the minibus are four young Japanese, five telescopes, and the entire contents of a Nikon warehouse: flashes, autowinds, tripods, monopods, telescopic lenses. Most of the equipment hasn't shed its cellophane wrapping. Atsuko says the lights from the Ayers Rock resort made it difficult for them to see the comet, much less photograph it. So they're hoping to find a remote spot between here and Alice to set up camp again.

"Many people out there?" she asks me, pointing at a blank spot on the map. It is as thickly settled as a Siberian missile range. When I shake my head, she smiles and communicates the news to the rest of the van.

It is the first hopeful moment of their Australian expedition. They had expected to see kangaroos everywhere and have spotted only one, flat on the bitumen. They'd hoped to feast on inexpensive lamb and beef, but couldn't afford the Rock's pricey restaurants and had to settle for meat pies instead. As for the comet, well, the comet has been no more spectacular in the Australian desert than it was in suburban Tokyo.

"The comet my grandmother see in 1910, she say it was a fire in the sky," Atsuko tells me. So bright and close in fact, that the Japanese worried that the comet's vapors might poison them. Atsuko's family filled up bicycle tubes with spare oxygen, just in case.

"But this time, the comet, it is all head and no tail." Atsuko says. "We think if we go bush, maybe the comet grow some tail."

Atsuko puts a hand on my arm as the van skids to a halt. There, a hundred yards into the scrub, a big red kangaroo is sniffing at the ochre-colored earth. Within seconds the van's arsenal of photographic gear is wheeled into action. High-powered lenses poke out the windows like guns along a firing squad. Click. Wind. Click. Wind. Reload, Click. Click. The van fires off a few dozen rounds of film before the kangaroo hops out of range. Everyone is smiling now and chatting with excitement. Proof of their Australian journey is well in hand.

At a roadhouse by the Stuart Highway, two hours east of Ayers Rock, their path leads north to Alice; mine south toward Adelaide. But not before we've climbed out of the van and lined up so a camera on a tripod can snap a time-release photograph: four Japanese and one American, standing against a backdrop of empty scrub. We shake hands and they drive away, leaving me to imagine myself a few weeks hence, projected onto a living room wall in Tokyo between three dozen slides of the big red kangaroo and one slide of a dim, blurry fuzzball called Halley's Comet. "This hitchhiker, he go bush. . . ."

The chronicle of my own journey is in a holding pattern over the center. I had planned to be chugging into the sunset west of Docker River by now, or firing up a billy of tea with Afghan camel drivers (who, I fantasized, still roam the desert out there). Instead, I've retreated 125 miles east, in time to watch the sunset turn the Desert Oasis Roadhouse from gray to brown to black.

Even more distressing is a message flashing by the roadside like so many dots and dashes on the Overland Telegraph. Scratched,

painstakingly, onto fifteen separate rocks, it reads: C-O-O-B-E-R
P-E-D-Y P-L-E-A-S. Decoded into hitch-speak, that means "God help
me, I've been sitting here for days and I think I'll spend a few hours
scratching my destination onto stones so I don't go crazy or worse."

It seems the poor bastard couldn't spell, unless he got a ride before completing the "pleas." Either that or the heat finished him
off and a pack of dingoes picked his corpse clean before I got here.

I have just begun scratching an "e" onto a nearby stone when
another messenger of doom appears, this time in person. Emerging
from the Desert Oasis is a scruffy-looking man about my own age,
with a rucksack over his shoulder and a cardboard sign under his
arm. He is the first hitchhiker I've seen in the three months since
Phil "Boots" Harris hustled me at cards in rural New South Wales.

Fortunately, he's headed the other way, toward Alice. Unfortunately, he's just come from South Australia and he can't wait to
tell me all about it.

"Mate," he says, crossing the highway to greet me, "mate, if you
have any sense, you'll turn around. I spent sux days getting from
Adelaide to here. Worst sux days of my life."

The hitchhiker's accent tells me he's from New Zilind. The
hitchhiker's stench—and the battalion of flies buzzing around his
head—tells me he knows of what he speaks.

"Mate," he says, sitting down on his pack now, "it was horrible,
let me tell you." And he does. Two days in Port Augusta, in burning sun, with no one stopping to pick him up. A ride finally to
Coober Pedy—"hell on earth, mate, hell on earth." Stuck there for
another two days. Then a ride with two Aborigines who broke an
axle in the middle of nowhere, and just abandoned the car—and
him—to wander off into the scrub. He finally flagged down a car
for the last stretch, which was the worst of all. "Mate, imagine a
bedspread that's all crumpled, except that it's made of rock, and
you're driving over it. That's what the road is like. I needed back
surgery by the time we reached the Northern Territory."

There's more ("plenty of it, mate"), but a car is coming the other way. So he crosses the highway and sticks his finger out. When the car stops, he chats with the driver a minute, then comes over and asks if I want to go to Alice. No thanks, I tell him. He shakes his head as if seeing me off to the front line of some distant battlefield.

"Take this," he says solemnly, handing me a road map and tourist guide to outback South Australia. "And take care, mate. I hope you make it."

With that he vanishes toward Alice, leaving me with his flies, which busily begin crawling into my eyes and up my nose.

As twilight descends, c-o-o-b-e-r p-e-d-y p-l-e-a-s takes on the eerie aspect of a headstone. I retreat to the roadhouse, but no one's there to ask for a ride. So I settle in over a beer and begin a crash course on South Australia, which I hadn't planned to travel through at all. The fine print of the Kiwi's road guide makes for a grim introduction: "Coober Pedy to Kulgera: 465 kms—100 kms bitumen and 344 kms gravel and earth road in fair condition only, with bad corrugations, thick bulldust, loose sand and stony surface a hazard."

Dislocated vertebrae. Bruised coccyx. Emphysema from the dust. No wonder there's no traffic on this road.

I'm interrupted by two girls, aged about seventeen, coming in for a cup of coffee. They flash me friendly smiles so I wander over and inquire which way they're headed.

"Darwin," they answer in unison. "How about you?"

"Darwin, but I'm going the long way around."

They look at each other and shrug. Crazy Yank.

When I ask about their plans, I get a bubbly report about how they just left Tasmania and are on their way to work on a cattle station near Darwin. Jo likes to cook. Maryanne does laundry, but she wants to be a "jillaroo," which seems to be the female equivalent of a cowboy, or "jackeroo." Except that on this particular station, there are a whole lot of jacks and no other jills.

"Three hundred and sixty blokes, and just the two of us." Jo giggles. "Can you imagine?"

"I'm just hoping to find one guy to go out with," she says, her mouth wrinkling into a serious, meditative knot. "What do you think?"

I think I would vote this comely Tasmanian most likely to succeed of any woman in Australia, and I tell her so.

Jo, the flirt of the pair, breaks into a toothy smile. "Sure you don't want to go to Darwin the direct way? We've got plenty of room."

Bloke number three hundred and sixty-one. No thank you. I just wish my own prospects were that good: car upon car, headed south, and I the only hitchhiker to choose from a zillion empty seats.

The seat I finally get, two hours later, consists of a few inches of vinyl, wedged between 500 pounds of baby food and a lifetime's supply of diapers. And Ken and Anna and baby in the front seat, driving home to South Australia from a shopping expedition to Alice.

"The stores aren't much in our town," Ken explains, shouldering aside a mountain of shopping bags to make room for me in the back. "So once or twice a month we go for a big splurge in the city."

The city being Alice, being only an 800-mile round trip from their home in Mintabie, South Australia. Not much worse than popping around to the corner deli, once you get used to it.

Shopping isn't the only thing that's a bit limited in Mintabie. Strapped to the car roof is a pile of timber, fresh from an Alice lumber yard. "That's for our walls," Ken says. "Right now all we've got is corrugated iron." Apparently, the few hundred inhabitants of Mintabie are too busy mining opal to worry much about what their houses are made of. Anyway, they'll strike it rich any day now, which means they can move out of Mintabie. So why bother building a real home?

Ken sold his farm near Adelaide a year ago to buy mining equipment for digging opal. "You don't make a million dollars talking about it at the pub," he says of the career change. You don't make it digging for opal either, or at least Ken and Anna haven't. But everyone they know seems to be hitting it big.

"They don't actually say so, but you can kinda smell it on their trousers when they've found something," Anna says. A new truck, maybe. An aerial sticking up from the corrugated iron. Then the final tip-off: They leave Mintabie altogether. That's what keeps the rest of the miners scratching in the desert soil. Maybe one day they'll get lucky and then they can leave Mintabie, too. In the meantime, well, there's always the fifteen-hour drive to Alice and back for entertainment.

"We've got all our money sunk into the mining now anyway," Ken says. "We couldn't leave if we wanted to."

Around midnight, Ken pulls in at a roadhouse near the South Australian border to secure the rooftop cargo before plunging into 125 miles of gravel and bull dust. He tells me that the turn-off to Mintabie "is about as lonely a place as a man would ever want to see" and recommends I bed down here instead. "At least you can get some water at the roadhouse if you're stuck." Then, unable to resist adding one more blighted thought for me to sleep on, he says; "Anna and I will be back up this way in a week or so. If you're still here, we'll pick you up."

The roadhouse is shut; there's not even a light in the back to hint at any humans about. Just me, a gas pump, and a night sky as un-polluted by smog and city lights as any I've ever gazed at. As soon as Ken's headlights disappear, a brilliant tapestry of stars opens up overhead. Even the comet is a bit more of a smudge tonight—a piece of lint, say, instead of a speck of dust.

Most travelers dream of rolling out their swag in unspoiled bush like this. Not me. Sleeping out has never been one of my talents; nor, for that matter, has sleeping in. Outdoors, my natural insom-nia is compounded by a stunning ineptitude for the basics of camp-ing. I'm hopeless at pitching a tent, unless there are floodlights and a civil engineer on hand. Nor do I have much hope of starting a fire without a quart or two of lighter fluid.

I toss down my rubber mat and blanket, then lie on my back, gazing up at the brilliant night sky. Let's see now . . . Halley's . . . the Southern Cross . . . the Trifid Nebula. For the first time all day I am comfortable and contented. Back in the bush, a free bird, with only the constellations for company. The shooting stars become sheep, and counting them I begin to drift slowly off to sleep. Who knows, I wonder dreamily, an eye movement away from unconsciousness, maybe I'll turn over a new leaf. . . .

A new leaf . . . a leaf . . . a leaf blowing in the wind . . . a wind blowing me like a leaf to South Australia. . . .

I jolt awake to discover huge clumps of roly-poly gusting past. My blanket is wrapped around my ankles, and a collection of clothes and books are scattered across the scrub downwind of me, like fuselage from an airplane crash. Only my rucksack, half-emptied, is lying on its side where I left it a few hours before.

I sit up and the blanket takes off after the rest of my gear. The foam pad rolls itself and blows up against my pack. I stand up and am blown back to the ground again. Half-naked and shivering, I start crawling around the scrub collecting my scattered possessions. A shirt is lying at anchor in a pile of cow dung. My blue jeans have thrown themselves against a barbed wire fence. T. S. Eliot is doing slow, awkward somersaults across the wasteland. "What are the roots that clutch, what branches grow out of this stony rubbish?"

On the other side of the barbed wire I find a shallow trench and throw myself in. The wind still gusts across my scalp but at least my torso is protected. I prop my pack against the fence as a windbreak. Huddled behind it, I pull on two pairs of pants, three shirts, four pairs of socks—my entire wardrobe in fact, except for the dung-covered shirt and five pairs of elastic-waisted underwear. No room for dignity here, at the center of a cyclone. I put the jockey shorts over my head, one pair at a time, fitting the fly over my nose to let a little oxygen in.

A soothing calm envelops me with each added layer of cotton. I lie down, stop shivering, and listen to my own heavy breathing and the muffled gusts of the wind above. Much better than the hard ground, this trench. This underwear trick's not bad either; I'll have to give it a try on an insomniac night in Sydney.

12

Elvis Presley Boulevard

Mark Winegardner

When the groan of an idling Peterbilt woke me, I was still wearing the same clothes I'd danced in at the Urban Men's League. My tie was stuffed in my shirt pocket, though, and my blazer was draped not over a chair back but over me, a poor substitute for a blanket. In the front seat Bob, his head supported by the steering column, rubbed his eyes and whimpered.

"God, I miss David's floor," I said, opening the car door and waiting for enough energy for me to emerge into the morning sunlight of an anonymous rest area. "Is this Iowa? It looks like Iowa. It's Iowa, isn't it?"

"Illinois," Bob said. "Western, I think. I'm pretty sure. I hope. Can you drive?"

I asked for the trunk key, then foraged through my suitcase in search of deodorant, fresh underwear, a semiclean T-shirt, and torn, ratty jeans. "Back in a sec," I said, heading to the men's room to change.

The night before Bob had decided that rather than fight traffic, we ought to wait until near midnight to leave town. We wound up back in the Rush Street singles bars—sans Kirsten this time— standing around and, in my case, trying to function despite an abrupt, inexplicable but certain loss of 67 IQ points. Unfortunately I wasn't drunk enough to blame this loss on alcohol. At one point I asked a tall redhead to dance to an undanceable current song. After shucking and weaving my way through it, I asked where she was from.

"Oh, I'm from a little town a half hour from here called Romeoville."

"How far is that from here," I asked.

"About a half hour, like I said."

"Oh yeah, right. Hmm. You know, I've read *Romeo and Juliet*."

"Well, isn't that nice for us both." She reached under the table for her purse. "Good-bye."

After two hours of that, I bagged it. I found a corner barstool and—looking straight ahead, speaking to no one but the bartender—got stinking drunk.

Bob found me soon after the lights came up for last call. He had a very pretty, very busty brunette in tow. I remember being surprised, since the singles-bar scene is hardly Bob's element. She walked with us to El Basurero, and while I dove into the back to pass out, they kissed and swapped addresses.

Other than a vague sensation of motion and a dim awareness of tires singing and thumping against the worn and periodically pitted interstate, that was my final image of Chicago and the last thing I laid bleary eyes on until that western Illinois rest area.

I stuck my head under the faucet of the men's room's lone sink, clamping my eyelids shut as the cold water shocked my scalp. Then I quickly changed clothes, shook the excess water from my hair and donned a Cincinnati Reds ballcap. I checked the red "You Are Here" dot on the glass-encased roadmap: we were indeed in the western part of the state, about 13 miles from Ohio, Illinois.

"Move over," I said to Bob, still in his defeated, head-against-the-wheel pose. "I'm driving."

"I have to change."

"Well, hurry up. We don't have all day."

Bob Wakefield snickered. "Yes, we do. We have all day, and then some."

The Eight Most Unpleasant and Least Topographically Interesting States to Drive Through East to West in One Sitting (Or: These Are Drives That Try Men's Souls):

1. Kansas
2. Nebraska
3. Iowa
4. Oklahoma
5. Pennsylvania
6. North Dakota
7. South Dakota
8. Ohio

As a native of one of those states, I'm acutely aware how condescending the list is. Real life is more complex than passers-through might imagine among these glacially scrubbed plains, often hundreds of miles from the nearest on-ramps. But the dignity and curious interest these states engender are best recorded by sociologists, backroads reactionaries, and other people with time on their hands, tenure and grant money in their pockets. That work, once published, may hold great fascination for people with real jobs, Americans whose two weeks of summer vacation don't allow enough time for first-hand observation of noble farmers and above-average children, soybean festivals and hamlets where no one speaks French or pays to park. For those of us on our way to the more immediate pleasures of Disneyland and Universal Studios, the Grand Canyon and the Rocky Mountains, the Midwest is something to be endured, an object lesson in delayed gratification.

What this has created in these states is a parallel-universe community—a ramshackle cement ditch bisecting the state, filled with sleepy truck drivers and out-of-state leadfoots, lined with one hundred gas stations, fireworks sales, and fast-food emporia that are repeated in endless, predictable cycles, like the background animation in a low-budget cartoon. The citizens of this long, thin town steer their vehicles with one finger, adjusting for deficiencies in wheel alignment while dreaming of the horizon, passing the time by mentally calculating gas mileage or trying to set a new personal record for miles traveled during the playing time of a Supremes tape. People in the filling stations here have a desperate look in their eyes, born of too many hours with wailing children and the onus of having gotten a late start. The law here brandishes a gun that shoots bullets of radar, and he accepts Visa. No one in this long, thin town has clean hair.

All because this is the second-fastest and by far the cheapest way to get from Point A to Point B.

We were making good time, so we rewarded ourselves.

I drove all the way to Des Moines, where we stopped for gas and lucked into an all-you-can-eat, family-style Sunday buffet at a restaurant featuring Bavarian decor, a waitress with an Australian accent, and steaming piles of roast beef and green beans. Bob drove from there to Lincoln, where we stopped to see a movie, choosing the just-released *Ghostbusters*. This was a loud theater, dominated by two rows of teenagers shouting instructions at the screen—"Don't go in *there*—couldn't *pay* me to go in there."—and a few dozen VCR owners too dim to realize they'd left home and come to a large, dark, public room where not everyone needed to be told, "That guy was on 'Saturday Night Live'" or "Here comes the good part." I must confess, however, that Bob and I did do some talking ourselves. At one point in the film, when the titular characters are being celebrated for busting ghosts, they're asked this question by New York talk-show host Joe

Franklin: "Well, I guess there's one question all of America wants to know: have you been in contact with Elvis?"

Whereupon Bob and I, in disbelief and unison, said, "Give us this day our daily Elvis," and executed a high-five.

"We almost missed today," I said after the movie, driving toward Colorado and a drab red sunset. "Jeez, that was close, but our record's still perfect."

"I'd have to say it *is* pushing the outer limits of coincidence." Bob rattled through the tape box. "Have you seen Wall of Voodoo?"

The Mileage Chart in our map indicated 1,021 miles between Chicago and Denver, which—by means of comparison—is 113 miles shorter and 114 times less interesting than the drive between Los Angeles and Seattle. Piled on top of the horrible stasis of I-80 through Iowa and Nebraska, eastern Colorado's I-76 seems a cruel joke, particularly the stateline sign: a rough hewn log affair, painted brown, surrounded by sunbaked weeds, distant fencing, and powerlines, reading WELCOME TO COLORFUL COLORADO. Sure, pal. You bet, and thank you.

Bob knew the ride well. He'd been here in 1969, when his mother conducted a prototypical post-divorce pile-the-kids-in-the-Pontiac-and-see-America trip. He returned for a few weeks in 1975 to visit his second-eldest sister, Joan, who'd moved there. And the summer before he'd worked for a month as a waiter—serving monied vacationers $18 plates of curried elk—in the Black Canyon Lodge, which Joan manages. So, like most travelers who haven't been all that many places, Bob took obvious pleasure in recognizing *everything*: fast-food places where he'd eaten, filling stations where he'd refueled, exits where a member of his family had demanded restroom stops.

By the time we got off I-76, we could see the Rockies, though they were still more than 100 miles away. Through Greeley, then on to Loveland, U.S. 34 ran us through a gauntlet of the New West, which is to say, small towns which feature the juxtaposition of Jeep dealerships and Westernwear outlets with computer supermarkets and Italian bicycle shops—all the while with the Rockies suspended over the hood of El Basurero like a gorgeous threat.

Yet our rusty steed made it huffing and clacking up the 31 miles from Loveland to Estes Park without incident, albeit also without ever reaching 30 miles per hour. The tension that marked previous climbs through the Appalachians was absent this time, ostensibly because we were preoccupied with running out of gas ("There's a gas station right when we get to Estes," Bob said, "I'm pretty sure I've made it with this much gas before"), but more likely because of the prospect of a non-metal roof over our heads and free eats.

We made the Estes Park Texaco just before noon, Mountain Standard Time. Bob told me that the tourist season hadn't started here yet, wouldn't start until after the 4th of July. The main intersection —which has a slot in its traffic-light cycle reserved solely for pedestrians, during which they may walk any whichway, including diagonally—was no more bustling than the intersection of High and Main in Bryan. The Ripley's Believe It Or Not Museum was closed for remodeling.

The Black Canyon Lodge abutted the northern edge of Estes, far enough from touristy downtown and close enough to Rocky Mountain National Park to charge exorbitant rates. Set in a stand of hearty conifers off the main road, the Black Canyon complex included the restaurant, housed in a gable-ceilinged lodge with a mortared-rock porch, and a series of cabins tucked into boulder-strewn recesses in the mountainside. The owners and/or guests must have been persnickety in the extreme, since the first thing Joan did when she saw Bob was tell him to park El Basurero at the bottom of the driveway, out of sight.

When Bob and Joan first saw one another, they neither hugged nor kissed. They spoke as if Bob lived a half hour away and had swung by for a beer, a conversation full of odd, elliptical pauses and sentences completed by committee. After the exchange of how-was-your-trip pleasantries, Bob asked if there was a waiter's job open. Joan wasn't sure.

Bob and I each took a quick shower in Joan's cabin, then went with Joan into town to lunch with the remainder of the Estes Park Wakefield contingent.

I come from a tiny family, the nuclear kind you hear so much about: a mommy and a daddy and a brother and a sister. I have an aunt, an uncle, three cousins, and two surviving grandparents. Period. Consequently I have an outsider's interest in the machinations of large families, especially those made yet more scattered, diversified and complex by the lingering effects of divorce. At the end of the summer I would marry into such a family, fraught with divorced and remarried parents, married and unmarried siblings and half-siblings, three sets of grandparents, and a formidable array of aunts, uncles, and cousins.

Even though big families capture my imagination, I confess that I have more trouble keeping them straight than I do sorting out the dramatis personae in Russian novels. With the seven Wakefield siblings, this problem is compounded by their soundalike names: Blaine, Bill, and Bob; Jane, Joan, and Jean. I find it easiest to keep track of the youngest, Polly, if only because of the breach her first name causes in the alliterative gender lines. But on the whole, during their mealtime conversations, I might as well have been watching random episodes of an unfamiliar soap opera.

That first lunch set the tone. In an open-air Estes restaurant, Bob and his three sisters and two of their boyfriends caught up on recent news and put forth the blasé front of the native. I was startled to hear them call my friend "Robby," the only people on the planet to do this. For everyone else, it's "Bob" first and "Robert" second. "Robby," in fact, had never occurred to me.

I was brought into the fold to discuss our trip-to-date (though by now we were already embellishing). But for the most part, I spent lunch gawking at the entertainment—a guitarist who ached to be John Denver—and drinking a yard of ale: a conspicuous 3-foot-high beaker that, when not in use, is supported by a large wooden holder. This contraption makes the consumer look lost and ridiculous, like a Tyrolean shepherd who has wandered into the café to sound his horn.

Like Gatlinburg, Estes Park is a National Park fringe town, if a less entrenched one, and it seems to fulfill a roughly approximate function. Though the gourmet taffy shoppes, rubber-reptile boutiques, and Believe It Or Not Museum clearly mark Estes as a fringe town, there are touches that one could hardly imagine in a place like Gatlinburg. The fortune teller in the lobby of one of the town's two movie theaters, for example. Or the presence of a pretty good bookstore: dominated, admittedly, by regional histories, guides to indigenous flora and fauna, and compendia of gruesome campfire tales, but nevertheless a place where one might buy the collected poems of Yeats or the latest *New Yorker*. Estes Park is, at once, more frontier and more upscale than most fringe towns, though the understandable pull exerted by the majesty of the bordering Rockies makes me suspect that "frontier" and "upscale" are not, in 1984, mutually exclusive. In Estes Park, Colorado, perhaps even in the whole of the much-ballyhooed New West, "frontier" and "upscale" are becoming synonymous.

Since sitting still in Estes Park didn't fulfill my original idea for this trip, I really wanted to get going. After dropping our film off at a one-day photo developer, I gamely spent an afternoon poking through curio shops and a few hours catching lazy hatchery bass in a one-acre pond. Though diverting, this wasn't fishing—not when you rent a rod and pay by the hour. Nor was it sufficiently touristy: tourists should walk away with felt pennants or painted shot glasses, not bloated, squirming smallmouths.

But I understood that Bob wanted to spend some time with his sisters, so I tried not to act restless, even as he cloaked himself in dignity and professed to be embarrassed when I played with various bits of displayed trinketry—embarrassed, he said, because he lived here. Had lived here, anyway. Might live here in the near future.

"I'm out of money," he told me on our way to dinner one night with Polly and her boyfriend Doug.

"All out? Or just really-low out?"

"Out-out. Two dollars and change. My mom was supposed to forward my last assistantship check, but Joan said it hasn't come yet."

"Oh." We wound out of Estes to Polly and Doug's in silence, save for the transmission straining to make it halfway up Giant Track Mountain. I knew that if a cushy waiter's job opened up, Bob might well abandon me. But Joan had told him not to count on anything, and I figured the trip was a lock. Now, for the first time, I realized that Bob might well stay in Estes, job or no.

The meal was really more of a party—a festive and convenient excuse for Bob and I not to talk to each other for several hours.

Afterward we sat on the hood of El Basurero, 6,500 feet above sea level, and looked across a sky full of moonlit snowcaps. Without looking at me, Bob outlined contingency plans. He said he'd drive me to the nearest airport and I could fly home. Or, he said, he had this friend in Denver—a guy I'd never met—who might want to take a trip. Or maybe once the tourist season got underway, we both could find jobs in Estes. Or maybe I could even take his car, though he said he'd have to mull that one over.

Polly and Doug let us stay at their place that night. Bob and I flipped for the sofa bed, and I lost.

In the morning we climbed Giant Track Mountain. With tennis shoes and no climbing experience, we had little hope of reaching the 9,300-foot summit. But it was a perfect morning—even though we got temporarily stranded on the sheer face of a cliff, learning the hard way that it's easier to climb up than down—that gave us a chance to work off a little aggression, and to think.

I sat with my feet dangling off a cliff, trying to decide what Bob would do. A hawk flew past, no more than 10 feet from my face. I'd have made a pathetic Indian, I thought, having no idea what to make of this particular omen.

When we finally made it down, the tension between us had entirely eased. We agreed to go into town to pick up our photos and have a few beers, and that's when we first saw the Miracle Photo.

The rest of the photos were pleasant, if ordinary: shots of the Ruby Falls trash can, a Memphis shop window full of black mannequin heads, our new haircuts in Chicago; driving pictures featuring drivers unkempt, unshaven, and resolute; amateurish attempts at picture-postcards. As a whole, they were conclusive proof that the camera worked fine, but the flash was finished.

And the Miracle Photo? Well, this was a shot of the Pigeon Forge Elvis Presley Heartbreak Motel. Over the Elvis Presley Boulevard sign, there was a double exposure of three nuns, one of whom brandished what appeared to be a set of hedge clippers.

"Did you take any pictures of nuns," I asked.

Bob shook his head. "No. And I'm sure I didn't photograph any hedge clippers."

I didn't know whether to laugh or be amazed. The Miracle Photo, I decided, was conclusive proof that there's something to this Elvis thing.

I watched Bob study the nuns, and resisted the temptation to offer him money for his analysis.

13

Down and Out in Alaska

Whit Deschner

There are two theories to bush flying. One, go with a pilot who has never crashed, reasoning that they never—knock on wood, rub rabbit's foot, keep fingers crossed—will. Or two, go with an "experienced" pilot, one who has crashed and lived, because at least they know *how* to crash and survive.

Ted fit in the latter category. He fished out of the same camp I did, in Earth-left-field, Dillingham, Alaska. The first time I saw Ted's Piper Cub wrecked (though not the first time it had been in such a condition) was shortly after he buzzed the camp. The plane climbed, then started doing things I know Orville and Wilbur would not have endorsed. It spun and looped, emulating a county fair ride that spins you dizzy while hanging you upside down, until all the loose change is emptied from your pockets, before returning you to earth where you can throw up. When the plane finished this unwholesome behavior it returned to camp—and crashed.

As it turned out, Ted wasn't flying. At the controls was an old crop duster who hadn't flown in decades, whom Ted had inveigled into the pilot's seat. The duster remembered the aerobatics but forgot that he now wore bifocals and, misjudging the beginning of the camp runway, hit short, knocked the landing gear off, bounced

157

airborne, leapfrogged the camp's fuel tanks that were kept in the runway's dogleg (not your normal runway), then returned to earth. Besides the crumpled landing gear, the impact bent the prop and scuffed up the underbelly. Otherwise the plane was intact. Unfortunately, this was not the last time I was to see the plane wrecked.

In subsequent years a few more mishaps occurred, like Ted failing a take-off here, flipping the plane beachcombing there, nothing much, just a few entries in a log book that was now looking like a catalog of disasters. Besides beachcombing, Ted actually did use the plane as a legitimate tax write-off, for example, to drop eggs on rival fishing boats.

On occasion, I had accompanied Ted on excursions and had actually survived, but the odds against me were growing. Ted would ask me to go with him on some new mission and I'd have to think up novel excuses to parry these invites, like, "Sorry, Ted, I've got to go see about this broken arm."

"But you don't have a broken arm."

"No, I'm about to go break it."

Ted was also a card-carrying gold junkie and he used his plane for prospecting. Often, while showing me his new riches, Ted would unscrew the cap on a vial no larger than a well-used pencil, then carefully spill the contents onto a piece of paper for me to admire. A single sneeze would have wiped out his earnings, along with our friendship. He'd always say, "There's more where this comes from."

Which was a relief, because what he always had wasn't much. What he was really hinting at, however, was for me to embark on some new airborne adventure with him, a hint I just plain ignored. Regrettably, he knew I possessed a weakness, too: I was a sucker for whitewater. Exploiting my addiction he nonchalantly inquired one day, "You want to go flying?"

I replied, "Ted, since it seems to be in the best interest of my continued existence, I've decided never to go flying with you again."

"Never?"

"Ever!"

"How about if I show you a creek that's never been run?"

"OK."

To get there, we flew over lakes and over alder- and spruce-brushed hills, then over hills that turned mountainous, jagged, and near-vertical. We were climbing and following a small creek when Ted, through the headset, voiced doubts about the weather and about a hide-and-go-seek hole in the cloud we needed to have open so we could clear the pass we were headed for. The rock shepherding our passage closed in. Ted said, "This is our last chance to turn around." But he kept going. Soon I was seeing details in the rock off both wing tips—details that I really didn't want to see. Buzzing just off the ground, we cleared the pass with our tail slicing the mists.

The land opened up, and Ted said, "Look on the map and see where we are now."

"Don't *you* know?"

"I haven't a clue."

"You mean we're lost?"

"No. We're not lost. I've been lost before and it looked nothing like this."

We followed a ribbon of a stream down until it petered out into a beaver-infested swamp.

"See where we are now."

"Don't you know yet?"

"Well we crossed some mountains back there."

This sort of conversation was normal with Ted. But every once in a while he dropped a bomb, like, "Just wait until you see where we're going, then you'll know why I didn't file a flight plan."

"You didn't file a flight plan?"

"You kidding? I didn't want anyone to know where we're going."

"Because of this unrun creek?"

"Well, no, not the creek. I didn't want anyone to know about this hot gold-panning spot we're heading to."

"You mean we're not headed for this creek?"

"Well, yes, but you don't just want to look at that."

"I don't?"

In time we arrived over, and correctly identified, Ted's unrun piece of water, Trail Creek. Its valley was broad, one large wrestling mat of tundra with a hundred-and-fifty-foot crack down its middle through which the creek ran. Heavily escorted by alder, the creek had the velocity of an excited slough.

"What do you think?" Ted asked.

"I think I'm going to throw up all over your back if you keep cranking turns like this."

After checking out Trail Creek we hopped over some hills, landing on a strip called Canyon Creek, and arriving at a recently abandoned mine. We walked to an upthrust vein jutting through a small drainage. This was Ted's hot mother lode. Somehow I thought gold panning should be different. There was too much labor-intensive sloshing for the end product, which Ted referred to as "color," flecks of gold the size of fly poop that he painstakingly extracted with his forefinger. My idea was that if I couldn't extract the nuggets using my thumb and forefinger they weren't worth keeping. After half an hour of numbing my hands to such a state that I would never regain full control of my fingers, we extracted enough color to melt into a small nugget—not exactly enough to overburden and sink a Spanish galleon.

When at last our entire bodies were immobilized to the exact responsiveness of an ice cube (and richer by at least thirty-seven cents), we returned to the plane. Ted dumped a quart of oil in the engine and we took off. We flew south across a wind-blown ridge and Ted commented that it wouldn't be a bad place to land. It was too bad Ted didn't switch fuel tanks there, because, shortly after, over a place that *wasn't* good to land on, he did switch the fuel, and the engine quit.[1]

Dead.

In the void of the reassuring engine noise came the insidious sound of wind brushing the cabin as we began our disturbingly quick return to earth. But if I thought this sound was the lone thing that would unravel my composure I was wrong because suddenly I heard heavy breathing in the headset. Either Ted was practicing obscene phone calls or we were in for a heap of trouble. Then Ted, master of the understatement, announced, "This isn't good."

Time entered a new dimension. It ticked with rubber-second slowness, yet passed all at once. As we watched the unwelcoming terrain swell increasingly large we spotted a wind-eroded gravel ridge possibly big enough to accommodate a landing, a crash, or a combination of the two.

But Ted, with two hundred feet to go, suddenly veered from the ridge and opted for a sloping piece of tundra. As soon as we turned, we fell, accelerating like a roller coaster—but there was no track awaiting us at the bottom. Out of sheer boredom on jets, I've read the safety card a thousand times: Get in a tuck position so that on impact you can drive your head through the kidneys of the person seated in front of you. It is a fine position if you are a yoga expert. But as I tried pressing my knees into my eyes I realized that the twits who write such cards have never been augered in a plane before. The problem is, you can't see. As I rose to watch, we hit.

I know my life passed before my eyes but I couldn't see it: Ted, flopping around like a Raggedy Andy doll, was blocking my vision. Instead, in what could have been my last moment on earth—as we were colliding back with it—I saw something akin to an atomic period Salvador Dali painting; everything was in suspension, only

---

1. As Ted explained later, "There was probably too much gas in the water."

I was viewing it from inside a beer can being crushed. Plexiglass, a tire, and my hand all floated where plexiglass, a tire, and my hand shouldn't be; and these items were backdropped against a wing where a wing shouldn't be either. It was not a pretty picture, but one I came close to buying anyway.

Finally, the plane jarred to a stop, and quiet swelled around us. There seemed to be about a hundred-and-twenty-five decibels of it. Then Ted, wanting to make our exit as dramatic as possible, began smashing out the windshield with his fist—that is, until I opened the door.

We staggered from the wreck—25,000 uninsured bucks and now a useless crumpled heap. Ted shrugged and lamented, "Damn it, damn it, damn it! I just wasted a quart of oil!"

We sat there stunned, staring at the wreck, my knees clattering like castanets. At last I said, "Good thing for emergency locator transmitters."

"Oh yes!" Ted exclaimed, "I'd better turn it on!"

I said, "Let me get this straight. We have just crashed after not filing a flight plan and, on top of that, the E.L.T. wasn't armed?"

"Exactly. I never arm it. Every time I land too hard I set the darn thing off."

"Why weren't you born in the last century? You would have gotten on much better."

Ted turned the E.L.T. on, and our signal immediately snagged the attention of a passing satellite, which, in turn, immediately beamed the information to Control Central in France. France immediately exclaimed, "Voila! We have ze emarganzee sig-nal! Ted, ee must ave jaust land-ded hees plane ageen!" France immediately phoned Anchorage to let them know, and Anchorage immediately phoned Dillingham, which by this time had gone to bed. Dillingham, answering at last, said, "Do you know what time it is here?"

Late the following morning, above the cloud, we heard the distant drone of a plane circling. Ted grabbed the radio and, speaking in plane talk, said something like, "Distant drone of plane circling up there, this is voice of Piper Cub which has disassembled itself on the ground. Over."

"Yes, Piper Cub in pieces. Are you OK? Over."

"No. Situation critical. We need insect repellant immediately. Do you read?"

"Yes, copy that. Do you require anything else? Over."

"Yes. We're going to need some butter to fry these fish in."

Later in the day, having been given our coordinates, two friends, (in another Cub with no room for us), flew out to start our rescue. We flagged off a runway for them—the one we could have used. They brought us a loaf of bread, bug juice, a cube of butter, a can of Norwegian fish balls, and a 30-30 rifle. The pilot said he'd fetch us the next day.

However, on the morrow, the weather packed in, and for six days we saw no one. In the mornings we hiked down to the nearby creek and began fishing, with the intention of showing no mercy to the fish. However, the fish had already decided to show no mercy to us. Catching only one fish a day, and having wolfed down the bread, we resorted to blueberries. Reduced now to the status of hunter/ gatherers, we immediately came across the fresh tracks of one of the local hunter/gatherers—tracks that one of our feet fit easily inside. We realized how inadequate our rifle was, should our competition decide to grow sensitive over the issue.

But later, starved, we came to realize that the rifle wasn't meant for bears at all but for use on ourselves, a realization that struck us when at last we opened the can of fish balls. We both swore we'd shoot ourselves before we were reduced to eating them.

Through the days of waiting, I began to comprehend that this fight for survival was something Ted had waited and practiced for his whole life. He was good at it, and if we'd stayed another week he would have constructed a five-bedroom log cabin, complete with a smokehouse and sauna. Ted caught all the fish. I lost the lures.

Ted—even in the pouring rain—would carefully construct his fires with shavings and twigs, trying miserably to light them with a flint. While he was busy at this task, I'd be draining gas out of the wing into an open container. Returning to Ted's fire, I'd say, "Watch this!" and dump my fuel onto his twigs, then jump-start the whole shebang with a tossed match. Ted regarded such behavior as sacrilegious and I imagine that if we had been marooned one more day, Ted would have tried out the rifle on me. But I was spared, for on the sixth day, even though planes were still unable to reach us, a helicopter from a luxury fishing lodge at last fetched us. Even industrial detergent couldn't have resurrected the leather seats after they were smeared by our grime-covered clothes.

Soon, we were back in the narrow confines of town, and the even narrower confines of the town's cafe—with several dinners stacked in front of us. There, a local asked what we were doing up Trail Creek. It was tough getting an answer out through all the food we were stuffing into our faces. But when he understood our reply, the local, firing a Parthian shot, informed us that we'd be hard pressed to make a first run down Trail Creek.

"Why's 'at?" I asked, filtering the words through a mouthful of whipped potatoes.

"Why, don't you know? Jacky Smeaton wrecked his plane up there years ago and made a boat out of a tarp and willows and floated out."

14

Transgressing the Laws

Mark Twain

All day Sunday at anchor. The storm had gone down a great deal, but the sea had not. It was still piling its frothy hills high in air "outside," as we could plainly see with the glasses. We could not properly begin a pleasure excursion on Sunday; we could not offer untried stomachs to so pitiless a sea as that. We must lie still till Monday. And we did. But we had repetitions of church and prayer meetings; and so, of course, we were just as eligibly situated as we could have been anywhere.

I was up early that Sabbath morning, and was early to breakfast. I felt a perfectly natural desire to have a good, long, unprejudiced look at the passengers, at a time when they should be free from self-consciousness—which is at breakfast, when such a moment occurs in the lives of human beings at all.

I was greatly surprised to see so many elderly people—I might almost say, so many venerable people. A glance at the long lines of heads was apt to make one think it was *all* gray. But it was not. There was a tolerably fair sprinkling of young folks, and another fair sprinkling of gentlemen and ladies who were non-committal as to age, being neither actually old or absolutely young.

The next morning, we weighed anchor and went to sea. It was a great happiness to get away, after this dragging, dispiriting delay. I thought there never was such gladness in the air before, such brightness in the sun, such beauty in the sea. I was satisfied with the picnic, then, and with all its belongings. All my malicious instincts were dead within me; and as America faded out of sight, I think a spirit of charity rose up in their place that was as boundless, for the time being, as the broad ocean that was heaving its billows about us. I wished to express my feelings—I wished to lift up my voice and sing; but I did not know anything to sing, and so I was obliged to give up the idea. It was no loss to the ship though, perhaps.

It was breezy and pleasant, but the sea was still very rough. One could not promenade without risking his neck; at one moment the bowsprit was taking a deadly aim at the sun in mid-heaven, and at the next it was trying to harpoon a shark in the bottom of the ocean. What a weird sensation it is to feel the stern of a ship sinking swiftly from under you and see the bow climbing high away among the clouds! One's safest course that day was to clasp a railing and hang on; walking was too precarious a pastime.

By some happy fortune I was not seasick—That was a thing to be proud of. I had not always escaped before. If there is one thing in the world that will make a man peculiarly and insufferably self-conceited, it is to have his stomach behave itself, the first day at sea, when nearly all his comrades are seasick. Soon, a venerable fossil, shawled to the chin and bandaged like a mummy, appeared at the door of the after deck-house, and the next lurch of the ship shot him into my arms. I said:

"Good-morning, Sir. It is a fine day."

He put his hand on his stomach and said, *"Oh,* my!" and then staggered away and fell over the coop of a skylight.

Presently another old gentleman was projected from the same door, with great violence. I said:

"Calm yourself, Sir—There is no hurry. It is a fine day, Sir."

He, also, put his hand on his stomach and said, *"Oh,* my!" and reeled away.

In a little while another veteran was discharged abruptly from the same door, clawing at the air for a saving support. I said:

"Good-morning, Sir. It is a fine day for pleasuring. You were about to say—"

"Oh, my!"

I thought so. I anticipated *him,* anyhow. I stayed there and was bombarded with old gentlemen for an hour perhaps; and all I got out of any of them was *"Oh,* my!"

I went away, then, in a thoughtful mood. I said, this is a good pleasure excursion. I like it. The passengers are not garrulous, but still they are sociable. I like those old people, but somehow they all seem to have the "Oh, my" rather bad.

I knew what was the matter with them. They were seasick. And I was glad of it. We all like to see people seasick when we are not, ourselves. Playing whist by the cabin lamps when it is storming outside, is pleasant; walking the quarter-deck in the moonlight, is pleasant; smoking in the breezy foretop is pleasant, when one is not afraid to go up there; but these are all feeble and commonplace compared with the joy of seeing people suffering the miseries of seasickness.

I picked up a good deal of information during the afternoon. At one time I was climbing up the quarter-deck when the vessel's stern was in the sky; I was smoking a cigar and feeling passably comfortable. Somebody ejaculated:

"Come, now, *that* won't answer. Read the sign up there—NO SMOKING ABAFT THE WHEEL!"

It was Capt. Duncan, chief of the expedition. I went forward, of course. I saw a long spyglass lying on a desk in one of the upper-deck staterooms back of the pilothouse, and reached after it—there was a ship in the distance:

"Ah, ah—hands off! Come out of that!"

I came out of that. I said to a deck-sweep—but in a low voice:

"Who is that overgrown pirate with the whiskers and the discordant voice?"

"It's Capt. Bursley—executive officer—sailing master."

I loitered about awhile, and then, for want of something better to do, fell to carving a railing with my knife. Somebody said, in an insinuating, admonitory voice:

"Now *say*—my friend—don't you know any better than to be whittling the ship all to pieces that way? *You* ought to know better than that."

I went back and found the deck-sweep:

"Who is that smooth-faced animated outrage yonder in the fine clothes?"

"That's Capt. L****, the owner of the ship—he's one of the main bosses."

In the course of time I brought up on the starboard side of the pilothouse, and found a sextant lying on a bench. Now, I said, they "take the sun" through this thing; I should think I might see that vessel through it. I had hardly got it to my eye when someone touched me on the shoulder and said, deprecatingly:

"I'll have to get you to give that to me, Sir. If there's anything you'd like to know about taking the sun, I'd as soon tell you as not—but I don't like to trust anybody with that instrument. If you want any figuring done—Aye, aye, Sir!"

He was gone, to answer a call from the other side. I sought the deck-sweep:

"Who is that spider-legged gorilla yonder with the sanctimonious countenance?"

"It's Capt. Jones, Sir—the chief mate."

"Well. This goes clear away ahead of anything I ever heard of before. Do you—now I ask you as a man and a brother—*do* you think I could venture to throw a rock here in any given direction without hitting a captain of this ship?"

"Well, Sir, I don't know—I think likely you'd fetch the captain of the watch maybe, because he's a-standing right yonder in the way."

I went below—meditating, and a little down-hearted. I thought, if five cooks can spoil a broth, what may not five captains do with a pleasure excursion.

III

Then the Wheels Fell Off

15

Not a Hazardous Sport

Nigel Barley

"**A**nthropology is not a hazardous sport." I had always suspected that this was so but it was comforting to have it confirmed in black and white by a reputable insurance company of enduring probity. They, after all, should know such things.

The declaration was the end result of an extended correspondence conducted more in the spirit of detached concern than serious enquiry. I had insured my health for a two-month field-trip and been unwise enough to read the small print. I was not covered for nuclear attack or nationalization by a foreign government. Even more alarming, I *was* covered for up to twelve months if hijacked. Free-fall parachute jumping was specifically forbidden together with "all other hazardous sports." But it was now official: "Anthropology is not a hazardous sport."

The equipment laid out on the bed seemed to contest the assertion. I had water-purifying tablets, remedies against two sorts of malaria, athlete's foot, suppurating ulcers and eyelids, amoebic dysentery, hay fever, sunburn, infestation by lice and ticks, seasickness, and compulsive vomiting. Only much, much later would I realize that I had forgotten the aspirins.

It was to be a stern rather than an easy trip, a last pitting of a visibly sagging frame against severe geography where everything would probably have to be carried up mountains and across ravines, a last act of physical optimism before admitting that urban life and middle age had ravaged me beyond recall.

In one corner stood the new rucksack, gleaming iridescent green like the carapace of a tropical beetle. New boots glowed comfortingly beside it, exuding a promise of dry strength. Cameras had been cleaned and recalibrated. All the minor tasks had been dealt with just as a soldier cleans and oils his rifle before going into battle. Now, in predeparture gloom, the wits were dulled, the senses muted. It was the moment for sitting on the luggage and feeling empty depression.

I have never really understood what it is that drives anthropologists off into the field. Possibly it is simply the triumph of sheer nosiness over reasonable caution, the fallibility of the human memory that denies the recollection of how uncomfortable and tedious much of fieldwork can be. Possibly it is the boredom of urban life, the stultifying effect of regular existence. Often departure is triggered by relatively minor occurrences that give a new slant on normal routine. I once felt tempted when a turgid report entitled "Applications of the Computer to Anthropology" arrived on my desk at the precise moment I had spent forty minutes rewinding a typewriter ribbon by hand because my machine was so old that appropriate ribbons were no longer commercially available.

The point is that fieldwork is often an attempt by the researcher to resolve his own, very personal problems, rather than an attempt to understand other cultures. Within the profession, it is often viewed as a panacea for all ills. Broken marriage? Go and do some fieldwork to get back a sense of perspective. Depressed about lack of promotion? Fieldwork will give you something else to worry about.

But whatever the cause, ethnographers all recognize the call of the wild with the certainty that Muslims feel about the sudden, urgent need to go to Mecca.

Where to go? This time, not West Africa but somewhere fresh. Often I had been asked by students for advice on where to go for fieldwork. Some were driven by a relentless incubus to work on one topic alone, female circumcision or blacksmithing. They were the easy ones to counsel. Others had quite simply fallen in love with a particular part of the world. They, too, were easy. Such a love affair can be as good a basis for withstanding the many trials and disappointments of ethnography as any more stern theoretical obsession. Then there was the third, most difficult group, into which I myself seemed now to fall—what a colleague had unkindly termed the SDP of anthropology—those who knew more clearly what they wanted to avoid than what they wished to seek.

When advising such as these, I had always asked something like: "Why don't you go somewhere where the inhabitants are beautiful, friendly, where you would like the food and there are nice flowers?" Often such people came back with excellent theses. Now I had to apply it to myself. West Africa was clearly excluded, but the answer came in a flash—Indonesia. I would have to make further enquiries.

I consulted an eminent Indonesianist—Dutch, of course, and therefore more English than the English with his hound's-tooth jacket, long, elegant vowels, and a Sherlock Holmes pipe. He pointed the stem of it at me.

"You are suffering from mental menopause," he said, puffing roundly. "You need a complete change. Anthropologists always go to their first fieldwork site and make the hard discovery that people there are not like the people at home—in your case that the Dowayos are not like the English. But they never get it clear that *all* peoples are unlike each other. You will go around for years looking at everyone as if they were Dowayos. Do you have a grant?"

"Not yet. But I can probably sort out some funding." (The saddest thing about academic research is that when you are young you have plenty of time but no one will give you any money. By the time you have worked a little way up the hierarchy, you can normally persuade someone to fund you but you never have enough time to do anything important.)

"Grants are wonderful things. I have often thought that I would write a book about the gap between what grants are given for and what they are actually spent on. My car,"—he gestured through the window—"that is the grant to get my last book retyped. I sat up all night for six weeks and did it myself. It is not a very good car, but then it was not a very good book. I got married with a grant to enable me to study Achinese. My first daughter was a grant to allow me to visit Indonesian research facilities in Germany." Academics. The culture of genteel poverty.

"You got divorced recently. Did you get a grant for that?"

"No. . . . That one, I paid for. But it was worth it."

"So where should I go?"

He puffed. "You will go to Sulawesi. If anyone asks why, you will explain it is because the children have pointed ears."

"Pointed ears? Like Mr. Spock?"

"Just so. We have him too."

"But why?"

He puffed smoke like an Indonesian volcano and smiled mysteriously. "Just go and you will see."

I knew I was hooked. I would go to the island of Sulawesi, Indonesia, and look at the pointed ears of the children.

There may be pleasure in the remote anticipation of a journey. There is none in its immediate preparation. Injections. Should one really believe that smallpox has been "eradicated"?—a nice, clean, hard-edged word that was infinitely suspicious. Rabies? How likely were you to be bitten by a rabid dog? Yes, but you can catch it by being scratched by a cat or pecked by a bird. Gammaglobulin? The Americans swear by it. The British don't believe in it. Ultimately, you make an arbitrary choice like a child grabbing a handful of sweets. How many shirts? How many pairs of socks? You never have enough to wear but always too many to carry. Cooking pots? Sleeping bags? There will be moments where both will be indispensable but are they worth the suffering involved in carrying them across Java? A review of teeth and feet, treating one's body like a troublesome commodity in a slave market. A time to look at guidebooks and the previous works of ethnography.

Each seemed to tell a different story. Planning a route was impossible. They could not be reconciled into a unified vision. According to one, Indonesian ships were floating hellholes, the nadir of degradation, filthy and pestilential. Another viewed them as havens of tranquillity. One traveler claimed that he had traveled tarmac roads which another traveler declared to have been cancelled. Travel books were as much works of fantasy as grant applications. My Dutchman probably wrote them. A secondary problem was that you could never be sure of the values of the writer. One man's "comfortable" was another's "absurdly expensive." In the end, the only thing to do was go and look.

There is a stage at which maps appear essential. In fact, they merely give a spurious sense of certainty that you know where you are going.

Map men are the true eccentrics of the book trade—wild-haired, glasses-pushed-up-on-forehead sort of people.

"A map of Sulawesi? Charlie, we've got one here wants a map of Sulawesi." Charlie peered over a stack of maps at me. Apparently, they didn't get the Sulawesi type here every day. Charlie was the glasses-pushed-down-to-tip-of-nose sort.

"Can't do you one. We'd love one for ourselves. Do you a pre-war Dutch one with nothing on it. Indonesians have the copyright you see. Frightened of spies. Or you can have an American Airforce

Survey but it comes on three sheets six foot square. Lovely bit of cartography."

"I'd hoped for something a little more convenient."

"We can do you East Malaysia Political. You get the rest of Borneo Physical Features up the far end and four inches of South Sulawesi to make up the square. But I suppose if you want to go more than ten miles from the capital, that's not much use. We can do you a street map of the capital with directory."

I looked at it. How often had one studied these ambitious tangles of streets and avenues that resolved themselves on the ground into hot, dusty little villages with only one real road.

"No. I don't think so. Anyway, the name's changed. It's not called Macassar any more. It's Ujung Pandang."

Charlie looked shocked. "My dear sir. This is a 1944 map." It was too. The directory was in Dutch.

Money being, as ever, in short supply, it was time to phone around the bucket-shops for a cheap ticket. One could not reasonably hope to find one to Sulawesi. The best thing would be to get to Singapore and hunt around.

What is astonishing is not that fares should vary from one airline to another, but that it is virtually impossible to pay the same fare to fly by the same airline on the same plane. As the trail cleared and the prices declined, the names of airlines seemed less and less real and more and more revealing. Finnair suggested a vanishing trick. Madair was expensive but suggested a bout of wild adventure. In the end, I settled for a Third World airline described as "all right once you're in the air." In an attic above Oxford Street, I rendezvoused with a nervy little man who looked like a demonstration of the disastrous effects of stress—wizened, twitchy, biting nails, chain-smoking. He was surrounded with huge heaps of paper and a telephone that rang incessantly. I paid my money and he began writing out the ticket. Ring, ring.

"Hallo. What? Who? Oh dear. Ah, yes, well. I'm sorry about that. The problem is that at this time of the year all the traffic is going East so there *will* be a problem in getting a seat." There followed five minutes of placatory explanation to someone on the other end of the line who was manifestly very annoyed. He hung up, bit his nails, and returned to writing out the ticket. Immediately, the phone rang again.

"Hallo. What? When? Oh dear. Ah, well. The problem is that at this time of year all the Asians are heading West so there will be problems getting a seat." Another five minutes of soothing noises. He sucked desperately on a cigarette. Ring, ring.

"Hallo. What? Oh dear. I am sorry. That's never happened before in all the years I've been in this business. I certainly posted the ticket to you." He picked through a wad of tickets, put one in an envelope and began scribbling an address.

"The trouble is that at this time of year, most of the Post Office is on holiday, so there will be delays."

It was with the direst forebodings that I pocketed my ticket and left the office.

And so I arrived at predeparture depression. Having taken a turn about the room with the beetle-carapace rucksack, I unpacked it and threw half the contents out. I needn't have bothered. When I arrived at the airport, there was no room on the plane and no other plane for a week. I rang the pre-stressed travel agent.

"What? Who? Well, that's never happened before in all the years I've been in the business. The problem is that at this time of year the extra planes are held up by the monsoon. But I'll give you a full refund. I'm putting it in an envelope now." When the check arrived, several weeks later, it bounced.

It is said that every positive term needs its negative to sharpen its definition and fix its place in the wider system of things. This is

perhaps the role of Aeroflot in the airline world—a sort of antitheti-
cal airline. Instead of effete stewards, burly mustachioed wardresses.
Instead of the fussy congelations of aircraft cuisine, fried chicken.
Between London and Singapore, we ate fried chicken five times,
sometimes hot, sometimes cold, always recognizable. Rather than
lug my luggage back home, I had opted for the only cheap flight
that day—on Aeroflot.

Some strange smell like oil of cloves had been introduced into
the air supply. It was particularly pungent in the lavatory—a place
entirely devoid of paper—and as a result of it, people would emerge
red-faced and gasping. At moments of stress, such as landing, cold
air streamed visibly from vents in the ceiling as off dry ice in a the-
atrical production. This terrified the Japanese who thought it was
fire and whimpered until a wardress shouted at them in Russian.
Thereafter they were not convinced but at least cowed.

The only relief from the bouts of fried chicken was the changing
of planes in Moscow. Emerging in late evening from the miasma
of cloves, we were made to queue on the stairs under 20 W bulbs
as in a municipal brothel. Wardresses rushed among us inquisitori-
ally shouting "Lusaka!" Or was it "Osaka!"? Japanese and Zambians
jostled each other without conviction. Our tickets were minutely
examined. Our luggage was searched. A scowling young man
checked our passports, reading them line by line with moving lips.
He insisted on the removal of hats and glasses. Myself, he measured
to check my actual height against that alleged in my passport. I
cannot believe that the figures matched.

The girl behind me was French and garrulous, eager to tell her
life story. She was going to Australia to get married. "I expect it
will be all right when I get there," she said gamely. Having a well-
developed sense of humor, she found my being measured exquis-
itely funny. "They measure you for a coffin?" she suggested cheerfully.
The scowling young man did not appreciate her levity and sent her
to the back of the queue to stand in line again. It was just like being

back at school. In fact the whole transit area recalled drab, postwar school days. Stern ladies wheeled trolleys of chipped cream enamel, meaty faces set in disapproval. Surely these were the very women who had dispensed fatty mince at my primary school while discussing the problems of rationing. The broken lavatories of the airport recalled the outhouses of the school.

Younger women in olive-green uniforms saluted soldiers sauntering about with rifles. They had the air of those on important state business. An air of guilt and insecurity seemed to invade the Westerners. We all felt improperly frivolous and facetious, like gigglers at a funeral. One day, perhaps, we would grow up into sober citizens like these people.

All the shops were shut, thus preventing us rushing in to buy nests of Russian dolls and books on Vietnamese collectivization. More adventurous souls discovered a bar upstairs where fizzy mineral water could be bought from a dour man with no change.

We had all been issued with squares of cardboard on which someone had written "diner 9:00." There was an area of tables and chairs so here we all sat down looking more and more like refugees. At ten o'clock the school-dinner-ladies emerged, adjusting their headscarves for action. But, alas, there was no mince for us. They served a copious and leisurely meal to themselves, consumed before our envious eyes with great lip-smacking gestures of content. For once, no chicken seemed to be involved. The ladies disappeared and went into a prolonged bout of off-stage plate-clattering. Shortly before our plane was due to leave, they surged out triumphantly with the enamel trollies. One served us two slices of bread, a tomato, and black coffee while two others shooed us into tight groups and examined tickets. When all expectation of more had been abandoned, we were served a single biscuit on magnificent china.

Beneath us, in the space before the departure gates, a lively floor-show was in progress. Two tourists, English by the sound of them, were banging on the glass door of the immigration office. They had tried pushing it. They had tried pulling it. They did not know it was a sliding door.

"Our plane!" they shouted, indicating what was indeed a large aircraft parked just the other side of the plateglass window. Passengers could be seen embarking. A rotund official in a sackcloth uniform stared out of the window, his back turned towards them, and worked hard at ignoring the noise they were making.

"You phoned us to come to the airport," they cried. "We've been waiting a week for a plane."

Finally, the disturbance grated on his nerves and, unwillingly, he slid the door open an inch to peer at them like a householder wakened by knocking in the small hours. They thrust tickets at him in justification. This was a mistake. He took them, peacefully closed and locked the door, set the tickets on the end of his desk and resumed his untroubled contemplation of the plane. A wardress appeared at the top of the steps, looked briefly around, shrugged, and went back inside.

"Call someone," the travelers pleaded. "Our luggage is on that plane."

In response, the official deftly slid the tickets back under the door and turned his back again. The hatch of the plane was closed, the steps wheeled away. The travelers began hammering on the door in renewed desperation. The official began to smoke. We watched for a full ten minutes before the plane finally roused itself to trundle off. By then, the travelers were sobbing.

Pharisaically, we turned away. Our own plane had finally been called. Following this little morality play, no one wanted to be late. We bayed around the doors like pagan hordes at the gates of Rome. Occasionally, a wardress would appear behind the glass doors and we would surge forward. Then she would disappear again and leave us stranded in foolishness.

The resumed flight brought no relief, only more fried chicken. A bumptious Indian paced the plane, telling all and sundry that he was an admiral in the navy and only traveled by Aeroflot for security reasons, not out of parsimony. In one corner sat a Seasoned Traveler. She dismissed all offers of chicken with a disdainful wave of the hand, having had the foresight to provision herself with a selection of cheeses and a good loaf. At her feet stood a bottle of wine. On her lap rested a stout novel. Most outrageous of all, she had soap and a toilet roll. We regarded her with the undisguised resentment of those faces at the windows of old folks" homes. We took pleasure in the fact that, as we began our descent to Singapore, a green-faced man emerged from the lavatory and kicked her wine over.

16

Assassination Vacation

Sarah Vowell

One night last summer, all the killers in my head assembled on a stage in Massachusetts to sing show tunes. There they were—John Wilkes Booth, Charles Guiteau, Leon Czolgosz—in tune and in the flesh. The men who murdered Presidents Lincoln, Garfield, and McKinley were elbow to elbow with Lee Harvey Oswald and the klutzy girls who botched their hits on klutzy Gerald Ford, harmonizing on a toe-tapper called "Everybody's Got the Right to Be Happy," a song I cheerfully hummed walking back to the bed-and-breakfast where I was staying.

Not that I came all the way from New York City just to enjoy a chorus line of presidential assassins. Mostly, I came to the Berkshires because of the man who brought one of those presidents back to life. I was there to visit Chesterwood, the house and studio once belonging to Daniel Chester French, the artist responsible for the Abraham Lincoln sculpture in the Lincoln Memorial. A nauseating four-hour bus ride from the Port Authority terminal just to see the room where some patriotic chiseler came up with a marble statue? For some reason, none of my friends wanted to come with.

Because I had to stay overnight and this being New England, the only place to stay was a bed-and-breakfast. It was a lovely old country mansion operated by amiable people. That said, I am not a bed-and-breakfast person.

I understand why other people would want to stay in B&Bs. They're pretty. They're personal. They're "quaint," a polite way of saying "no TV." They are "romantic," i.e., every object large enough for a flower to be printed on it is going to have a flower printed on it. They're "cozy," meaning that a guest has to keep her belongings on the floor because every conceivable flat surface is covered in knickknacks, except for the one knickknack she longs for, a remote control.

The real reason bed-and-breakfasts make me nervous is breakfast. As if it's not queasy enough to stay in a stranger's home and sleep in a bed bedecked with nineteen pillows. In the morning, the usually cornflake-consuming, wheat-intolerant guest is served floury baked goods on plates so fancy any normal person would keep them locked in the china cabinet even if Queen Victoria herself rose from the dead and showed up for tea. The guest, normally a silent morning reader of newspapers, is expected to chat with the other strangers staying in the strangers' home.

At my Berkshires bed-and-breakfast, I am seated at a table with one middle-aged Englishman and an elderly couple from Greenwich, Connecticut. The three of them make small talk about golf, the weather, and the room's chandeliers, one of which, apparently, is Venetian. I cannot think of a thing to say to these people. Seated at the head of the table, I am the black hole of breakfast, a silent void of gloom sucking the sunshine out of their neighborly New England day. But that is not the kind of girl my mother raised me to be. I consider asking the Connecticut couple if they had ever run into Jack Paar, who I heard had retired near where they live, but I look like I was born after Paar quit hosting *The Tonight Show* (because I was) and so I'd have to explain how much I like watching tapes of old programs at the Museum of Television and Radio and I don't want to get too personal.

It seems that all three of them attended a Boston Pops concert at Tanglewood the previous evening, and they chat about the conductor. This, I think, is my in. I, too, enjoy being entertained.

Relieved to have something, anything, to say, I pipe up, "I went to the Berkshire Theatre Festival last night."

"Oh, did you see *Peter Pan?*" the woman asks.

"No" I say. "*Assassins!*"

"What's that?" wonders the Englishman.

To make up for the fact that I've been clammed up and moping I speak too fast, merrily chirping, "It's the Stephen Sondheim musical in which a bunch of presidential assassins and would-be assassins sing songs about how much better their lives would be if they could gun down a president."

"Oh," remarks Mr. Connecticut. "How was it?"

"Oh my god," I gush. "Even though the actors were mostly college kids, I thought it was great! The orange-haired guy who played the man who wanted to fly a plane into Nixon was hilarious. And I found myself strangely smitten with John Wilkes Booth; every time he looked in my direction I could feel myself blush." Apparently, talking about going to the Museum of Television and Radio is "too personal," but I seem to have no problem revealing my crush on the man who murdered Lincoln.

Now, a person with sharper social skills than I might have noticed that as these folks ate their freshly baked blueberry muffins and admired the bed-and-breakfast's teapot collection, they probably didn't want to think about presidential gunshot wounds. But when I'm around strangers, I turn into a conversational Mount St. Helens. I'm dormant, dormant, quiet, quiet, old-guy loners build log cabins on the slopes of my silence and then, boom, it's 1980. Once I erupt, they'll be wiping my verbal ashes off their windshields as far away as North Dakota.

I continue. "But the main thing that surprised me was how romantic *Assassins* was."

"Romantic?" sneers a skeptic.

"Totally," I rebut. "There's a very tender love scene between Emma Goldman and Leon Czolgosz."

Blank stares.

"You know. He was the anarchist who killed McKinley. Buffalo? 1901? Anyway, the authorities initially suspected Goldman had helped him, but all it was was that he had heard her speak a couple of times about sticking it to The Man. He'd met her, but she wasn't his coconspirator. Anyway, the play dramatizes the moment they meet. He stops her on the street to tell her that he loves her. The guy who played Czolgosz was wonderful. He had this smoldering Eastern European accent. Actually, he sounded a lot like Dracula— but in a good way, if you know what I mean." (They don't.)

"He told her, 'Miss Goldman, I am in love with you.' She answered that she didn't have time to be in love with him. Which was cute. But, this was my one misgiving about the performance, I thought that the woman playing Goldman was too ladylike, too much of a wallflower. Wasn't Emma Goldman loud and brash and all gung ho? Here was a woman whose words inspired a guy to kill a president. And come to think of it, one of her old boyfriends shot the industrialist Henry Frick. Maybe I'm too swayed by the way Maureen Stapleton played Goldman in the film *Reds*. She was so bossy! And remember Stapleton in that Woody Allen movie, *Interiors*? Geraldine Page is all beige this and bland that so her husband divorces her and hooks up with noisy, klutzy Maureen Stapleton, who laughs too loud and smashes pottery and wears a blood-red dress to symbolize that she is Alive, capital A. Wait. I lost my train of thought. Where was I?"

Englishman: "I believe Dracula was in love with Maureen Stapleton."

"Oh, right. I haven't even mentioned the most touching part. Squeaky Fromme and John Hinckley sing this duet, a love song to Charles Manson and Jodie Foster. Hinckley and Squeaky sang that they would do anything for Charlie Manson and Jodie Foster. And I really believed them! Squeaky's like, 'I would crawl belly-deep through hell,' and Hinckley's all, 'Baby, I'd die for you.' It was adorable."

Mr. Connecticut looks at his watch and I simultaneously realize that I've said way too much and that saying way too much means I might miss my bus back home. And I really want to go home. I yell, "Nice meeting you!" and nearly knock down the teapot collection in my rush to get away from them. Though before I can leave, I have to settle up my bill with the friendly B&B owner. His first name? Hinckley.

On the bus home, I flip through my *Assassins* program from the night before and read the director's note. Of course talking about the murders of previous presidents is going to open the door to discussing the current president. That's what I like to call him, "the current president." I find it difficult to say or type his name, George W. Bush. I like to call him "the current president" because it's a hopeful phrase, implying that his administration is only temporary. Timothy Douglas, the *Assassins* director, doesn't say the president's name either, but he doesn't have to. Clearly, Douglas is horrified and exasperated by the Iraqi war. He writes,

> Proportionate to my own mounting frustrations at feeling increasingly excluded from the best interests of the current administration's control in these extraordinary times helps me toward a visceral understanding of the motivation of one who would perpetrate a violent act upon the leader of the free world. My capacity for this depth of empathy also gives me pause, for I have no idea how far away I am from the "invisible line" that separates me from a similar or identical purpose. . . . Please allow me to state for the record that I am completely against violence of any kind as a way of resolving conflicts.

That crafty explanation slaps me in the forehead with all the force of "duh." Until that moment, I hadn't realized that I embarked on the project of touring historic sites and monuments having to do with the assassinations of Lincoln, Garfield, and McKinley right around the time my country iffily went to war, which is to say right around the time my resentment of the current president cranked up into contempt. Not that I want the current president killed. Like that director, I will, for the record (and for the FBI agent assigned to read this and make sure I mean no harm—hello there), clearly state that while I am obsessed with death, I am against it.

Like director Tim Douglas, my simmering rage against the current president scares me. I am a more or less peaceful happy person whose lone act of violence as an adult was shoving a guy who spilled beer on me at a Sleater-Kinney concert. So if I can summon this much bitterness toward a presidential human being, I can sort of, kind of, see how this amount of bile or more, teaming up with disappointment, unemployment, delusions of grandeur and mental illness, could prompt a crazier narcissistic creep to buy one of this country's widely available handguns. Not that I, I repeat, condone that. Like Lincoln, I would like to believe the ballot is stronger than the bullet. Then again, he said that before he got shot.

I am only slightly less astonished by the egotism of the assassins, the inflated self-esteem it requires to kill a president, than I am astonished by the men who run for president. These are people who have the gall to believe they can fix us—us and our deficit, our fossil fuels, our racism, poverty, our potholes and public schools. The egomania required to be president or a presidential assassin makes the two types brothers of sorts. Presidents and presidential assassins are like Las Vegas and Salt Lake City that way. Even though one city is all about sin and the other is all about salvation, they are identical, one-dimensional company towns built up out of the desert by the sheer will of true believers. The assassins and the presidents invite the same basic question: Just who do you think you are?

One of the books I read for McKinley research was Barbara Tuchman's great history of European and American events leading up to World War I, *The Proud Tower*. Her anarchism chapter enumerates the six heads of state who were assassinated in the two decades before Archduke Ferdinand was murdered in 1914: McKinley, the president of France, the empress of Austria, the king of Italy, a couple of Spanish premiers. Her point being, it was an age of assassination. Well, I can come up with at least that many assassinations off the top of my head from the last two years alone as if playing some particularly geopolitical game of Clue: Serbian prime minister (sniper in front of government building in Belgrade), Swedish foreign minister (stabbed while shopping in Stockholm), the Taiwanese president and vice president (wounded when shots were fired at their motorcade the day before an election), two Hamas leaders (Israeli missile strikes), president of the Iraqi Governing Council (suicide bomber). And, in May 2004, an audio recording surfaced from Osama bin Laden promising to pay ten thousand grams of gold (roughly $125K) to assassins of officials in Iraq representing the United States or the United Nations.

"I'm worried about the president's safety," I said at a Fourth of July party in 2004 when this guy Sam and I were talking about the upcoming Republican National Convention here in New York. "I think you've seen *The Manchurian Candidate* too many times," said Sam. Guilty. Still, I dread bodily harm coming to the current president because of my aforementioned aversion to murder, but also because I don't think I can stomach watching that man get turned into a martyr if he were killed. That's what happens. It's one of the few perks of assassination. In death, you get upgraded into a saint no matter how much people hated you in life. As the rueful Henry

Adams, a civil service reform advocate who marveled at his fellow reformers' immediate deification of President Garfield after that assassination, wrote, "The cynical impudence with which the reformers have tried to manufacture an ideal statesman out of the late shady politician beats anything in novel-writing."

Somewhere on the road between museum displays of Lincoln's skull fragments and the ceramic tiles on which Garfield was gunned down and McKinley's bloodstained pj's it occurred to me that there is a name for travel embarked upon with the agenda of venerating relics: pilgrimage. The medieval pilgrimage routes, in which Christians walked from church to church to commune with the innards of saints, are the beginnings of the modern tourism industry. Which is to say that you can draw a more or less straight line from a Dark Ages peasant blistering his feet trudging to a church displaying the Virgin Mary's dried-up breast milk to me vomiting into a barf bag on a sightseeing boat headed toward the prison-island hell where some Lincoln assassination conspirators were locked up in 1865.

I remembered that my friend Jack Hitt had written a book called *Off the Road* in which he retraced the old pilgrimage route to Santiago de Compostela in Spain. So I floated my pilgrimage theory to him in an e-mail and he wrote back that at one point on his Spanish trip, he saw "the flayed 'skin' of Jesus—the entire thing, you know, with like eyeholes and stuff, mounted on a wooden frame." Cool. His e-mail went on to say that in the Middle Ages:

> Relics were treasured as something close to the divine. Often when a great monk died and there was a sense that he might be canonized, the corpse was carefully guarded in a tomb—often twenty-four hours a day. Visitors could come to the tomb. Most of the funeral vaults of potential saints had a small door, like you might have in your suburban house for cats. Visitors could poke their heads in the

little door and breathe in the holy dust. Most people thought that such dust had curative powers since it was associated with a near-saint whose corporeal matter had been directly blessed by God. So, getting near a relic, touching it, being near it was considered extremely beneficial and treasured.

Curative powers? I wondered how taking the train to Philadelphia to look at a sliver of the Garfield assassin's brain floating in a jar is supposed to fix me. "There was a late Renaissance king of Spain whom I loved," Jack went on.

He was so inbred and crazy, incapable of eating food or reproducing that he was called *El Hechizado*—the bewitched. He was probably retarded. After destroying the world's largest empire (ever, in all history) and bankrupting a nation drowning in New World gold, he came to die. Half the College of Cardinals arrived to recite prayers over his feeble frail body. They split a live dove over his head every morning. And they had brought with them the most powerful curative tool then known to man, the putrefying, stinking rotting corpse of Saint Francis of Assisi, then (and maybe now) the greatest saint ever. It was laid in the bed next to *El Hechizado* and for the rest of his days, the King of Spain shared his bed with the greatest relic ever in the hopes that it would restore his health and grant him the potency to generate an heir. Neither happened and the empire eventually dissolved into warfare with England around 1588 and became a backwater.

I can relate. (Not to being retarded, though it has been my experience that if you go on your historical pilgrimage while wearing your *Jackass: The Movie* ball cap some people look at you like you are.) I crave my relics for the same reason Señor Bewitched bunked with the late saint. We're religious. I used to share the king's faith. And while I gave up God a long time ago, I never shook the habit of wanting to believe in something bigger and better than myself. So I replaced my creed of everlasting life with life, liberty, and the pursuit of happiness. "I believe in America," chants the first verse of one of my sacred texts, *The Godfather*. Not that I'm blind to the Psych 101 implications of trading in the martyred Jesus Christ (crucified on Good Friday) for the martyred Abraham Lincoln (shot on Good Friday).

One thing the Spanish king's Catholicism and my rickety patriotism have in common, besides the high body count, is that both faiths can get a little ethereal and abstract. Jesus and Lincoln, Moses and Jefferson can seem so long gone, so unbelievable, so dead. It's reassuring to be able to go look at something real, something you can put your hands on (though you might want to wash them afterward). "What's that smell?" wondered the bewitched king. Actual Saint Francis, staining the sheets. Did a fellow as shrewd and sad and poetic and miraculously the right man for the right job at the exact right moment as Abraham Lincoln truly walk the earth until gunned down? Well, come along on one of these We Cannot Escape History weekend escape packages and we'll genuflect before the bone from inside his head *and* the hats he wore on top of his head. The Declaration of Independence, the Constitution, the Civil War—when I really think about them they all seem about as likely as the parting of the Red Sea. But somehow, jumping up a foot to stare at my own face framed in Lincoln's Springfield shaving mirror makes the whole far-fetched, grisly, inspiring story of the country seem more shocking and more true. Especially since when I jumped up to the mirror, I set off a super-loud alarm.

Jack's e-mail about the relics ended with an aside about how he had just been shopping on eBay and stumbled onto "a guy selling tiny specks of 'George Washington's hair.' Literally, these clippings were nothing more than single strands of hair less than a quarter of an inch long. They came in little ampoules and with documentation."

I looked away from my computer and over at a frame on my wall and wrote Jack back that my twin sister Amy had given me a teensy eyelash-size hair of John Brown as a Christmas present. She settled on the more affordable tresses of the abolitionist guerrilla warrior Brown because Lincoln's hair was out of her price range. That is the kind of person I have become, the kind of person who rips open a package in snowman wrapping paper to discover that her only sibling has bought her an executed slavery hater's hair. (I got her a DVD player.)

As I learned that morning at the bed-and-breakfast while I was going on and on about the singing Squeaky Fromme, most people don't like to talk about violent historical death over muffins. I would come to find out that's also true about lunch and dinner, too. When my friend Bennett and I were trying to decide where to have brunch he suggested a dim sum place in Chinatown. He asked me if I had ever tried bubble tea. I said yes, that I think a better name for the tea afloat with tapioca globules is tea 'n' dumplings and that I had it at the Chinese restaurant in D.C. that used to be the boarding-house where Booth and his coconspirators met to plan the Lincoln assassination.

Bennett asked, "You know that Kevin Bacon game?"

"The one where he can be connected to every other movie star?"

"Yeah, that's the one. Assassinations are your Kevin Bacon. No matter what we're talking about, you will always bring the conversation back to a president getting shot."

He was right. An artist pal, marveling at the youth of a painter in the Whitney Biennial was subjected to the trivia, "Well, John Wilkes Booth was only twenty-six when he killed Lincoln." A gardener friend, bragging about his lilacs, was forced to endure a recitation of Walt Whitman's Lincoln death poem "When Lilacs Last in the Dooryard Bloom'd."

As Johnny Cash put it about how his Garfield assassination ballad went over at Carnegie Hall in 1962, "I did 'Mr. Garfield,' which isn't very funny if you're not on the right wavelength, and nobody was." Once I knew my dead presidents and I had become insufferable, I started to censor myself. There were a lot of get-togethers with friends where I didn't hear half of what was being said because I was sitting there, silently chiding myself, Don't bring up McKinley. Don't bring up McKinley.

The bright side to researching the first three presidential assassinations is that my interest is optional, a choice. One man who makes cameo appearances in all three stories was not so lucky. Abraham Lincoln's oldest son, Robert Todd Lincoln, was in close proximity to all three murders like some kind of jinxed Zelig of doom. The young man who wept at his father's deathbed in 1865 was only a few feet away when James A. Garfield was shot in a train station in 1881. In 1901, Robert arrived in Buffalo mere moments after William McKinley fell. Robert Todd Lincoln's status as a presidential death magnet weighed on him. Late in life, when he was asked to attend some White House function, he grumbled, "If only they knew, they wouldn't want me there."

On July 2, 2003, the 122nd anniversary of the Garfield assassination, my friend Nicole and I rented a car and drove up to Vermont to visit Hildene, Robert Todd Lincoln's estate in Manchester. His mansion is a museum with landscaped grounds where, in the winter, there is cross-country skiing. I find it hard to stop myself from being unfair to Robert. Shown around the house, climbing the graceful staircase a guide proudly points out Robert himself designed, it's impossible not to compare him with his father: Abraham Lincoln freed the slaves, Robert Lincoln bought a nice ski lodge.

The person I'm really treating unfairly is Nicole, for talking her into the eight-hour round-trip drive to Hildene. I guess learning trivia about when the colossal William Howard Taft came to visit he slept on the floor because he was afraid of breaking the bed in Robert Lincoln's guest room isn't enough for Nicole, because at the end of the day, she pronounces the trip "kind of a bust." Ever polite, she hastens to add, "You brought really good snacks, though."

When we return the rental car on Thirty-fourth Street, the block is crawling with people filing into a concert at the Hammerstein Ballroom. The Foo Fighters are on the marquee. I walk Nicole to the subway, hoping she doesn't notice who's playing, because then she might remember tagging along as my plus-one to a Foo Fighters show seven years earlier, when I was still making a living as a rock critic, which I fear might remind her what I was like before I went off the historical tourism deep end, when tagging along with me to work used to be fun.

President Warren G. Harding, beware: the elderly Robert Lincoln was the guest of honor at the dedication ceremony at the Lincoln Memorial in 1922. (Harding, also in attendance, returned to the White House unscathed.) Robert died in 1926, but for the rest of his life, he made it a point to visit the memorial often, gazing into his father's marble eyes, saying, "Isn't it beautiful?"

A pilgrimage needs a destination. For medieval Christians, that was usually the cathedral of Saint James in northern Spain. This tour of the assassinations of Lincoln, Garfield, and McKinley ends up at the Lincoln Memorial because that's where I'm always ending up. It is the closest thing I have to a church.

On the National Mall in Washington, next to the Reflecting Pool, that shallow, rectangular pond in front of the Lincoln Memorial, the National Park Service has posted a sign. It features a picture of the protesters in the March on Washington listening to Martin Luther King Jr. deliver his "I have a dream" speech from the memorial's steps. The sign says, "The Pool reflects more than the sky and landscape. It mirrors the moods of America, from national celebrations to dramatic demonstrations." This reminds me of a photograph of the memorial's Lincoln sculpture that my tour guide held up at Chesterwood, Daniel Chester French's studio in the Berkshires.

French obsessed for years about how to sculpt Lincoln's peculiar face, fretting and reading and thinking before committing to the brooding, seated philosopher in the memorial. He received the commission in 1913. So by the time the memorial was finally dedicated nine years later, the sculptor was a little pent up worrying how his work would come off. Hoping to celebrate, French looked upon the final installation with horror. The problem with putting in a reflecting pool? The darn thing reflects. When the light off the Reflecting Pool bounced up onto Lincoln's face, it looked as if a flashlight had been held up under his chin. The Chesterwood guide described the photo as a "Halloween picture." Lincoln looks frightened, startled, confused—Edvard Munch's *The Scream* by way of Macaulay Culkin's *Home Alone*. Apparently, "hilarious" wasn't the aesthetic French had been going for.

Along with architect Henry Bacon, French tinkered with various solutions, concluding that only electric lighting placed above Lincoln's head could correct the travesty. For years, he pestered the government to pay to fix it. I'm happy for French that he lived long enough to see the ceiling lights installed so that his Lincoln is as dignified and pensive as he intended; otherwise the man might have died of embarrassment.

But I like that picture of the panicky Abraham Lincoln. Lately, I think I might prefer it. Given what that sign says about the Reflecting Pool mirroring American moods, and given that the current mood is on the edgy side what with all the new coffins being buried every day in the Arlington National Cemetery behind the statue's back, a freaked-out Lincoln gaping at the current government might look a little more true.

Then again, in the 1860s, at least half the country loathed Abraham Lincoln for filling up too many soldiers' coffins. Which is why Daniel Chester French isn't the only reason that marble likeness sits there on the Mall. John Wilkes Booth deserves some of the credit—a notion that would make the assassin want to throw up. After all, if no one had hated Lincoln, there would be no Lincoln Memorial to love.

17

Three Men in a Boat

Jerome K. Jerome

Then we discussed the food question. George said: "Begin with breakfast." (George is so practical.) "Now for breakfast we shall want a frying pan" (Harris said it was indigestible; but we merely urged him not to be an ass, and George went on) "a teapot and a kettle, and a methylated-spirit stove."

"No oil," said George, with a significant look; and Harris and I agreed.

We had taken up an oil stove once, but "never again." It had been like living in an oil shop that week. It oozed. I never saw such a thing as paraffin oil is to ooze. We kept it in the nose of the boat, and, from there, it oozed down to the rudder, impregnating the whole boat and everything in it on its way, and it oozed over the river, and saturated the scenery and spoilt the atmosphere. Sometimes a westerly oily wind blew, and at other times an easterly oily wind, and sometimes it blew a northerly oily wind, and maybe a southerly oily wind; but whether it came from the Arctic snows, or was raised in the waste of the desert sands, it came alike to us laden with the fragrance of paraffin oil.

And that oil oozed up and ruined the sunset; and as for the moonbeams, they positively reeked of paraffin.

We tried to get away from it at Marlow. We left the boat by the bridge, and took a walk through the town to escape it, but it followed us. The whole town was full of oil. We passed through the churchyard, and it seemed as if the people had been buried in oil. The High Street stank of oil; we wondered how people could live in it. And we walked miles upon miles out Birmingham way; but it was no use, the country was steeped in oil.

At the end of that trip we met together at midnight in a lonely field, under a blasted oak, and took an awful oath (we had been swearing for a whole week about the thing in an ordinary, middle-class way, but this was a swell affair)—an awful oath never to take paraffin oil with us in a boat again—except, of course, in case of sickness.

Therefore, in the present instance, we confined ourselves to methylated spirit. Even that is bad enough. You get methylated pie and methylated cake. But methylated spirit is more wholesome when taken into the system in large quantities than paraffin oil.

For other breakfast things, George suggested eggs and bacon, which were easy to cook, cold meat, tea, bread and butter, and jam. For lunch, he said, we could have biscuits, cold meat, bread and butter, and jam—but *no cheese*. Cheese like oil, makes too much of itself. It wants the whole boat to itself. It goes through the hamper, and gives a cheesy flavor to everything else there. You can't tell whether you are eating apple pie, or German sausage, or strawberries and cream. It all seems cheese. There is too much odor about cheese.

I remember a friend of mine buying a couple of cheeses at Liverpool. Splendid cheeses they were, ripe and mellow, and with a two hundred horse-power scent about them that might have been warranted to carry three miles, and knock a man over at two hundred yards. I was in Liverpool at the time, and my friend said that if I didn't mind he would get me to take them back with me to London, as he should not be coming up for a day or two himself, and he did not think the cheeses ought to be kept much longer.

"Oh, with pleasure, dear boy," I replied, "with pleasure."

I called for the cheeses, and took them away in a cab. It was a ramshackle affair, dragged along by a knock-kneed, broken-winded somnambulist, which his owner, in a moment of enthusiasm, during conversation, referred to as a horse. I put the cheeses on the top, and we started off at a shamble that would have done credit to the swiftest steamroller ever built, and all went merry as a funeral bell, until we turned a corner. There, the wind carried a whiff from the cheeses full on our steed. It woke him up, and, with a snort of terror, he dashed off at three miles an hour. The wind still blew in his direction, and before we reached the end of the street he was laying himself out at the rate of nearly four miles an hour, leaving the cripples and stout old ladies simply nowhere.

It took two porters as well as the driver to hold him in at the station; and I do not think they would have done it, even then, had not one of the men had the presence of mind to put a handkerchief over his nose, and to light a bit of brown paper.

I took my ticket, and marched proudly up the platform, with my cheeses, the people falling back respectfully on either side. The train was crowded, and I had to get into a carriage where there were already seven other people. One crusty old gentleman objected, but I got in, notwithstanding; and, putting my cheeses upon the rack, squeezed down with a pleasant smile, and said it was a warm day. A few moments passed, and then the old gentleman began to fidget.

"Very close in here," he said.

"Quite oppressive," said the man next to him.

And then they both began sniffing, and, at the third sniff they caught it right on the chest, and rose up without another word and went out. And then a stout lady got up, and said it was disgraceful that a respectable married woman should be harried about in this way, and gathered up a bag and eight parcels and went. The remaining four passengers sat on for a while, until a solemn-looking man in the corner who, from his dress and general appearance, seemed to belong to the undertaker class, said it put him in mind of a dead baby; and the other three passengers tried to get out of the door at the same time, and hurt themselves.

I smiled at the black gentleman, and said I thought we were going to have the carriage to ourselves; and he laughed pleasantly and said that some people made such a fuss over a little thing. But even he grew strangely depressed after we had started, and so, when we reached Crewe, I asked him to come and have a drink. He accepted, and we forced our way into the buffet, where we yelled, and stamped, and waved our umbrellas for a quarter of an hour; and then a young lady came and asked us if we wanted anything.

"What's yours?" I said, turning to my friend.

"I'll have half a crown's worth of brandy, neat, if you please, Miss," he responded.

And he went off quietly after he had drunk it and got into another carriage, which I thought mean.

From Crewe I had the compartment to myself, though the train was crowded. As we drew up at the different stations, the people, seeing my empty carriage, would rush for it. "Here y'are, Maria; come along, plenty of room." "All right, Tom; we'll get in here," they would shout. And they would run along, carrying heavy bags, and fight round the door to get in first. And one would open the door and mount the steps and stagger back into the arms of the man behind him; and they would all come and have a sniff, and then drop off and squeeze into other carriages, or pay the difference and go first.

From Euston I took the cheeses down to my friend's house. When his wife came into the room she smelt round for an instant. Then she said:

"What is it? Tell me the worst."

I said: "It's cheeses. Tom bought them in Liverpool, and asked me to bring them up with me."

202

And I added that I hoped she understood that it had nothing to do with me; and she said that she was sure of that, but that she would speak to Tom about it when he came back.

My friend was detained in Liverpool longer than he expected; and three days later, as he hadn't returned home, his wife called on me. She said:

"What did Tom say about those cheeses?"

I replied that he had directed they were to be kept in a moist place, and that nobody was to touch them.

She said: "Nobody's likely to touch them. Had he smelt them?"

I thought he had, and added that he seemed greatly attached to them.

"You think he would be upset," she queried, "if I gave a man a sovereign to take them away and bury them?"

I answered that I thought he would never smile again.

An idea struck her. She said:

"Do you mind keeping them for him? Let me send them round to you."

"Madam," I replied, "for myself I like the smell of cheese, and the journey the other day with them from Liverpool I shall ever look back upon as a happy ending to a pleasant holiday. But, in this world, we must consider others. The lady under whose roof I have the honor of residing is a widow, and, for all I know, possibly an orphan, too. She has a strong, I may say an eloquent, objection to being what she terms 'put upon.' The presence of your husband's cheese in her house she would, I instinctively feel, regard as a 'put upon'; and it shall never be said that I put upon the widow and the orphan."

"Very well, then," said my friend's wife, rising, "all I have to say is, that I shall take the children and go to an hotel until those cheeses are eaten. I decline to live any longer in the same house with them."

She kept her word, leaving the place in charge of the charwoman, who, when asked if she could stand the smell, replied, "What smell?" and who, when taken close to the cheeses and told to sniff hard, said she could detect a faint odor of melons. It was argued from this that little injury could result to the woman from the atmosphere, and she was left.

The hotel bill came to fifteen guineas; and my friend, after reckoning everything up, found that the cheeses had cost him eight- and-sixpence a pound. He said he dearly loved a bit of cheese, but it was beyond his means; so he determined to get rid of them. He threw them into the canal; but had to fish them out again, as the bargemen complained. They said it made them feel quite faint. And, after that, he took them one dark night and left them in the parish mortuary. But the coroner discovered them, and made a fearful fuss.

He said it was a plot to deprive him of his living by waking up the corpses.

My friend got rid of them, at last, by taking them down to a seaside town, and burying them on the beach. It gained the place quite a reputation. Visitors said they had never noticed before how strong the air was, and weak-chested and consumptive people used to throng there for years afterward.

Fond as I am of cheese, therefore, I hold that George was right in declining to take any.

"We shan't want any tea," said George (Harris's face fell at this); "but we'll have a good round, square, slap-up meal at seven—dinner, tea, and supper combined."

Harris grew more cheerful. George suggested meat and fruit pies, cold meat, tomatoes, fruit, and green stuff. For drink, we took some wonderful sticky concoction of Harris's, which you mixed with water and called lemonade, plenty of tea, and a bottle of whiskey, in case, as George said, we got upset.

It seemed to me that George harped too much on the getting-upset idea. It seemed to me the wrong spirit to go about the trip in.

But I'm glad we took the whiskey.

We didn't take beer or wine. They are a mistake up the river. They make you feel sleepy and heavy. A glass in the evening when you are doing a mooch round the town and looking at the girls is all right enough; but don't drink when the sun is blazing down on your head, and you've got hard work to do.

We made a list of the things to be taken, and a pretty lengthy one it was before we parted that evening. The next day, which was Friday, we got them all together, and met in the evening to pack. We got a big Gladstone for the clothes, and a couple of hampers for the victuals and the cooking utensils. We moved the table up against the window, piled everything in a heap in the middle of the floor, and sat round and looked at it.

I said I'd pack.

I rather pride myself on my packing. Packing is one of those many things that I feel I know more about than any other person living. (It surprises me myself, sometimes, how many of these subjects there are.) I impressed the fact upon George and Harris and told them that they had better leave the whole matter entirely to me. They fell into the suggestion with a readiness that had something uncanny about it. George put on a pipe and spread himself over the easy chair, and Harris cocked his legs on the table and lit a cigar.

This was hardly what I intended. What I had meant, of course, was, that I should boss the job, and that Harris and George should potter about under my directions, I pushing them aside every now and then with, "Oh, you—!" "Here, let me do it." "There you are, simple enough!"—really teaching them, as you might say. Their taking it in the way they did irritated me. There is nothing does irritate me more than seeing other people sitting about doing nothing when I'm working.

I lived with a man once who used to make me mad that way. He would loll on the sofa and watch me doing things by the hour together, following me round the room with his eyes, wherever I went. He said it did him real good to look on at me, messing about. He said it made him feel that life was not an idle dream to be gaped and yawned through, hut a noble task, full of duty and stern work. He said he often wondered now how he could have gone on before he met me, never having anybody to look at while they worked.

Now, I'm not like that. I can't sit still and see another man slaving and working. I want to get up and superintend, and walk round with my hands in my pockets, and tell him what to do. It is my energetic nature. I can't help it.

However, I did not say anything, but started the packing. It seemed a longer job than I had thought it was going to be; but I got the bag finished at last, and I sat on it and strapped it.

"Ain't you going to put the boots in?" said Harris.

And I looked round, and found I had forgotten them. That's just like Harris. He couldn't have said a word until I'd got the bag shut and strapped, of course. And George laughed—one of those irritating, senseless, chuckle-headed, crack-jawed laughs of his. They do make me so wild.

I opened the bag and packed the boots in; and then, just as I was going to close it, a horrible idea occurred to me. Had I packed my toothbrush? I don't know how it is, but I never do know whether I've packed my toothbrush.

My toothbrush is a thing that haunts me when I'm traveling, and makes my life a misery. I dream that I haven't packed it, and wake up in a cold perspiration, and get out of bed and hunt for it. And, in the morning, I pack it before I have used it, and have to unpack again to get it, and it is always the last thing I turn out of the bag; and then I repack and forget it, and have to rush upstairs for it at the last moment and carry it to the railway station, wrapped up in my pocket handkerchief.

Of course I had to turn every mortal thing out now, and, of course, I could not find it. I rummaged the things up into much the same state that they must have been before the world was created, and when chaos reigned. Of course, I found George's and Harris's eighteen times over, but I couldn't find my own. I put the things back one by one, and held everything up and shook it. Then I found it inside a boot. I repacked once more.

When I had finished, George asked if the soap was in. I said I didn't care a hang whether the soap was in or whether it wasn't; and I slammed the bag to and strapped it, and found that I had packed my tobacco pouch in it, and had to reopen it. It got shut up finally at 10:50 p.m., and then there remained the hampers to do. Harris said that we should be wanting to start in less than twelve hours" time and thought that he and George had better do the rest; and I agreed and sat down, and they had a go.

They began in a light-hearted spirit, evidently intending to show me how to do it. I made no comment; I only waited. When George is hanged Harris will be the worst packer in this world; and I looked at the piles of plates, and cups, and kettles, and bottles, and jars, and pies, and stoves, and cakes, and tomatoes, etc., and felt that the thing would soon become exciting.

It did. They started with breaking a cup. That was the first thing they did. They did that just to show you what they *could* do, and to get you interested.

Then Harris packed the strawberry jam on top of a tomato and squashed it, and they had to pick out the tomato with a teaspoon.

And then it was George's turn, and he trod on the butter. I didn't say anything, but I came over and sat on the edge of the table and watched them. It irritated them more than anything I could have said. I felt that. It made them nervous and excited, and they stepped on things, and put things behind them, and then couldn't find them when they wanted them; and they packed the pies at the bottom, and put heavy things on top, and smashed the pies in.

They upset salt over everything, and as for the butter! I never saw two men do more with one-and-twopence worth of butter in my whole life than they did. After George had got it off his slipper, they tried to put it in the kettle. It wouldn't go in, and what *was* in wouldn't come out. They did scrape it out at last, and put it down on a chair, and Harris sat on it, and it stuck to him, and they went looking for it all over the room.

"I'll take my oath I put it down on that chair," said George, staring at the empty seat.

"I saw you do it myself, not a minute ago," said Harris.

Then they started round the room again looking for it; and then they met again in the center and stared at one another.

"Most extraordinary thing I ever heard of," said George.

"So mysterious!" said Harris.

Then George got round at the back of Harris and saw it.

"Why, here it is all the time," he exclaimed indignantly.

"Where?" cried Harris, spinning round.

"Stand still, can't you?" roared George, flying after him.

And they got it off, and packed it in the teapot.

Montmorency was in it all, of course. Montmorency's ambition in life is to get in the way and be sworn at. If he can squirm in anywhere where he particularly is not wanted, and be a perfect nuisance, and make people mad, and have things thrown at his head, then he feels his day has not been wasted.

To get somebody to stumble over him, and curse him steadily for an hour, is his highest aim and object; and, when he has succeeded in accomplishing this, his conceit becomes quite unbearable.

He came and sat down on things, just when they were wanted to be packed; and he labored under the fixed belief that, whenever Harris or George reached out their hand for anything, it was his cold damp nose that they wanted. He put his leg into the jam, and he worried the teaspoons, and he pretended that the lemons were rats, and got into the hamper and killed three of them before Harris could land him with the frying pan.

Harris said I encouraged him. I didn't encourage him. A dog like that don't want any encouragement. It's the natural, original sin that is born in him that makes him do things like that.

The packing was done at 12:50; and Harris sat on the big hamper, and said he hoped nothing would be found broken. George said that if anything was broken it *was* broken, which reflection seemed to comfort him. He also said he was ready for bed. We were all ready for bed. Harris was to sleep with us that night, and we went upstairs.

We tossed for beds, and Harris had to sleep with me. He said:

"Do you prefer the inside or the outside, J.?"

I said I generally preferred to sleep *inside* a bed.

Harris said it was odd.

George said: "What time shall I wake you fellows?"

Harris said: "Seven."

I said: "No—six," because I wanted to write some letters.

Harris and I had a bit of a row over it, but at last split the difference, and said half past six.

"Wake us at 6:30, George," we said.

George made no answer, and we found, on going over, that he had been asleep for some time; so we placed the bath where he could tumble into it on getting out in the morning, and went to bed ourselves.

18

French Revolutions

Tim Moore

It was interesting to note how unremarkable I felt waiting on the platform for the 11:39 to Paris. Cyclists from Lance Armstrong to Terry Davenport invariably discovered at least one inner truth about themselves in the eye of some desperate ordeal. "I met a guy up on that mountain who I grew to kind of like, and do you know who that guy was? That's right: it was me." That sort of thing. But looking back over the already slightly unreal events of the past twenty-four hours, the only epiphany I could claim to have experienced was this: some mornings, even five croissants are not enough.

Though actually there was something else. Wheeling ZR back out through the Holiday Inn's automatic doors and into the misty sun I'd seen a roomful of sales-conference delegates staring bleakly into their Styrofoam cups as a bald man drew pie charts on an overhead projector; one of them turned to me as I cleated up and as our eyes met we both understood an important truth: however wretched my day might be, even if it meant going back to Belfort and back his was going to be far worse.

Troyes had not surprised me by looking rather better by day: haphazard, half-timbered streets opening into well-scrubbed, geometric boulevards, a Gothic cathedral, market squares—a proper

French town; the kind of place you wouldn't mind being twinned with, especially because every time the maire came over you'd be able to go on about the post-Agincourt Treaty of Troyes that recognized our own Henry V as heir to the French throne.

There were two tourist offices, and lured by window displays of bikes and jerseys and ville d'étape posters I visited them both. I didn't expect much, and I didn't get it—not even a souvenir bidon. But at least this time the ignorance was cheerful, and the lady at the second place did endeavor to help by telling me I'd got my helmet the wrong way round, even though I hadn't.

It was here I learned that it might indeed be possible to take my bike on the train, and so at least vaguely emulate the Tour riders, who would transfer by Orient Express to Paris for the final stage, a circuitous roam about the capital followed by the traditional mad scramble of laps up and down the Champs-Elysées. After painstaking ticket-office conversations and timetable consultations, I established with as much certainty as any tourist can hope for that the 11:39 to Paris Est was a service on which accompanied bicycles could be carried free of charge.

The 11:39 was one of those sixties efforts with a windscreen that sloped the wrong way, the only sort I'd imagined being allowed to take a bike on, but it creaked up to the almost deserted platform on the dot and with difficulty I bundled ZR aboard.

"Eh! Non! Eh! Monsieur! C'est interdit!"

There were rapid footsteps and further cries and suddenly two inspectors were outside on the platform, gesticulating at the driver and yanking my door handle. Someone had already blown a whistle and there we were, having a tug of war through an open door with ZR as the rope. I'd been wondering when the monstrosities of yesterday would catch up with me, and now I knew. There was little physical resistance and less mental: a four-armed yank and ZR was on the platform; a slight shove from an onboard official behind and I joined her.

"Oh, c'est joli, le maillot," said one of the inspectors, dusting off my jersey as the train awoke with a long, rusted yawn and moved slowly away. "Un rétro?"

His kind, trustworthy voice was so unexpected and disarming that I somehow found myself quietly discussing Merckx, Simpson, Bernard Thévenet, and other Peugeot riders of yore when by rights I should have been well entrenched in a physical confrontation whose final scene would see me bellowing the terms of the Treaty of Troyes as the gendarmerie dragged me down the platform by my ankles. As the pair gently escorted me out of the station I did halfheartedly draw their attention to my pocket timetable, and in particular the little bicycle symbol next to the 11:39, but they both just smiled and nodded like uncles being shown their small nephew's inept artwork. It didn't really matter. There was an Avis office almost next door and in half an hour I was shooting past fields of lilac opium poppies, a handlebar in my ear, hairless thighs sticking to the hot upholstery of an Opel Corsa.

In one way it was a shame not to be cycling into Paris, not to see the Eiffel Tower taking shape on a hazy horizon and gradually reeling it in with each portentous turn of the pedals, but in most ways it was not. Everyone was getting sweaty and bad-tempered as I approached the outskirts—it was no place to be on a bike. The signs warned pedestrians to cross in two stages, but the way things were going it was more likely to be two pieces. After turning off the périphérique ring road it got worse, and the apparently straightforward task of finding a hotel and parking the car required me to commit several dozen motoring offenses, from illicit U-turns to driving the wrong way down a one-way street. On the pavement.

The hotel, near the Place d'Italie in the city's unfashionable south, was unsatisfactory to the point of outrage. It looked no worse than grubby from the outside, set in a street behind an enormous hospital and flanked by the sort of dirty-windowed, faceless government offices you could only imagine being responsible for the most obscure bureaucratic pedantries: issuing crab licenses, approving artichoke export quotas, plotting the wholesale assassination of environmental activists.

A big-faced man with a moist neck made me pay up front before entering my name with difficulty in his soiled register of the damned; as I trod carefully toward the lift he issued a two-tone grunt of dissent and without looking up thumbed at a dark stairwell. My fourth-floor window overlooked a forgotten courtyard full of dead pigeons and an avant-garde installation entitled One Hundred Years of the Fag End. Inside, the view wasn't much better. The wardrobe was the size of a child's coffin and contained a vegetable. Rolling back the tramp's blanket on a bed of institutional design, I beheld a pillowcase that might have been used to filter coffee. But of course it hadn't: after all, what's the bathroom towel for? Still, clicking off the Bakelite switch with wet hands I wished I'd used it. The shock was so violent it flung me halfway to the bed—not bad seeing as the bathroom was a shared one right down the end of the corridor.

But do you know what? I simply didn't care. I didn't care because it reminded me of the tawdrily romantic hotels I'd patronized during my first teenage visit to Paris. I didn't care because it was cheap. But mainly I didn't care because I was setting out into a flawless summer evening with a bottle of pink champagne inside me, and because having put it there in a very small number of minutes I was already strangely untroubled by the negative aspects of my environment, and because the reason I had put it there was because I had done it. I had gone all the way round an enormous country, all the way across Europe's hugest range of mountains: 2,952 kilometres, with almost 10 percent of them in a single historic day. I had done all these things, and here was the bit I still couldn't get over as I jostled out into the zigzagging scooters and the apple-polishing Turkish grocers and the mincing old women walking their Pekineses: I had done them on a stupid bloody bicycle.

Feeling smug and splendid and world-famous, I promenaded luxuriously up to the Place d'Italie. It was remarkable that somewhere so humdrum by Parisian standards—this was just one of the minor étoiles, those vast roundabouts where boulevards converge— could seem the epitome of Continental sophistication in British terms. The nearest equivalent in London would be some brutalist concrete nightmare, a gyratory wasteland such as the Elephant & Castle. But here there was space and light and the huge glass wall of a daring new cinema complex and cobbles and ashlar and bars with outside tables: a proper urban focus for a proper urban community.

Sweden were playing Turkey and the local supporters of the latter team were out in force, filling the bars to the rafters and standing on chairs outside to get a view of the telly. It was all terribly exciting. I had a peek through one door and in seven loud seconds established that far post was "deuxième poteau" and that Ross from *Friends* was playing on the left side of the Turkish midfield. And it was good to hear that even in such an environment, "ooh la la" remains the exhilarated Parisian's default expression.

I found an outside table at a bar that wasn't showing the game, next to two old men almost inevitably playing chess. Lovers were sitting on the statues around us, stroking each other's warm faces in the 9 p.m. sun, and as my tall glass of cold beer arrived I surveyed the scene with the avuncular fondness of the reasonably plastered. But then, succumbing to this same group's vulnerability to wild swings of emotion, I suddenly felt a profound sadness. A snapshot photographed by my eyes the previous day was belatedly developed in my brain, and as it took shape I found myself looking at three teenage girls silently sharing a Coke outside a bar flanked by abandoned homes in a decaying rural town strung carelessly along both sides of a thundering main road.

How could you expect any young person to put up with a life like that when they could be having a life like this? The girls were mentally thumbing a lift from anything that passed—they even plotted my weary passage through their lives with glum envy—and one day soon someone would stop and pick them up and they'd be off. It was tragic to think that when the Tour first visited Londun or Obterre, or Carpentras or Chaumont or a thousand semi-derelict towns in between, each had been as vibrant as this in its own modest way, each had its own thronging Place d'Italie. But industrialization and social mobility and any number of other de-mographic phenomena had lured people away to the cities, and even those rural towns that weren't just slinking off to die alone were doomed. They'd pay their million francs and string up their bunting and resurface their miniroundabouts, but when the Tour came to town, that one day of sex and speed would only serve to highlight the snail-paced, strait-laced parochialism of the other 364.

I made my way back to the hotel, as wistful as it's possible to be with a leaking kebab in your mouth. The traffic was still insane at 10:30 and I knew that my final trans-Parisian stage would be feasible only at dawn, and that consequently I should go to bed straight away.

Bed was one thing; sleep was another. The sackcloth sheets were too short for the mattress and against my shaven shins the horse-hair blanket felt like the rough grope of a lust-fogged drunk. That was how it started. The night before I had fallen immediately into a fatigued coma; only now, as the bedding rasped against my silken skin, did I notice how peculiar it felt to have hairless legs. Suddenly I couldn't keep my hands off them. Wobbling the firm, smooth bulk of those enormously bulked-up calves, as meaty and sculpted as granite chicken breasts; prodding and tracing the outlines of the entirely new front-thigh muscles that spilt over my kneecaps like double chins; stroking the thick and toughened tendons, still sore from the (how could it only have been yesterday?) massage.

It was like a variant of that joke about the reason men didn't have breasts: because if they did they'd just stay in and play with them all night. I kept expecting to be slapped in the face. Even after I finally stopped fondling myself and dropped off it wasn't over—twice that night (and there'd be many more such nights in the weeks ahead) I awoke with a start: What the bloody hell was this knobbly-kneed woman doing in my bed?

When it happened the third time I couldn't get back to sleep. My legs were now twitching spasmodically, wondering why they weren't pedaling—the legacy of a day spent cycling 279.7 kilometers followed by one sitting in traffic jams and getting drunk. With daylight sneaking in through the filthy curtains I creaked stiffly out of bed and stood before the wardrobe mirror. Even at this time of day, even with a slight hangover, it was a spectacle so frankly ludicrous that I barked out a single, mad guffaw.

Those legs, still blotched from their therapeutic ordeals, looked like champagne flutes: wrist-thin at the ankles, they progressively flared out on their way up to a set of mighty hams, thunder thighs indeed. Halfway up these the smooth, red-brown pint-of-best tan abruptly gave way to varicose magnolia and Puckish wire wool, as if I was wearing hairy white shorts. My similarly bleached torso, graced with its new—and hideous—stomach hairs, was topped by a zip-scarred neck and a gaunt, broiled head with singed and flaking extremities; from its sides dangled two thin arms whose tan-line apartheid had been brutally enforced. I might never leave my mark on the Tour, but that didn't matter. It had left its mark on me.

The final chlorinated bidon, the final night-dried Lycra taken down from the final hotel curtain rail, the final fistful of vitamins, the final slathering of the arse. Du pain, du vin, du Savlon—as silly and vile as they might be, I knew I would miss my routines. At 5:30 a.m. I clacked down four flights of dark stairs, dropped my key on the empty reception desk, bullied free several recalcitrant bolts and locks and stepped out into what I could already see, with a sort of mournful glee, was going to be a gorgeous day.

Any European city where a man can walk down a major thoroughfare at dawn wearing a string vest with his head held high is

OK in my book. He walked past with a brisk nod as I leant against the car finishing my breakfast—three cellophane packets of biscuit crumbs stolen in rather better condition from the Holiday Inn. ZR stood ready beside me, assembled with practiced hands; I chucked the panniers in the boot, cocked a leg, and rolled off down an empty boulevard.

I never expected to do the whole stage—the route before those laps of the Champs-Elysées was monstrously complex, its details still a mystery after prolonged, albeit fizz-fuddled, consultation of a detailed map of the capital. Forty-eight kilometers would do me fine: that would probably be enough to experience the trademark sensations—heat, fatigue, and fear—and, rather more importantly, certainly enough to bring up the momentous 3,000k. Gathering speed among the occasional taxis and police vans, I barreled up the boulevards toward the Eiffel Tower, starting point of the 2000 Tour de France's twenty-first and final stage. I swished past a bus with three people on, washed-out ravers silently wondering how it had all come to this; someone was playing a synthesizer four floors up; from a side street came a ragged, drunken roar: "Jean! Jean!"

I got to the Eiffel Tower as an enormous sun took shape behind it. The Eiffel Tower is one of the world's best things, and rolling to a halt in the center of its four iron feet I had it all to myself. I remembered that picture of Hitler standing in front of the Arc de Triomphe, grinning with disbelief that all this was his, and grinned with disbelief. I had made it to Paris. With my gleaming exoskeleton legs I looked the part, and now I felt it. Giant of the Road might be pushing it a bit, but cycling off across the Pont d'Iena I felt a twinge in my joints that could only have been growing pains.

The sky went from cream to blue as I rolled along the Seine, past houseboats with a view to die for, past joggers, past hot-dog vendors already warming up their Westlers at 6:15. At the fourth bridge down I turned left and headed out across the vast, cobbled no-man's-land of the Place de la Concorde. A plumb-lined kilometer to my right stood the scaffolded bulk of the Louvre; to the left, the same vista eased up to the tiny, sunlit keyhole that was the Arc de Triomphe, over two kilometers up the Champs-Elysées.

"There are no tired legs on the Champs-Elysées," they say, and though Paul Kimmage rather took the romance out of this by pointing out the absence of random dope controls on the final stage, I could see why they said it. Feeling exhilarated and tireless, up the mile-wide pavement I slalomed breezily between waiters putting out the first chairs and tables. On the way back down—the Tour riders would turn in front of the Arc de Triomphe ten times—I picked up speed with alarming ease. Thirty-five km/h. felt like 25; as I swished past the gendarmes questioning a van driver whose forlorn vehicle sat, front wheels splayed out, across the central reservation I gave Eddy Merckx an inner wink and hit 50.

I did a couple more Champs-Elysées laps, then arced off back to the Seine, bumping over the grilles that blasted weird wafts of hot Metro air up my legs. Past Notre-Dame, all the way back up to the Eiffel Tower, and all the way back. For another hour it was wonderful, but by 7:30 the magic had gone. Commuters were Henri Pauling it into the underpasses; van drivers parped and revved, and when I took refuge in the cycle lane they followed me. Hot, hounded, and hungry, I glanced down at the computer and did a quick perimeter tour of the Jardin des Plantes, and another, and another. It was enough. The 3,000 came up as I turned off the Boulevard Vincent Auriol, exchanged curt abuse with a jaywalking businessman and eased up to the car.

That was it. It was 15 June: I'd done nearly 1,900 miles in a month to the day. There should have been bunting and blondes and big bottles of bubbly, but I really didn't mind that there weren't. Eddy and Tom and my support crew had helped me up the Alps, and Paul Ruddle had helped me down them, but at heart mine had been a solo achievement, a 3,000-kilometer lone breakaway, and I was happy to celebrate its climax in an appropriate fashion.

In the final analysis, you see, because of what I had done I was simply a lot better than almost everyone else. With others around there would have been churlishness and jealousy; who knows, maybe even a couple of tiresome fans. Stalkers couldn't be ruled out. I took off my hot, wet gloves, opened the hatchback and, with a suitably epic commentary turning slowly through my mind, Moore's respectful hands began to strip down the machine that had been his slave, his master, his confidant and tormentor throughout a journey where suffering and glory had stood toe to toe and . . . and so on.

With my features settling into a happy, glazed reverie poorly suited to urban driving I set off into the rush hour, eventually finding myself amid the canoe-roofed British motorists piling back to Calais. The French were setting out deck chairs on the not enormously appealing beaches south of the ferry terminal, getting ready for summer, a summer of which the Tour would as ever be the cornerstone.

I parked in the hire-car compound, built my bike, and packed her bags, then pedaled across the hot tarmac to the Avis office.

"Voilà! You are return!" It was the man who had helped me dismantle ZR a month before.

"I am," I said, with simple dignity.

"Oh, your vélo. . . ." he said, peering over his desk at ZR's cleat-chipped crossbar and smutted tyres, ". . . your vélo 'as been doing many mileages, non?"

"Three thousand kilometers."

This information changed the shape of his face. "Sree souzand? Oh, c'est bien fait! Some montagnes?"

"Well, yes. I was following the Tour de France." I remembered telling him this before, and I remembered how he'd reacted when I'd done so. He seemed to have forgotten.

"So . . . le Mont Ventoux?"

"Yes." Well, near enough.

"L'Aubisque?"

I issued a sort of puff and rolled my eyes in an expression of partial conquest, hoping he wouldn't ask about Hautacam. He didn't.

"L'Izoard? Le Galibier?"

That was better. "In the same day."

"Eh bien," he said with a smile, then pinched the brim of an imaginary trilby and raised it. "Chapeau!"

Two hats in three days—it was a good feeling. And ten minutes later I almost made it a—woo-hoo—hat trick, defying the gloomy predictions of the girl at the ticket desk by covering the vast acreage of tarmac between her office and the ferry in less than the ninety seconds she had given me to get there before the ramp was raised. After an all-hands-on-sundeck crossing I whisked through the customs at Dover, waved past by officers who clearly couldn't imagine an earnest sportsman like that shoving a condom full of Kruggerands up his jacksy. More fool them!

On the way out, the route from station to ferry had seemed a white-knuckled, knee-buckled roller coaster of mountains; on the way home, I honestly didn't even notice the change in gradient. The same Victorian guard's van and the same rattling progress, the scenery dribbling by when the noise and commotion implied an indistinguishable blur of greens and browns. We went through Staplehurst, and as I said this name to myself I somehow knew that my former sloth was already beckoning, that my endeavor had not been a turning point in my life, just a memorable detour, and that a lot of this might be because cycling around Avignon had something about it that cycling around Staplehurst did not.

And two hours later I was cycling up my road, oblivious to the highway hazards that had so unsettled me as I'd set off for London Bridge. Birna opened the door and smiled, then looked down at the flesh between shorts and socks and stopped.

"Oh, you *haven't*," she said.

19

Malaria Dreams

Stuart Stevens

The problem was the sand ladders. They kept digging into the deep drifts, causing the Land Cruiser to buck and snort. There was a certain irony to this as the sole reason one carried sand ladders was to *extricate* not impale.

The theory is that when you travel through the desert you should carry these huge, awkward things called sand ladders designed to go under a vehicle's wheels when stuck in the sand. "Drive up onto the sand ladders and use them as a short piece of artificial road to give the vehicle a run and sufficient momentum to get through more sand," advises the *Sahara Handbook,* warning, "To get out of a large stretch of soft sand it may be necessary to use the sand ladders several times."

The theory, I'll grant, is impressive. But as far as I was concerned, simply carrying the devices—or trying to carry them—created an instant crisis.

The *Handbook* features pictures of neatly rigged vehicles with sand ladders attached in ingenious manners. Bolting the long metal strips to the roof rack is the most common method. The ladders in the photos are handsome devices made of aluminum that, as one picture demonstrates, a woman can easily carry.

While I am willing, if begrudgingly, to admit that the photos are genuine, I promise that nothing of the sort can be had in N'Djamena. In fact, it took a massive search to locate the frustrating substitute we finally acquired. It was a big long steel plank intended for use with the semitrailers that ply, perilously, the desert routes. We acquired it from a truck driver who lived on the edge of town in a small mud brick hut with a courtyard. He had been using it quite effectively as a perch for roosting chickens ever since he acquired it from a Japanese relief organization that had abandoned N'Djamena during the last fighting.

It was a single, fifteen-foot-long piece of metal perforated with holes. We needed two smaller lengths.

"No problem," the truck driver exulted, "my brother will cut in half."

His brother was a junk dealer who worked out of a walled compound stacked with dead cars and various military vehicles punctured with violent holes. He examined the merchandise and announced that it would take an hour to cut. He also wanted a small fortune for the job.

"An hour?" I gasped. I was very hot and covered in chicken shit from wrestling with the plank. For days I had wandered N'Djamena trying to locate the essential items to cross Lake Chad: additional jerricans for water and fuel, tire tubes, a rear spring, food, and, alas, a pair of sand ladders. I had begun to feel like an automotively obsessed Don Quixote.

Once he had payment in hand, the junk dealer sliced through the metal in less than five minutes. "Not so hard," he said, trying to muster his most convincing tone of surprise. I groaned, rolling over in my mind a phrase popular with the American embassy crowd: WAWA—West Africa Wins Again.

Figuring out how to transport the sand ladders was the next urgent problem. We decided to hang both sections from a single hook that juts from the front bumper of the Land Cruiser as a tow-ing aid. The end result resembled a lethal battering ram, an effect I rather enjoyed. Unfortunately, as we learned that first morning out of N'Djamena, in practice it worked more like a scoop than a ram.

Contemplating Lake Chad, I'd always envisioned a flat expanse of deep sand, like the bottom of a dry pond. But the reality was a constantly shifting terrain of rolling sand hills. As the Cruiser crested one rise and started up the next, the sand ladder jammed into the ground. In essence we were digging up a large portion of Lake Chad. I thought of what our tracks must look like from the air, the trail of some wounded beast rolling through the sand.

After a morning of this, something had to be done. At the top of a rise, Ann, Bertrand, and I dismounted. Bertrand took a look at the front of the Cruiser, shook his head, and walked off to squat in the sand, his long white bou-bou draping on the ground. He smiled pleasantly but with an air that indicated fixing sand ladders was not in his job description. He was a guide.

Bertrand lived in a village on the far side of Lake Chad. He'd guided the Belgians across the lake to N'Djamena and now was returning home with us.

The economics of our arrangement baffled me. For the privilege of chauffeuring the amiable teenager back to his village, he wanted to charge us a staggering fee. The Belgians had encountered a similar situation when they employed Bertrand for the trip to N'Djamena.

It was a function of supply and demand. All travelers across Lake Chad passed through N'Guigmi, Bertrand's village. The guiding business was a local monopoly controlled by a union of sorts; the locals knew their services were essential for the inexperienced and that no guides were available other than those in N'Guigmi. All they had to do was stick together to demand a high price.

The Belgians were not loose with money. For two days they had sat in N'Guigmi refusing to pay the going rate (about three hundred dollars), threatening either to go it *sans* guide or to retreat the way they had come. And then they found Bertrand.

Actually, he found them. One morning he turned up at their camp on the edge of town to volunteer his services for only a "small" fee. Bertrand needed to go to N'Djamena to pick up a new identity card, having lost his old one. After hours of discussion over many cups of coffee, a deal was struck for Bertrand to guide them for a mere third of the normal fee. (Bertrand neglected to mention that his lack of an identity card meant that he would be harassed at each of the numerous checkpoints along the way, delaying the crossing several days.)

Having acquired his new papers in N'Djamena, Bertrand appeared at the mission and asked the Belgians if they would like to take him back home. They demurred but suggested he talk to Ann and me. We needed a guide and Bertrand wanted a ride home—it seemed a fair enough swap. But when I suggested to Bertrand that he should consider making the trip without a fee, he erupted into a pout that lasted two days. It was all a bit strange. Instead of making a simple arrangement with a teenager, I felt as if I were trying to coax Greta Garbo out of retirement.

Finally we came to terms and Bertrand became our guide—but not, apparently, a sand ladder repairman. He squatted and watched while Ann and I worked on the problem.

In N'Djamena, I had secured the metal planks to the bumper hook with a cable and padlock. The locking cable was one of the gadgets I'd brought from America and, as was the case with all my toys, I was inordinately proud of it. But what had seemed so clever in N'Djamena had been transformed by the desert into a mistake; sand clogged the lock, making it inoperable.

While struggling with the lock, the sand whipping into my eyes and mouth, a figure appeared on horseback. He—or she—was dressed in a flowing white robe, a brimmed straw hat, and a scarf wrapped around the face, hiding all features. In other circumstances, the garb would have seemed fantastical but here I merely thought about how practical it was and envied the person for his or her superior protection from the elements. The figure waved and continued over a rise. A moment later I wondered if I'd imagined the scene.

By pouring water into the keyhole of the frozen lock, we eventually freed the cable and secured the sand ladders next to the Cruiser's grille. Bertrand rose, nodding his approval. We followed him back into the Cruiser.

When I turned the key, nothing happened. We got back out and raised the hood, trying to figure out whether it was a bad connection or faulty battery. We poked and pulled to no avail. Positioned at the crest of a small hill, I assumed it would be a simple matter to push the Cruiser down the slope, jump-starting the engine. But I failed to consider the weight of the fully loaded vehicle and the adhesive qualities of sand. With our hands, we dug the hot sand away from the wheels; we pushed, sweated, dug, and pushed some more. Twice the Cruiser started to roll and twice, as we jumped in, it ground to a halt.

I began to think about how long we might have to wait until another vehicle chanced our way. Now I envied our visitor on horseback, not only for his clothes but for his more dependable transportation as well.

We dug and pushed again; this time when the car began to move, Ann leaped in while Bertrand and I pushed. Just as the hill began to bottom out, the engine fired.

"What did he say?" I asked Ann, who could vaguely understand Bertrand's twisted French. We were back in the Cruiser now, jolting over the sand.

"I think he said not to turn off the engine."

That night when we camped, we left the Cruiser idling contentedly. We were in a little grove of trees, scrub thorns that had grown up in the ten years or so since this section of the lake had lost its water. Above the low grumble of the Cruiser's diesel, voices floated across the sand. It would have been difficult to imagine a spot that appeared more isolated, but I had grown accustomed in Africa to the inevitable presence of others, however unlikely and surprising. It was a hard place to be alone.

The sky presented its usual spectacular display of stars. I had the aching exhaustion I'd come to expect on the road. Africa was turning me from an insomniac into a narcoleptic. Under me, the sand radiated a soothing heat. For a moment I ran through a list of nagging difficulties: the faltering battery and the electrical gremlins, the grinding sounds of the transmission in low gear, the scores of acacia thorns sticking from the tires that made them look like black porcupines with crew cuts, the questionable amount of fuel left in the tank and jerricans.

But I was happy, deeply happy, falling asleep in this strange place with a contentment I'd rarely known.

If one were looking to shoot a film at a location that epitomized a bedraggled, fly-ridden, godforsaken desert border station, Bol would do nicely. It was the last official town in Chad, though the actual border lay somewhere beyond at a point that once was the middle of Lake Chad.

The look of the crowd hanging around the customs house made it seem an evil place. A sullen bunch, they stared at us with bored disgust.

The customs office was a mud building surrounded by acacia trees that cast a thin shade over the tin roof. Ann went inside with our papers while I opened the hood of the Cruiser and fiddled with the battery and starter, still puzzled by its intermittent response. A tall man with tribal scars inquired as to the problem and volunteered his services. Perhaps, I thought, I was wrong about this place. Maybe it was not so bad.

The volunteer mechanic requested tools, and I brought out the odd-fitting nonmetric set I'd stolen from Lucien. He grunted and went to work with a set of pliers. After a few minutes of messing about, he rose and said, simply, "Fifty thousand."

"I'm sorry?" I asked, not understanding.

"Fifty thousand CFA to fix the car."

That was almost two hundred dollars. I wanted to laugh but felt somehow that wasn't the prudent response. My suggestion of an alternative, say ten dollars, was met with a sudden burst of anger. He threw the pliers into the dirt and stormed away to pace in front of the customs office. Low-voiced invectives flew back and forth between him and his friends.

The outburst caught me by surprise. Almost without exception, the Africans I'd met had a gentle manner that usually left me feeling loud and insistent. Often preposterous sums of money were demanded but only a few times had anyone responded with true anger when I'd pushed a more reasonable price.

This did not seem like the best place to incur hostility. I'd heard stories of travelers stranded at borders for days, even weeks. It was a fear Ann accelerated when she emerged fuming from the customs office.

"We have to wait. The commandant"—she rolled the title around with relish—"has left for the day. He might be back tomorrow. He might not."

The commandant, Ann explained, and *only* the commandant could stamp our passports. I looked over at the would-be mechanic and his friends. It was a smug bunch.

"Look," I said, with some heat, "what you have to do is go back inside and tell them that we must send a message to the U.S. embassy explaining that we will be late for our meeting in N'Guigmi because the commandant will not stamp our passports. Show him Tim Whitset's letter."

This, of course, was a lie. It was the sort of vague threat I often bandied about with officials. "I'll need to contact the embassy. . . ." To date, no one had seemed to care in the least.

Ann groaned. "Look around," I suggested, "and think about spending the next week here."

Glumly she tramped back inside the office.

When I turned to work more on the car, I had this sudden paranoid rush that the thwarted mechanic had sabotaged the machine. I stared at the hot, sand-encrusted engine, wondering if those loose wires had dangled as uselessly this morning.

Ann returned from the customs hut with a smiling official in a long white robe. He wore tennis shoes and carried a plastic briefcase.

"We go to the commandant," the man said blithely.

"It worked," Ann whispered as she walked around to get into the car.

"We should help our American friends," the official pronounced. "You are working for the embassy. You are my friends."

The magic letter had worked again. I knew Tim Whitset, sitting in his vault-office plotting against the African bureaucracy, would be chuckling.

"I'm not sure I'd get in the car just yet," I warned, as Ann and the official began to squeeze into the front seat.

"Why?"

I turned the key and pushed the starter. Silence.

"Those guys didn't fix it?" Ann asked, gesturing toward the gloating mechanic.

"We have to talk about that," I answered dryly.

Fortunately the customs office sat on a slight hill. We got out and pushed. Ann stood by the open driver's door while the official and I worked from the rear, our feet digging into the hot sand. The engine fired suddenly, lurching forward, leaving the officer and me sprawled in the sand.

"We are friends," the official repeated with only a slight waver. We looked at each other and nodded while picking acacia thorns out of our palms. "We are friends."

Bol has few streets; all are deep sand, affording a natural advantage to the small donkeys that move people and goods at a pace suited to the rhythms of Bol life. We passed the skeleton of a Land

Rover, its aluminum frame, stripped by the sand and wind of all paint, gleaming in the sun. The houses were mud brick, jammed one against the other.

We found the commandant in a dark room strewn with rugs sitting cross-legged like a pasha. A veiled woman moved through the rear of the two-room house.

The commandant was a shrewd man. As our escort from customs explained our story, stressing that we were traveling on official United States embassy business and had an important meeting to attend in N'Guigmi, the commandant nodded with the hint of a smile. It was not, I believe, my imagination that his eyes lingered over my attire before he asked in a quiet voice, "You travel on official business?"

Ann and I both were filthy. I wore torn red shorts and an Ole Miss T-shirt encrusted with sweat and sand. My knees, jutting noticeably in the squatting position I'd assumed, bled from scores of sand scrapes. Swirls of grease decorated my face like war paint; my hands were mostly black.

"This meeting in N'Guigmi. Tell me more about this meeting. Your letter does not mention a meeting."

We were a bit of amusement for the commandant. Two oddball Americans washed up to relieve the tedium of a fiery afternoon. He wanted us to understand that he was no backwater fool to be awed by a thin piece of paper no matter how many seals or signatures shouted for attention.

In the end, reluctantly, he let us go, sorry to see the finish of such sport. From a little wooden box, he produced a metal seal and stamped our passports, adding under his name an admirably ironic note: "Important visitors."

Driving back to the customs post, where, not surprisingly, there was more stamping and signing to be done, the official asked if we needed fuel. In the middle of Lake Chad, the answer to such a question is invariably yes.

"You sell fuel as well as do customs duty," Ann teased. With the commandant's signature in hand, we were in a good mood.

He looked confused. "I have no customs duties," he answered.

Why, I asked, was he at the customs office when we arrived?

"It is very cool with the shade of the trees. And I meet friends there. Like my American friends!"

We bought the fuel from fifty-gallon drums on the back of an ancient Land Cruiser pickup. It was bootlegged fuel from Nigeria, dyed a wine red and speckled with clumps of dirt and thorns. I strained it through a metal strainer and an old baseball hat. The price, at least, was reasonable.

"Do you stay with the Italians tonight?" the customs official/fuel salesman asked us.

Ann and I looked at each other. Italians? There were Italians in Bol?

"There are many Italians," he answered. "I will show you. I am also a guide," he added, casting a jealous eye at Bertrand, who seemed unfazed by the potential competition.

There were moments traveling with Ann when I expended great energy contemplating exotic ways to do away with her. (There were more times—and for infinitely better reasons I'm sure—when she pursued similar lines of thought about me.) But often she proved invaluable, and I wouldn't have traded her for a carload of trilingual mechanics.

Meeting the Italians was one such moment.

Our new guide, bouncing happily on the seat between Ann and me, directed us to a large compound on the edge of Bol. It looked like a military base: a collection of buildings behind a high hurricane fence topped with barbed wire. Some of the buildings rose two and three stories, while others were like Quonset huts, lined barracks-style in a row. A swamp of sorts lay to the side of the installation, a remnant of the disappearing waters of Lake Chad. A sign read, "Calabrase Construction."

Enhancing the military effect, two Africans stood watch over the locked gates. Our guide, having delivered us here, did not seem to know what to do next. I stopped the Cruiser and Ann approached the guards.

Their surprise was understandable: a white woman appearing from the desert? A discussion ensued. I wondered what language they were using: French? Italian? English? Eventually one guard left, leaving Ann standing at the gate: a small figure in dirty khaki pants and a Ralph Lauren shirt torn at the sleeves.

The guard returned with a white man who looked to be about fifty. He radiated cleanliness—clean in a way I had forgotten was possible. He wore pressed shorts and a white shirt, a neat, smiling man, deeply tanned, with a trim goatee. He reminded me of the sort of fellow one saw having lunch in Saint-Tropez with a bottle of cool white wine, a fresh salade Niçoise, and several pretty women; always the pretty women.

When Ann began talking the man stopped dead in his path and then rushed forward, hugging her. Inside the steaming Cruiser, Bertrand and our new guide looked at me, as if I were expected to explain. After more hugs, Ann started to walk inside the compound, led by the neat figure in pressed shorts. They had gone several yards when Ann, as if suddenly remembering us, jogged back to the Cruiser.

"You can come in now," she said, making it sound as if we were being invited into her house.

"You're sure?" I asked, trying to muster all my sarcasm.

"Sure. Fernando says it's fine."

"Fernando," I said flatly.

Fernando ran the Calabrase Construction complex. The Italians were in Bol building roads on a United Nations grant. Why someone thought it was a good idea to build roads in the middle of Lake Chad escaped my logical powers. There seemed to me two problematic questions. One: what happens if water returns? (I suppose the answer was fairly simple: the roads would be underwater.) And two: once constructed, who would use the roads? There were less than a dozen vehicles for two hundred miles in either direction.

But as far as I was concerned, it was a stroke of good fortune that someone at the UN was troubled by the state of local roads in the middle of Lake Chad. And that Calabrase Construction had been selected to improve the situation.

They loved Ann. That an attractive woman (albeit a bit dirty) speaking Italian had appeared in their midst must have seemed like a miracle, and the men—there were only men—responded like pilgrims blessed with a personal appearance by the Virgin Mary: reverential, thankful, gracious to the extreme. I mostly trailed around in Ann's wake enjoying the benefits.

When we explained our troubles starting the Cruiser, Fernando Diamond grew upset. "Oh, this is terrible," he said. "My best electrical mechanic is out in the field and this sounds like an electrical problem."

Ann and I exchanged glances. The luxury of choosing among mechanics with various specialties was like a dream from another life. It had, after all, been less than an hour since I was staring down at my engine with an old pair of pliers, praying for inspiration. "Electrical mechanic?" I asked. "You have other mechanics?"

He nodded vigorously. "We have many mechanics. Come, I will show you."

We followed him to one of the large metal structures. Inside was a replica of the CARE garages in N'Djamena: elaborate work stations with hydraulic hoists, tools galore, spare tires. We gawked.

For the rest of the afternoon, mechanics swarmed over the Land Cruiser. I watched, hoping to learn as much as I could. Ann wandered off, returning later with Perrier and cheese. At the time I was cleaning out the air filter caked with four or five inches of fine-grained sand.

"Would you like some lemon with this?" she asked, holding up a glass of Perrier.

An African mechanic who radiated competence removed the starter and disassembled it, cleaning each part in an oil bath. He made clucking sounds through his teeth as he worked.

"These springs are very poor." Fernando pointed to the Cruiser's rear springs.

"Yes."

"I wish we had some for you. But this model of Land Cruiser we don't use. You go across Lake Chad now, yes?"

We explained our route.

He shrugged. "Let us pray. But come now, first you take a hot shower and then a little espresso and a beer, then we have a real Italian meal. A big meal."

All of those things happened. Each was exquisite, but perhaps the shower emerged triumphant in the competition of the senses. The purifying event took place in Fernando's house, a metal three-room structure placed, as befitted his position, at the head of the row of sleeping accommodations. Most of the workers had roommates, but Fernando had the house to himself. The walls were covered with posters of Italy and Vargas drawings of pinup girls. Two black women, servants, I presumed, sat quietly in their veils, eyeing us with amusement. (It is an appealing side effect of wearing veils that it draws attention to a woman's eyes, which, in turn, appear uniformly more animated, as if in compensation for the masked features.)

One by one, including Bertrand, we took showers. By the time we finished, the bathroom resembled the site of a hotly contested mud pie war; crumpled towels once white, now a deep sienna, littered the floor. Fernando's servant took one look and giggled. Ann and I tried as best we could to clean up. It helped—a little.

Before dinner, we stopped for an espresso in the prefab building next to the prefab dining room. Though constructed like a house trailer, inside it had the feel of a working-class suburb of Milano. Freshly showered from their day in the desert, the sunburned men sat drinking beer or espresso from one of the two machines.

They were large men who talked about sports and debated fiercely the choice of movies for the night. (The videocassette player has permanently altered the Bol social scene.)

A friend of Fernando's named Marcus escorted us to the bar. Marcus's nickname was Little Valentino, a tribute to his good looks and elegant clothes. Marcus was an accountant, with the smooth hands of an office worker. There were others like him, the front office executives of Calabrase Construction. Though they looked and talked like Florentine intelligentsia, Marcus and his friends mixed easily with the other workers. The conditions of employment in Bol blurred management and labor lines; everyone worked four-teen hours a day, ate the same food at the same time, had equal say in the vociferous arguments over the evening's film selections. (Marcus and friends wanted Bertolucci's *The Spider's Stratagem*; others lobbied for *Rambo III*.)

No one I met at Calabrase complained. Their salaries were triple what they would have been in Italy and, like the Frenchmen I'd met in the CAR, the Italians welcomed their African posting as a way to escape the "sameness" of European life. As Marcus put it, "Last year, after two years in West Africa, I went back home to work. At first it was wonderful: movies, ice cream, telephones. I saw my family every day. But after six months, it was *sooo* boring." Marcus sat upright in a rigid position. "Every morning, get in the car. Fight the traffic, work, come home."

As we walked to dinner, we watched the setting sun shoot red streaks across the shallow waters of Lake Chad. "Our Olympic pool," Marcus said. It was not a beautiful scene in any traditional sense—a muddy patch of water surrounded by scrub grass and thorn trees—but it had a quirky, rough appeal.

"I missed this," Marcus said after a moment.

"But not the mosquitoes," a friend laughed. They came off the lake like waves of suicide planes.

It was Fernando who reminded us it was Thanksgiving. He mentioned it in an offhand way while we stood at the head of the long buffet marveling at the pasta, the veal, the pastries. "An untraditional Thanksgiving, no?" he said. Ann and I looked at each other, not understanding what he meant, and then we both looked up at a wall calendar featuring a nude girl riding a tractor. He was right, it was Thanksgiving.

I gorged myself despite a stomach gone queasy for days. Later, I vomited wildly in the bathroom, while Marcus and his friends waited for me in their Toyota Hi-Lux pickups. We drove, whooping and hollering like teenagers heading home from a football game, to a modern ranch-style house not far from the compound. The Italians insisted Ann knock on the door, and when an attractive Italian came to the door and saw her, he gaped and stuttered. Everyone thought this very funny and Marcus and his friends erupted from the shadows in laughter.

20

"You're Lewis, I'm Clark"

W. Hodding Carter

"Look, I'm gonna say this for the last time," I said, sitting behind a two-foot-high stack of Lipton noodles-and-sauce and rice-and-sauce freeze-dried dinners. Preston and I were sorting our provisions and equipment in a downtown St. Louis hotel room the night before setting off. "You're Lewis . . . and I'm Clark. And I don't want any more joking about it."

"Sure thing, Lewis," he quipped, "anything you say."

"Up yours."

Neither of us wanted to be Lewis because he committed suicide three years after the expedition was completed. Rankled by accusations of embezzling government funds, Lewis determined to clear his name before Congress in the fall of 1809. Traveling from St. Louis, where he served as governor of the Louisiana Territory, by boat and then horseback, Lewis stopped at an inn along the Natchez Trace in Tennessee.

By most accounts, he arrived delirious and sick. The innkeeper's wife was the only person home, but she agreed to let him stay in an adjoining cabin. During the night she heard him pacing and talking to himself. Around three in the morning, she heard a gunshot and then Lewis uttering, "Oh, Lord." Then there was a second shot.

Later she heard him make his way to her door and beg for water. She was too afraid to open it, though, and waited until dawn to send for his servants, who were sleeping in the barn.

They found him in his cabin, wounded in the head and side. Lewis begged his servants to kill him. His last words were, "I am no coward, but I am so strong, it is so hard to die."

While there are those who believe he was murdered, suicide is the most commonly accepted conclusion. Both Thomas Jefferson and Clark believed that Lewis had taken his life, putting an end to his inner torment. Clark wrote, upon hearing the news, "I fear the weight of his mind has overcome him."

So I'd settled this many months before. As great as Lewis was, I didn't want to play him in our re-creation and therefore be compelled to kill myself a few years later. I would be Clark and Preston would be Lewis. Never mind that Lewis and I were closer in age and Preston and Clark were closer in age as well; that Lewis was anal and of the two of us I was more anal than Preston; and that Preston, like Clark, was more outgoing with strangers.

Preston walked past me to stuff something in a sack. He stunk. He was stripped to his shorts and sweating all too much considering the room's air conditioner was on high and the room was quite cool. I was stinky and sweaty, too, but that was different. I was used to myself. His scent was a completely different thing.

"I just want you to know how happy I am you asked me to go along," he said, turning to me as we continued to pack the dry sacks (rubber, waterproof packs). "This is going to be great."

We went to bed soon afterward. As I lay there, surveying all our goods, I wondered for the first time if all our equipment would fit in our twelve-and-a-half-foot rubber raft. The problem was that the boat really wasn't twelve and a half feet long on the inside. That wasn't a point the Zodiac Boat people had stressed when they sold it to me. The pontoons, when filled with air, had to expand somewhere, and inconveniently enough, they expanded inward. I guess, though, that if the pontoons expanded outward, then the overall length of the boat would be sixteen feet or so and some owners would be just as pissed about that. As it was, the actual size on the inside was only six feet three inches by two feet nine inches—smaller than a coffin. But I had told so many people that the boat was twelve and a half feet that I'd pushed the size of the usable space out of my mind. Anyway, who's going to take seriously a guy who only has a six-foot rubber raft ("inflatable boat" to the Zodiac people).

So there I was, the night before our departure (actually the morning of, as I'd fretted well past midnight), finally considering logistical problems. We had two large dry sacks—4 feet by 2 feet by 2 feet—weighing at least a hundred pounds each; a small dry sack—3 feet by 1½ feet by 1½ feet—weighing forty pounds or so. Two grocery bags of potatoes and rice that hadn't fit in the dry sacks. Three full backpacks. A six-gallon gas tank. A five-and-a-half-gallon plastic gas can. Two cases of sixteen-ounce motor-oil cans. Five gallons of water. A first-aid kit. A repair kit. And numerous loose articles, including life preservers, auxiliary paddles, binoculars, books, a camera, etc. Could it all fit? Would Preston and I really be able to sit on the side pontoons for twenty-eight straight days (that's how long I figured we'd be on the Missouri)? Why hadn't I thought of any of this before?

We woke at six-thirty the next morning—August 24, Departure Day—and drove our gear over to the concrete-covered levee that stands below the St. Louis Gateway Arch. The arch commemorates the westward expansion of the United States, and since Lewis and Clark opened up the West for the United States, it was only fitting that we began our journey in the arch's shadow.

We unloaded everything only a few yards from the shore. A hundred feet north of us, a large, plastic Ronald McDonald stood guard before the floating McDonald's barge/restaurant that waited to feed the expansion-hungry tourists.

I'd planned on our departing within an hour. At nine-thirty, we'd barely begun inflating the boat. Never mind, I thought, that'd only take a few minutes and then I'd return the rental car, grab a few last-minute items, and head back to the levee. I was in charge of reading the instructions and directing our efforts. At first it appeared that the pressure gauge for the pontoons wasn't working.

"Oh, God, what are we going to do?" I pleaded. "I can't believe I didn't pump up the boat in New York for a trial run. What a damn idiot. Jesus, I've got to go call the Zodiac company. We won't be able to leave until tomorrow."

"Wait, let me try something," Preston said.

"No, no, it's broken. Just leave it alone."

"Maybe we haven't pumped it up enough. The gauge doesn't begin until two sixty. Let's just give it a try," he suggested. Yeah, right, I thought. We'll burst the pontoon and then we'll have to postpone our departure even longer, but I let him try anyway.

He was right.

After that, we couldn't fit the floorboards in the bottom. We struggled with them for more than hour. It was already eighty-five degrees out and humid. Our hands kept slipping and we both cut ourselves with the screwdriver we were using to wedge the boards into place. Finally, I let Preston see the directions. He saw that I had us attempting to assemble the floor out of sequence. A few minutes later the floorboards were in place. We finished pumping her up. It was eleven o'clock.

While Preston guarded our stuff, I went for the last-minute articles: a knife, toothbrush, rat traps ("I need those for hunting," Preston said. "You can catch all kinds of birds with them"), pencils, notebook, pancake mix, pens, extra cotter pins (something for the engine that Preston said we needed), beef jerky, pepperoni, and a new water bag because our collapsible one had burst during the night.

The errands took two and a half hours, and I was unable to find the cotter pins, pepperoni, rat traps, or even a cheap enough knife.

When I returned at two, Preston was burned bright red. It was ninety-two degrees and the humidity was nearly as high. But he was undaunted. We were more than six hours behind.

"Hod, I think we need a final meal," he said, nodding to the McD's. "My treat." We gorged ourselves. Big Macs, large fries, fish fillets, extralarge iced teas. There was, I hypothesized as the Special Sauce slipped down my throat, no better salute to Lewis and Clark than the open arms of Ronald McDonald. He was America's modern-day adventurer. Also, this would be our last meal that wasn't cooked by either of us for quite a while.

We returned to the boat and loaded her with all of our equipment, packing the craft from bow to stern. I had worried for good reason. Would it still float? We pushed and lifted it into the water, scraping the rubber bottom along the rough concrete. It floated. We picked up a cup of iced tea that we'd carried over from McD's.

"With this tea, we christen thee *Sacagawea*. May our trip be successful," I said, and together we bashed the cup against her bow. We shoved off at 3:25 p.m.—seven and a half hours behind schedule. *Sacagawea* kept us afloat, and we even started the engine with only a couple of pulls on the cord. Preston seemed touched that I let him drive the boat first, which meant that I must really have been a controlling ogre ever since his arrival the night before. I'd have to improve.

A plump man and his two sons waved from the railing of the McD's barge as we motored by. "That's Joe," Preston explained. "I met him while you were gone. He thinks we're crazy." Joe and the kids yelled to us, but we couldn't hear them. Preston idled the engine.

"Good luck, Lewis and Clark," they screamed. It was nice to have an audience, although it was somewhat less noble than L&C's departure and less dramatic than the chiropractor and the teacher's departure.

The chiropractor and the teacher were two men who had retraced the Lewis and Clark Trail earlier in the summer. I had originally learned about them from a past president of the Lewis and Clark Trail Heritage Foundation. My intention—before I had to postpone our departure—had been to leave at the same time and playfully antagonize them along the way. Although we didn't know these men, we considered them rivals. They had traveled in a jet boat.

Before heading out, Tom Warren, the chiropractor, and John Hilton, the teacher, spoke to the press. *USA Today,* UPI, *The Washington Post,* and various other news agencies were on hand.

"People often think of the environment as something outside their house," Warren said. "I want them to realize that it's something inside their hearts."

"Lewis and Clark saw what was there," Hilton added, "and we're going to find out what's left." Not only did Warren and Hilton speak more nobly than Preston and I, but they were also better equipped. Their twenty-one-foot jet boat was powered by a 270-horsepower engine. They had two mountain bikes, two canoes, a cellular telephone, a global positioning system that used satellites, packaged meals provided by Nutri Systems, and a "support" van driven by John Hilton Jr., who met up with them at the end of each day's journey. They nicknamed John Junior "York" after Clark's slave, who was a member of the original expedition. All of their gear rode in the van with Johnnie. They were well prepared and had sponsors up the wazoo. They began their trip back at the beginning of June and finished a few days before we began ours.

We'd seen pictures in *People* magazine of them standing behind their boat's windshield. Both of them wore safari-type hats. They stared purposefully ahead.

"The proctologist and his buddy were shit," Preston said. He'd changed Warren's profession. "This is the way to travel. They sped right by all of this." He gestured to the thick-leafed trees that hung over the river's bank and also to the various smokestacks that stood along the shore. We'd quit counting the factories after half a dozen.

Most of them were burning either clear or white, but one had been yellow and brown—a bad polluter. A spokesman for American Rivers, the conservation group that helped organize Warren's crusade, told me that the lower Missouri and Mississippi were akin to toxic waste dumps. Pollution threatened the rivers from every direction: agricultural chemicals, industrial waste, road and highway runoff (oil and gas), mines that spewed out heavy metals and mercury, and cattle grazing (erosion of entire soil levels). We passed some large drainage pipes that were gushing with yellow, frothy liquid, which we hoped was only sewer water.

It began raining—a hard, heavy summer downpour. The water bit into our skin and we were soaked. Would it do this every day? I couldn't handle day after day of rain. But twenty minutes later, the storm clouds had traveled on. The river was flat from the rain and the deep, strong current. Now and again an unruly whirlpool would appear and give our little boat a good shaking, but we were able to keep heading north on the mighty Mississippi. Six miles above St. Louis we'd head west into the mouth of the Missouri, but for now we were on Old Man River.

Around 5 p.m. we came upon what appeared to be a four-to-five-foot-high wall of water stretching the entire width of the river. I figured we needed to acquaint ourselves with breaching rough water sooner or later, so I headed *Sacagawea* right into the heart of the fall. Our speed decreased even as I revved the engine higher. By the time we neared its base, we were at a standstill. I kept pushing her. The flood forced us sideways. Preston was almost flung from the boat. Water poured in over his side.

We allowed the current to carry us back.

"Should we try it again?" I asked.

"Yeah," he answered. We tried a different spot. Same results. We crossed back and forth the width of the fall, looking for an easier ascent. The west bank appeared weaker; the water looked lower and less powerful.

We made it higher than before, slowly inching our way through the waterfall. The motor was at full throttle. Suddenly, the boat and the motor were shaken. The engine popped out of the water and painfully whined at a trillion rpm as the prop cut through the air.

As we drifted back once again, we lifted the propeller completely out of the water. It was pretty banged up. Those had been rocks shaking the boat. So it was either flip the boat underneath the cataract or mangle the propeller on the rocks. We put the propeller back in the water and started the engine. It could still propel us forward.

A few hundred yards offshore, two men and a boy were fishing, anchored against the current. We motored over to them.

"Excuse me," I yelled, trying to hide my desperation, "do you know how we can get over this thing? We've been trying for the last hour."

"I know," one answered. A small smile crept across his face. "We've been watching. It's impossible."

"Maybe you could do it in the spring at high water, but even then it's tough," the man standing at their boat's wheel said. "There's only a ten-foot gap that lets you through, and you have to hit it just right. Some people who've been on this river their whole lives can't find it. If you try it now, you're taking your life into your own hands." They suggested we attempt the weak side again.

We decided to walk it over the rocks near the shore. I pulled on the bow line and Preston pushed from behind. The water was anywhere from two to four feet high, depending on the rocks. If I fell, I kept thinking, the boat would knock into Preston, drag him underwater, and probably pull him, tangled in a rope, a mile downstream. Or if none of that happened, it would at least knock him out. I walked very carefully.

Painfully, I recalled sitting at home, feet propped up on my desk, chuckling at all the times the Lewis and Clark men had had to pull their boats through the water. It had seemed so amusing and fun. "We'd never have to do that," I'd thought.

"We're going to be changed men after this," Preston announced as we stood in the water, physically holding the boat steady against the rushing current. After thirty minutes we made it past the rocks. We high-fived each other—a queer gesture but heartfelt. We'd made, at the most, five miles since leaving St. Louis.

A blue heron lifted off from the western shore a little later. Preston identified it. The bird slowly and awkwardly flapped its way skyward, then glided more smoothly between the trees. It seemed so prehistoric with its neck all bent on top of itself. The heron reminded me of Preston and me—ungraceful at first but able to get the job done. And a little later the soft light of the descending sun settled on an entire family of great blue heron wading in the shadows. They all stood in an upright, head-down position searching for food.

We began looking for a secluded place to camp. At seven-thirty—two hours later than I'd planned—we gave up and pulled *Sacagawea* up onto a sandy beach. It appeared to be the worst-possible spot. There were no rocks or trees to tie the boat to, a problem I'd never considered. I always imagined there would be a convenient tree for mooring the boat along with some convenient rocks to climb onto and unload our equipment.

We jumped into the water with our new hiking boots on (why were we wearing hiking boots in the boat? I don't know. It had seemed like the right, explorer type of thing to do) and pretty soon had the boat completely out of the river and water on the inside of our boots—where they weren't waterproof. "What if it rains upstream tonight, and the water comes flooding down here, sweeping sweet *Sacagawea* back down to St. Louis?" I asked Preston.

So we unloaded the boat completely—she was too heavy to drag on the sand—carrying all of the bags one hundred yards up the beach to our campsite.

"Maybe we should anchor it," Preston suggested. Counting on convenient trees and rocks, I hadn't brought an anchor.

We hauled the large yellow dry sack back down to the boat and tied the bow line to it. It held most of the sixty days' worth of food and weighed more than one hundred pounds.

We might still have the same trouble Lewis and Clark encountered on the river. "At half past one o'clock this morning the Sand bar on which we camped began to under mind and give way," Clark recorded on September 21, 1804. " . . . I ordered all hands on as quick as possible & pushed off, we had pushed off but a few minutes before the bank under which the Boat & perogus lay gave way . . . by the time we made the opsd. [opposite] Shore our Camp fell in."

Things weren't looking good.

Considering the distance we'd traveled and the amount of gas used (half a tank), I began to reconsider how long the trip would really take. On our first day we'd covered at the most five miles and it took four hours. We'd have to make many more stops for gas than I'd originally anticipated, and we'd only get gas if we could find it. We'd been told there weren't very many marinas along the lower Missouri. It would probably take us two extra months, I guessed.

At that moment, as we stood along the Mississippi, watching a swarm of tugboats across the river, I wanted to quit. This wasn't fun. We weren't prepared. The propeller was already busted. I could hear my adventurous stepbrother's warning echoing in my head: "The two things you've got to do, weasel-breath, are get a gun and an extra propeller. You've done that, right?" Was he going to be right about the gun also? Just how humiliating would it be if we quit right now? I wondered. I'd be in debt, yes, but I wouldn't be stuck attempting a hopeless cause.

Our first day had been only slightly similar to Clark's—Lewis was attending to some last-minute business in St. Louis. "I set out at 4 oClock p.m., in the presence of many of the neighbouring inhabitents," Clark recorded for May 14, 1804, "and proceeded on under a jentle brease up the Missourie to the upper Point of the island 4 miles and camped on the Island which is Situated Close on the right Side, and opposit the mouth of a Small Creek called Cold water, a heavy rain this after-noon."

Yes, we'd both had rains, but enough points were different. Many "neighbouring inhabitents" saw them off. In other words, their voyage meant something to other people.

They'd reached the Missouri and we hadn't even made it off the Mississippi.

They had a gentle breeze, pushing their keelboat upstream. That alone made me want to quit. Here we were with a gasoline engine, finding the going almost impossible. Lewis and Clark had two canoes and one fifty-five-foot keelboat with sails and forty-odd men to row and pull the boats when the wind died down. They were expecting hardships.

Most of all, though, they knew what they were doing. Lewis and Clark were experienced outdoorsmen and soldiers. Working with nature was their life. Preston and I, well. . . .

I began figuring how much money I'd be able to sell the equipment for. Would it be enough to pay my debts and send Preston and me home?

No. We'd have to go on until I could figure out a way to end this mistake.

"Preston, you know that itinerary I worked up for us? Well, I believe it'll be off by a few months," I said. "I don't think we'll be finishing this thing until January—the middle of the winter. Is that all right? You can think about it some, you know what I mean?" Please, please, back out, I thought.

"In for a dime, in for a dollar," he said, not missing a beat, and headed up toward camp to begin dinner.

After a miserable meal of boiled potatoes and onions that he cooked (I promised myself that I'd be the chef from then on) and a few slices of melting summer sausage, we sat around our gas lantern taking notes and listening to the night. The light attracted a lot of bugs, as well as a small green frog. It looked to be a southern leopard—the most common frog in the East—but it was difficult to tell in that light. I pointed it out to Preston.

"I wish I had my slingshot," he said. His weapon was packed away in the blue dry sack. I'd pressed the point about him being the hunter on the expedition a little too hard.

The frog leaped within three feet of the lantern. Was he excited about the light or all of the kamikaze bugs dying on the surrounding sand? He moved closer to the light and continued to stare at it. A few seconds later he turned, took a short hop, and shot out his tongue, nabbing some gnats. He was ideally situated for bug eating, well hidden in a valley between two three-inch-tall mountains of sand. His gullet continually quivered but everything else stayed absolutely still. His tongue shot out again.

"You know what we can do when we're up there on those lakes?" Preston said. He was referring to the lakes that the Army Corps of Engineers had created in South Dakota, North Dakota, and Montana. Huge dams blocked the flow of the Missouri to provide a constant supply of water for the farmers and cattle ranchers. "We can hitch a ride with some old fishermen or even some pleasure boats. There ought to be plenty of both around. We'll make up a lot of time that way."

The frog crouched down even lower behind one of the mountains, waiting for his turn at more bugs. It was eleven o'clock. Whipped by the long day, I barely noticed that the stars were magnificent, covering the sky in one huge Milky Way.

21

The Years of Wonder

E. B. White

R ussia's foolish suggestion that a dam be thrown across Bering
Strait brings back happy memories of that body of water and
of certain youthful schemes and follies of my own. I passed through
the Strait and on into the Arctic many years ago, searching for a
longer route to where I didn't want to be. I was also in search of
walrus. A dam, I am sure, would have been an annoyance.

I was rather young to be so far north, but there is a period near
the beginning of every man's life when he has little to cling to except his unmanageable dream, little to support him except good
health, and nowhere to go but all over the place. This period in my
life lasted about eight years, and I spent the summer of one of those
years in and around Alaska. It was the summer of 1923. In those
days, I kept a diary, entering in it whatever was uppermost in my
mind. I called it my journal; the word "journal," I felt, lent a literary and manly flavor to the thing. Diaries were what girls kept. A
couple of years ago, when Alaska achieved statehood, I began digging into my journal for the year 1923, hoping to discover in its faded
pages something instructive about the new state. This account,
then, is a delayed account—some thirty-seven years late. I doubt
that the reader will be able to put together a picture of Alaska from

reading it, but he may catch a glimpse of the young diarist. And of the 1920s, that notorious decade that was almost a delirium.

My trip to Alaska, like practically everything else that happened to me in those busy years, was pure accident. I was living in Seattle; I was unemployed, my job on a newspaper having blown up in mid-June; and although I had no reason for going to Alaska, I had no reason for staying away, either. The entries in my journal covering the four-week period between the loss of my job and the start of my trip to the north reveal a young man living a life of exalted footlessness. I was a literary man in the highest sense of the term, a poet who met every train. No splendor appeared in the sky without my celebrating it, nothing mean or unjust took place but felt the harmless edge of my wildly swinging sword. I walked in the paths of righteousness, studying girls. In particular, I studied a waitress in a restaurant called the Chantecler. I subscribed to two New York dailies, the *World* and the *Evening Post*. I swam alone at night in the canal that connects Lake Union and Lake Washington. I seldom went to bed before two or three o'dock in the morning, on the theory that if anything of interest were to happen to a young man it would almost certainly happen late at night. Daytimes, I hung around my room in Mrs. Donohue's boarding house, reading the "Bowling Green" and the "Conning Tower," wondering what to do next, and writing.

My entry for June 15, 1923, begins, "A man must have something to cling to. Without that he is as a pea vine sprawling in search of a trellis." Obviously, I was all asprawl, clinging to Beauty, which is a very restless trellis. My prose style at this time was a stomach-twisting blend of the Bible, Carl Sandburg, H. L. Mencken, Jeffrey Farnol, Christopher Morley, Samuel Pepys, and Franklin Pierce Adams imitating Samuel Pepys. I was quite apt to throw in a "bless the mark" at any spot, and to begin a sentence with "Lord" comma.

On June 19, I recorded my discharge from the *Times* and noted that the city editor said it was "no reflection on my ability." I didn't believe then, and do not believe now, that it was no reflection on my ability. As a newspaper reporter, I was almost useless, and it came as no surprise when one more trellis collapsed on me. When I left the *Times* office with my final pay check in my pocket, I "sauntered" down Pine Street. I can still recall experiencing an inner relief—the feeling of again being adrift on life's sea, an element I felt more at home in than in a city room. On June 25, I clipped a sonnet sequence by Morley from the "Bowling Green" and pasted it in the journal. The second sonnet began, "So put your trust in poets." As though I needed to be told that!

On July 2, I entered in my journal a copy of a poem I had written and mailed anonymously to the Reverend Mark A. Matthews, pastor of the First Presbyterian Church, who had preached a sermon I found offensive. A resume of the sermon had appeared in the Monday morning paper. Dr. Matthews had attacked non-churchgoers, of whom I was one. On the following Sunday, I departed from my usual stance and became a churchgoer, attending the morning service at the First Presbyterian to make a routine check on my man. "The smugness of his doctrine," I wrote in my journal, "made the air stifling." Probably what really made the air stifling for me was that in his sermon the minister made no mention of having received my stinging communication.

For one week I worked on Hearst's *Post-Intelligencer,* commonly called the *P.I.,* substituting for a reporter on vacation. My entry for July 18 (1:30 a.m.) begins, "A man scarce realizes what a terrible thing scorn is until he begins to despise himself." I doubt that I found myself despicable; I simply found life perplexing. I did not know where to go. On Friday, July 20 (3 a.m.), appears the abrupt entry, "I sail Monday on S.S. Buford for Skagway." No explanation or amplification follows, only an account of an evening spent with a girl who lived on Lake Union. (She fed me bread and apple jelly.)

I did, however, clip from the *P.I.* and paste into my journal the item that started me on my way to Alaska. The story was headed and began:

> The resources and trade conditions of Alaska will be studied by a
> delegation from the San Francisco Chamber of Commerce, which
> will leave San Francisco today on the steamer *Buford* for an 8,300
> mile trip to Alaska and Siberia, via Seattle. The group will also in-
> clude citizens of other cities, among them ten Boston capitalists, and
> the trip will be in charge of B. S. Hubbard, vice president of the
> Schwabacher-Frey Stationery Company.

A number of things must have attracted me to this item in the
news. First, the ship was to call at Seattle. I was a dockside regular
at this period, and any ship at all was of interest to me. Second,
Alaska was in the opposite direction from home, where I considered it unsuitable to be at my age. Third, a Chamber of Commerce
was involved, and this opened up familiar vistas. As a reporter, I
had spent many a lunch hour covering the noonday gatherings of
fraternal and civic groups; Seattle was a hotbed of Elks, Eagles,
Moose, Lions, Kiwanians, Rotarians, and members of the Young
Men's Business Association. I had broken the hard roll countless
times with Chamber of Commerce people, had laughed courteously at their jokes and listened patiently to their tales of industrial
growth. I was under the influence of Mencken and Lewis, and felt
proud disdain for business and for businessmen. It was important
to me at that time to move among people toward whom I felt aloof
and superior, even though I secretly envied their ability to earn a
living.

Perhaps the clincher in the news story of the *Buford* was the list of
the ports of call, names that were music to the ear of youth:
Ketchikan, Taku Glacier, Juneau, Skagway, Sitka, Cordova, Seward,
Kodiak, Cold Bay, Lighthouse Rocks, Dutch Harbor, Bogoslof Island,

the Pribilof Islands, Cape Chaplin, Anadir. "From Nome, they [the voyagers] will pass the ice pack, proceeding to East Cape, Siberia, and then return to Nome. On the home trip they will stop at St. Michael, Akutan and Seattle, the entire trip requiring forty days."

Forty days! To me, forty days was a mere siesta in time's long afternoon, and I could cling, for lack of anything else, to the ship. The Pribilof Islands with ten Boston capitalists—sheer enchantment! All I needed was a job on the ship, and this I determined to get. The *Buford* arrived in due course and tied up to Pier 7. Every day while she was there, I sneaked aboard and hung about the corridors, waylaying ship's officers and offering my services in any capacity. When, after three days, I found no taker, I made inquiries and learned that for $40 I could sail as a first-class passenger as far as Skagway, which is at the head of the Inside Passage. This enabled me to shift my strategy; I *had* $40 and I decided to launch myself in the direction of the Arctic by the sheer power of money. Once firmly entrenched in the ship, I could from that vantage point pursue my job-hunting. The second steward gave me a bit of encouragement. "Anything can happen in a ship," he said. And he turned out to be right.

To start for Alaska this way, alone and with no assurance of work and a strong likelihood of being stranded in Skagway, was a dippy thing to do, but I believed in giving Luck frequent workouts. It was part of my philosophy at that time to keep Luck toned up by putting her to the test; otherwise she might get rusty. Besides, the 1920s, somehow or other, provided the winy air that supported dippiness. The twenties even supported the word "dippy."

You might suppose that the next few entries in my journal, covering the days when I must have been winding up my affairs and getting ready to sail on a long voyage of discovery, would offer a few crumbs of solid information. Not at all. From Friday morning, when I announced that I would soon be off, until the departure of the *Buford*, several days later, my journal contains no helpful remarks, no hint of preparation, no facts about clothes, money, friends, family, anything. A few aphorisms; a long, serious poem to the girl on Lake Union ("Those countless, dim, immeasurable years," it begins); a Morley clipping from the "Bowling Green" about writing ("A child writes well, and a highly trained and long-suffering performer may sometimes write with intelligence. It is the middle stages that are appalling. . . ."); a short effort in vers libre written on Sunday morning and describing my boardinghouse slatting around in the doldrums of a summer Sabbath—that is all I find in these tantalizing pages. Mr. Morley was right; the middle stages are appalling. As a diarist, I was a master of suspense, leaving to the reader's imagination everything pertinent to the action of my play. I operated, generally, on too high a level for routine reporting, and had not at that time discovered the eloquence of facts. I can see why the *Times* fired me. A youth who persisted in rising above facts must have been a headache to a city editor.

Memory helps out on a couple of points. I recall that winding up my affairs was chiefly a matter of getting a Ford coupé repossessed by the finance company. My other affairs were portable and would go along—a Corona typewriter, a copy of *Lyric Forms from France,* and my wardrobe, which fitted cozily into one droopy suitcase. I owned an unabridged Webster's, but I am quite sure I did not take it—probably placed it in safekeeping with a friend. The luckiest thing that happened to me was that my wardrobe included a very old and shabby flannel shirt and a dirty pair of dungarees. Without these I would have been in some difficulty later on.

The *Buford* did not get away until almost ten on Tuesday evening, thirty-four hours behind schedule. As the lines were cast off, I stood at the starboard rail and watched the lights of the city—the Bon Marché sign, the tower of the Smith Building—and was shaken by the sudden loud blast of the whistle giving finality to my adventure. Then, it would appear, I sat right down and wrote what was for me a fairly lucid account of the departure. I listed some of the items that had come aboard: beeves, hams, nuts, machinery for Cold Bay, oranges, short ribs, and a barber's chair. I noted that when this last item was carried up the plank, the passengers lining the rail broke into applause. (Already they were starved for entertainment.)

At sundown the following evening, July 25, we passed a tall gray ship that rode at anchor in a small cove near a fishing village. On board was President Harding, homeward bound from Alaska. A band on his ship played, and the President came to the rail and waved a handkerchief borrowed from his wife. The incident caused a stir among the passengers and crew of our ship; seeing the President of the United States in such an unlikely spot, on our way to the mysterious North, was reassuring. About a week later came the radiogram telling of his death.

The voyage of the *Buford* carrying the men of commerce to the Arctic wasteland was an excursion both innocent and peculiar. It inaugurated a new steamship line, the Alaskan-Siberian Navigation Company, and I think the company had been hard up for passengers and had persuaded the Chamber to conduct a trade tour and bring wives. The *Buford* herself, however, was in no way peculiar; she was a fine little ship. She had been a troop carrier in the war, and afterward had been reconverted to carry passengers and freight. She was deep, was not overburdened with superstructure, and had a wide, clear main deck. Painted in tall block letters on her topsides and extending half her length were the words SAN FRANCISCO CHAMBER OF COMMERCE. This enormous label gave her a little the look of a lightship—all name and no boat—and in many a desolate northern port, where the only commerce was with Eskimos who swarmed aboard to peddle ivory paper cutters, the label acquired a bizarre and wistful meaning.

One of the things I know now, and did not know at the time, is that the *Buford* was being bought from the government on the installment plan. The owners never managed to complete their payments, and by 1925 she was being referred to in the San Francisco

Chronicle as "the hard-luck ship *Buford.*" Everything she touched turned to dross. The owners not only never completed their payments, they never fully completed the reconversion of the ship, either. I remember a room in the 'tween-decks that obviously dated from troop-carrying days. It was a spacious room furnished with a truly magnificent battery of urinals and toilets standing at attention and perfectly exposed—a palace of open convenience, seldom visited, except by me, who happened, at one juncture, to live close by. A lonely, impressive room. I have an idea that when the owners took possession of their ship, they must have taken one look at this panorama of plumbing and decided to let it stand. To have laid a wrench to it would have cost a fortune.

Our commander was Captain Louis L. Lane, a handsome, sociable man who delighted the ladies by his strong profile and reassured us all by his fine handling of the ship. He had been in the Arctic before, loved it, and was known and welcomed everywhere. I think he quite enjoyed the adventurous role he was cast in: shepherd of a crowd of landlubbers and dudes in wild, remote places where he had local knowledge and could display his special talents. No gunkhole was too small for Captain Lane to squeeze the *Buford* into. Before we were done with the voyage, though, I got the impression that our captain operated under unusual difficulties. The strong tides and treacherous currents of the Inside Passage, the cold, enveloping fogs of the Bering Sea, the shifting floes of the ice pack in the lonely, silent, too bright Arctic—these were strain enough on a man, but they were slight compared to the cold white bank of boredom that gradually enveloped the passengers, several of whom, I believe, would gladly have paid any reasonable sum to have the ship turn about and head back for the Golden Gate. Captain Lane in midpassage was the host at a party that was not going too well.

All pleasure cruises have moments of tedium, but usually the passengers can relax on sunny decks, swim in warm pools, go ashore every day or two where the ladies can plunder the shops and the men can stretch their legs and bend their elbows. The *Buford*, skirting the long coastline of Alaska in the early twenties, did not offer much relief of this sort. For some the *Buford* became a high-class floating jail—the food good, the scenery magnificent, but no escape. A hundred and seventy-odd passengers did a six-week stretch, and their spirits sagged as the scenery became increasingly familiar. In the fog, the scenic effect was dampening to many a spirit; for long periods the forecastlehead was barely visible from the door of the main cabin. The horn sounded daylong and nightlong.

Whoever planned this odd voyage for the expansion of trade had, of course, foreseen the need of entertainment and had done his best. Provision had been made for music, dancing, gaming, and drinking. Music was in charge of the Six Brown Brothers, a saxophone combo that had once performed in a show with Fred Stone. I have a fine, sharp photograph of the Brothers taken at the Akutan whaling station; they are standing in front of a dead whale, their saxophones at the ready. Adventure was in charge of H. A. Snow, a big-game hunter, who brought along his elephant gun, his movie camera, and his son Sydney. The ship was well stocked with private supplies of liquor. One of the owners of the ship, J. C. Ogden, came along for the ride, and this gave the thing the air of a real outing. But although there was an occasional diversion, the days were largely without incident and without cheer. Even such advertised treats as the stop at the Pribilofs to see the seal rookeries proved anticlimactic to many of the students of trade conditions; the place smelled bad and the seals looked like the ones you had seen in zoos and circuses. Some of the passengers, having gone to the great trouble and expense of reaching the Pribilof Islands, chose, when they got there, to remain on board and play bridge. As for me, I never had a dull moment. I lived on three successive levels socially, a gradual descent that to me seemed a climb: first the promenade deck, then the main deck, then below. I was busy, but not too busy to journalize, and I was young enough to absorb with gratitude and wonder the vast, splendid scene of Alaska in the time before the airplane brought it to our door and when it was still inaccessible and legendary.

When, in Seattle, I presented myself to the purser as a paying passenger, he assigned me to a small room with another man. This fellow turned out to be an oddball like me—not a member of the Chamber. He was a Laplander, a short, stocky man with a long mustache. His clothes were rough; he had no white shirts and almost no English. "I go Nomee," was all he could tell me at first. His name was Isak Nakkalo, and he was a reindeer butcher on his way to a job. Isak and I dwelt in peace and in silence day after day, until life changed abruptly for me and I began my descent. All up the Inside Passage, while the *Buford* skirted headlands and dodged rocks and reefs, Isak took no part in the social life aboard ship, but I did. I struck up a few acquaintances, danced to the sweet jazz of the Brown Brothers, nursed my clean shirts to get the maximum mileage out of them, and displayed affability (if not knowledge) in the matter of trade relations. I also lived a secret life. At every opportunity, I bearded stewards, engineers, and deck officers, and asked for work. My encounters with these people must have mystified them; at sea, a first-class passenger looking for work is irregular. I was probably worse than irregular; I was annoying.

Ketchikan was our first Alaskan port of call and the scene of the passengers' first disillusionment. In the minds of most of us aboard was an image of Alaska formed by Robert W. Service and Jack London—a land of deep snow, igloos, Eskimos, polar bears, rough men, fancy women, saloons, fighting sled dogs, intense cold, and gold everywhere. Ketchikan as we rounded the bend, delivered a shattering blow to this fine image; the village was a warm, mosquitoey place, smelling of fish. Not an igloo was in sight, and on the dock to greet us was a small, moth-eaten band of Shriners in their caps. But, image or no image, this was our frontier, and long before the ship was close enough for voices to carry, the passengers began

shouting questions to the group ashore. One of our shipboard
Shriners ached to know whether there was going to be a ceremonial that night. The distant welcoming group cupped their ears. "I
say is there going to be a ceremonial tonight?" he bellowed. The
words were lost in air. Mr. Hubbard, our tour master, began bellowing, too. He wanted to know whether a representative of the
Ketchikan Commercial Club was on hand.

I sat on a bollard in the warm sun, watching these antics indulgently, I, a graduate of the University of Mencken and Lewis, studying the spectacle of Babbittry northbound—men visiting a strange
land yet craving not strangeness but a renewal of what was familiar. I can still recall the agitation of Mr. Hubbard on this occasion—
a pioneer in a sack suit glimpsing his frontier at last and taut with
emotion. As the ship was being warped alongside, Mr. Hubbard saw
the boatswain swing himself over the rail, grasp a hawser, and slide
down onto the dock. Eager to make contact with the Commercial
Club man, Mr. Hubbard stepped over the rail and took hold of the
hawser. But the dock was a long way down, and there was still an
ugly gully of water between ship and dock. Twice Mr. Hubbard
flexed his legs in a test take-off, both times lost his nerve. His face
wore a grim look, and he soon had an audience, just as a suicide on
a ledge gets one. For a few tense moments, the launching of
Mr. Hubbard into Alaska held everyone spellbound, but it never
came off. Prudence conquered zeal, and our first brush with the
frontier was a defeat for the spirit of San Francisco.

Later, when I went ashore, via the plank, I "lounged down the
street" (I was always "lounging" or "sauntering" in my journal) and
bought a copy of *Faint Perfume,* by Zona Gale. Because the town
smelled of fish, I considered this purchase clownish. Of such flimsy
delights were my days made in those delectable years.

That evening, the Shriners had their ceremonial, the Commercial Club had its meeting, the ladies from the ship bought great
numbers of Indian baskets, and one of the oilers from the *Buford*'s

engine-room crew managed to get ashore and establish trade relations with a half-breed girl. "Big, like that," he told me afterward.
(I was already cultivating the society of firemen and sailors, hoping to be admitted.) When everyone had satisfied his own peculiar
needs and refreshed himself in the way he knew best, the *Buford* let
go her lines and continued north through the tortuous straits of the
Alexander Archipelago. I was an extremely callow and insecure
young man, but as I examine my record of Ketchikan and translate
it from the Chinese in which it is written, I can see that I was not
alone in my insecurity; all of us were seeking reassurance of one
sort or another—some with mystic rites and robes, some with the
metaphysics of commerce, some with expensive Indian baskets and
inexpensive Indian girls. I was enraptured with my surroundings—
contemptuous of all, envious of all, proud, courageous, and scared
to death.

On the morning of Sunday, July 29, we sighted Taku Glacier, a
scheduled point of interest. When we brought it abeam, Captain
Lane stopped the ship and everyone rushed on deck. "The bride-
groom," I noted in my journal, "dashed to get his polo coat and his
yellow gloves. The bride put on her polo coat to match. Everybody
put on something special. Walter Brunt, potentate of Islam Temple,
put on his monkey cap in case he should get into a photograph with
the glacier in the background."

The whale boat was lowered and Sydney Snow was rowed off
to get pictures of the *Buford* against the glacier. But Captain Lane
was not easily satisfied; he wanted his charges to see that a glacier
is really a river of ice, discharging into the sea. Taku, in the manner of glaciers, was sulking in its tent and taking its own sweet time
about discharging into the sea; it needed prodding. Accordingly,
Mr. Snow was called on to stir things up. He hurried to the bridge
with his elephant gun and opened fire on Taku, while Sydney, in
the whaleboat, cranked away at his camera. Nothing happened. For
about an hour, there was desultory fire from the bridge while the

passengers hung expectantly at the rail. Then they wearied of the spectacle of a reluctant glacier, and most of them drifted away toward the dining saloon. A few minutes before noon, whether from rifle fire or from sheer readiness, a piece of ice did fall into the sea. It made a fine splash. Passengers who had deserted the deck rushed back but were, of course, too late.

As I stood at the rail studying Taku Glacier, I was joined by the *Buford*'s storekeeper, a solemn, thoughtful man. For a few moments he stared quietly at the great wall of ice. "How do you like it?" I asked, between volleys. He took my question seriously and his answer was slow in coming. "I don't care for it," he replied, at last, and walked aft to resume his duties. As our voyage progressed and we ventured farther and farther into nowhere, with sea and sky and fog and ice and the white wings of gulls for our backdrop, the storekeeper's measured words became more and more expressive of the inner feelings of many of the tourists; they did not care for it.

At Juneau, I watched one of the Brown Brothers fishing in the rain, and wrote an unrhymed poem: "Grapefruit and oranges in the green water off Juneau dock—grapefruit and oranges, part of the ship's scum." Sandburg had me by the throat in those days. Alaskan towns, I reported in my journal, "are just murmurings at the foot of mountains."

One of the faintest of these murmurings was Skagway, where my ticket ran out. The *Buford* tied up at the dock there on the last day of July. My search for a job on board had been vain. I put my Corona in its case, packed my bag, and went on deck to sit awhile in sorrow and in fear, delaying until the last possible moment my walk down the plank and into the forlorn street of Skagway—a prospector twenty-five years late and not even primarily interested in gold.

While I was sitting there on deck (my journal says I was "browsing" there), trying to sort out my troubles and wondering how I had managed to get myself into this incredible mess, I received a summons to the bridge. A Miss Linderman, according to my account, presented herself to me and delivered the message. "The captain wants to see you right away" was all she said. Oddly enough, I did not associate this summons with my job-hunting; I had no idea what was up, and felt like a schoolboy called to the principal's office. The message seemed ominous, but less ominous than the imminent trip down the gangplank into murmurous Skagway. I hustled to the bridge.

Captain Lane stared at me for a moment. Then he said, "We can put you on as night saloonsman for the remainder of the voyage—workaway passage. Is that satisfactory?"

"Yes, sir," I replied. I didn't know what a night saloonsman was, or a workaway passage, but I was in no mood for quibbling, and if Captain Lane had offered to tow me astern at the end of a long rope I would have grabbed the chance. I thanked my captain, reported to the second steward, and that night turned up in the dining saloon wearing a white jacket and carrying a napkin slung over my left forearm, in the manner of right-handed waiters the world over. The crisis of Skagway was behind me, and pretty soon Skagway was, too, as the *Buford* steamed west toward the Aleutians at her steady pace of eleven knots.

I cannot recall Miss Linderman—she is a name on a page, that is all—but among the handful of women who have distinguished themselves in some great way in my life she occupies a high position. I never found out exactly what happened; I never even tried to find out. This much is clear: the news that a job-hunter was loose on board finally reached the captain, just as the news would have reached him that a harmless snake was loose in the hold, and he reluctantly disposed of the matter in the easiest way, as he settled many another small but pesky problem in the business of running that crazy tour.

(Since beginning this account, I've been looking into the files of the San Francisco *Chronicle* for 1923 for news of the *Buford* and its company. One of the owners of the line, it appears, was a Mr. John Linderman, and the passenger list shows the presence on board of several Linderman girls—his daughters, I suppose. So I guess I was bailed out of Skagway by the daughter of an owner. Inasmuch as Mr. Linderman and his partner Mr. Ogden were buying the ship on the installment plan, and had slim prospects of making the thing pay, I think the management was foolhardy to take on another mouth to feed. But I still value Miss Linderman highly.)

Working in a ship is a far better life than sailing in one as a passenger. Alaska, the sea, and the ship herself became real to me as soon as I was employed; before that, all three had suffered from a sort of insubstantiality. Passengers never really come to know a ship; too much is hidden from their sight, too little is demanded of them. They may love their ship, but without their participating in her operation the identification is not established. As saloonsman, I was a participant—at first a slightly sick participant. I worked from eight in the evening till six in the morning. I set tables, prepared late supper for thirty, served it (sometimes carrying a full tray in a beam sea), cleaned the tables, washed the dishes, stropped the glasses, swept down the companionway leading to the social hall, and shined brass. This was hard work, dull work, and, until my stomach adjusted to the ripe smell of the pantry, touchy work. But when, at around three o'clock, I stepped out onto the forward deck for a smoke, with the sky showing bright in the north and the mate pacing the bridge and the throaty snores of the passengers issuing from the staterooms, the ship would throb and tremble under me and she was *my* ship, all mine and right on course, alive and purposeful and exciting. No longer was the *Buford* merely taking me from one benighted port to another; now she was transporting me from all my yesterdays to all my tomorrows. It was I who seemed to make her go, almost as though I were a quartermaster with my hand on the wheel.

My metamorphosis from passenger to saloonsman took the passengers by surprise and created a certain awkwardness at the late supper. A few of the first-class people knew me by name and most of them knew me by sight; naturally they felt uneasy when they found me at their service. There was the matter of tipping. Should a girl with whom I had danced between Seattle and Skagway leave a coin for me when I handed her a cold cut between Skagway and Cordova? A delicate question. One elderly female, flustered at seeing me in saloonsman's garb, cried, "Goodness! How long have *you* been a waitress?" I regarded my change in status as extremely comical, played it deadpan, and made quite a to-do about it in my journal, greatly exaggerating its comic value. Embarrassed at first, I soon felt an elevation of spirit and wore my white jacket like a plume. In my mouth was the taste of a fresh superiority over my fellow man; not only was I leading a secret literary life among the mercantile crowd but I was now a busy, employed man, gainfully occupied among wastrels and idlers. Always hungry myself and indulging in snacks at every opportunity, I nevertheless adopted a patronizing air toward those who appeared for the prebedtime meal, regarding their appetite at that hour as gross and contemptible. The hardest part of the job for me was remembering orders; I would stand attentively listening to a group of four telling me what they wanted, and by the time I reached the pantry the whole recital would be gone from my head. As a member of the Steward Department, I was permitted by the rules to go on deck to catch some air but was not permitted to sit down while on deck. I ceased mingling with the passengers and joined the much juicier fraternity of pantrymen and cooks, denizens of the glory hole in the stern of the ship next to the steering engine—a noisy, aromatic place, traditional seat of intrigue and corruption. I joined the glory-hole crowd, but I was not shifted to the glory hole itself; instead, I was assigned a bunk in a small, airless inside room, first class, with a young man named J. Wilbur Wolf. Wilbur was the other night saloonsman, and, like me, was burdened with a college education and an immaculate past. The second steward, a cagey man, chose not to inject Wilbur and me into the glory hole, where we properly belonged. The second may have feared that our morals would be corrupted, but I think he simply did not wish to disturb the gamy society of the hole by introducing two young dudes of almost unparalleled innocence. It would have made him uneasy.

Notes on the Contributors

Nigel Barley is a British anthropologist who has written several books, including *The Innocent Anthropologist, Adventures in a Mountain Hut*, and *White Rajah*.

Ludwig Bemelmans (1898–1962) was an American born in Austria, and he wrote and illustrated more than forty books including *Madeline's Rescue* and *My War With the United States*.

Bill Bryson, an American who has lived extensively in Britain, has penned such bestsellers as *A Walk in the Woods, In a Sunburned Country*, and *The Lost Continent*.

Christopher Buckley is a magazine editor and author of the novels *Thank You for Smoking, Florence of Arabia*, and *Little Green Men*, to name a few. He lives in Washington, D.C. with his wife and two children.

W. Hodding Carter has written for *Esquire* and *Smithsonian* magazines, and is the author of *A Viking Voyage* and *Westward Whoa*.

Whit Deschner's first book about kayaking was entitled *Does the Wet Suit You? The Confessions of a Kayak Bum*. He has paddled rivers around the world, and has gone on to become a novelist (*Burning the Iceberg*).

Tony Hawks is an English comic and songwriter, as well as the author of *A Piano in the Pyrenees* and *Playing the Moldovans at Tennis*.

Tony Horwitz is a Pulitzer Prize–winning journalist and author of *Baghdad Without a Map*. After years of traipsing through war zones as a foreign correspondent he returned to Virginia and wrote *Confederates in the Attic* and *Blue Latitudes*.

Pico Iyer is a British-born Indian and the author of *Video Night in Kathmandu, Falling Off the Map, Cuba and the Night, Tropical Classical*, and *The Lady and the Monk*.

Jerome K. Jerome (1859–1927) was an actor, teacher, and journalist before he turned to writing books. After the success of *Three Men in a Boat*, he and several friends founded *The Idler*, a magazine which ran stories by Robert Louis Stevenson and Mark Twain, among others. He also wrote *Three Men on the Bummel* and *Idle Thoughts of an Idle Fellow*.

John Krich writes for the *New York Times;* his books include *El Beisbol* and *Why Is This Country Dancing?*

Pete McCarthy is a writer and a producer of a travel series for radio and television in the United Kingdom. He also wrote *The Road to McCarthy: Around the World in Search of Ireland*.

Tom Miller is author of *On the Border, Jack Ruby's Kitchen Sink*, and *Trading with the Enemy*.

Tim Moore is an English humorist who writes for *British Esquire* and *Vanity Fair*, and has published *Travels With My Donkey*, and *The Grand Tour: The European Adventure of a Continental Drifter*.

Eric Newby is the author of more than fifteen travel books, among them *Slowly Down the Ganges, Love and War in the Apennines, The Last Grain Race*, and *A Small Place in Italy*. He lives in England.

P. J. O'Rourke has a long list of bestsellers to his credit: *Holidays in Hell, Give War a Chance, Eat the Rich, Parliament of Whores, All the Trouble in the World*, and *CEO of the Sofa*. He has homes in New Hampshire and Washington, D.C.

Stuart Stevens is an American political consultant and author of *Night Train to Turkistan*, *Feeding Frenzy*, and *The Big Enchilada*.

Mark Twain (1835–1910) was a renowned humorist, novelist, writer, and lecturer. His travel memoirs include *A Tramp Abroad* and *Following the Equator*.

Sarah Vowell is a journalist and writer whose works include *The Partly Cloudy Patriot* and *Take the Cannoli*.

E. B. White (1899–1985) was on the staff of *The New Yorker* for most of his career, and was the author of numerous books, including *Elements of Style*, *Charlotte's Web*, and *The Trumpet of the Swan*.

Mark Winegardner is a journalist and professor of English literature whose works include *Veracruz Blues*, *Crooked River Burning*, and *The Godfather Returns*. He lives in Florida.

Permissions

Permissions